D1565996

London, 1984

London, 1984

Conflict and Change in the Radical City

STEPHEN BROOKE

OXFORD
UNIVERSITY PRESS

OXFORD
UNIVERSITY PRESS

Great Clarendon Street, Oxford, OX2 6DP,
United Kingdom

Oxford University Press is a department of the University of Oxford.
It furthers the University's objective of excellence in research, scholarship,
and education by publishing worldwide. Oxford is a registered trade mark of
Oxford University Press in the UK and in certain other countries

Published in the United States of America by Oxford University Press
198 Madison Avenue, New York, NY 10016, United States of America

British Library Cataloguing in Publication Data
Data available

Library of Congress Control Number: 2023948501

ISBN 9780198862888

DOI: 10.1093/9780191895395.001.0001

Printed and bound in the UK by
Clays Ltd, Elcograf S.p.A.

to Theo and Eliza

Acknowledgements

This book could not have been written without the support of the Social Science and Humanities Council of Canada. I am grateful to my research assistants for their contributions: Hayley Andrew, Sage Milo, and Lisa Romano. Archival research is, of course, dependent upon archivists: the staff at the London Metropolitan Archives, Bishopsgate Institute, Black Cultural Archives, George Padmore Institute, and London School of Economics were unfailingly generous and helpful. I was very lucky to be able to work with Nadine Kolz, Thomas Deva, and Cathryn Steele at Oxford University Press. I am deeply indebted to those who were willing to be interviewed about Matrix and the Dalston Children's Centre. Those interviews were an extraordinary inspiration. For their feedback and the inspiration of their own work, I thank Lucy Robinson, Jordanna Bailkin, Matt Booi, Greig Dymond, Daisy Payling, Chris Moores, Kieran Connell, Catherine Ellis, Simeon Koole, Camilla Schofield, Kristine Alexander, Sarah Stoller, Judith Walkowitz, Gavin Shaffer, Becky Conekin, Matt Houlbrook, Anne Marie Rafferty, Glen Jeffery, Sally Alexander, Jess Clark, Jon Lawrence, Nick Garland, Matthew Hilton, Edward Jones-Imhotep, and James Vernon. At York University, I am indebted to Nicholas Rogers, Thabit Abdullah, Pablo Idahosa, and Kate McPherson for their friendship. I am fortunate to have Claire Langhamer, Martin Francis, and Christine Grandy as friends and colleagues who provided invaluable insight and kind encouragement at different stages of the present work. The anonymous reviewer of the manuscript made many helpful suggestions. Finally, I wish to thank Mary Brooke, Amy Black, Theo Brooke, and Eliza Brooke. *London, 1984* is about the past, but as for the present and the future, the book is dedicated to Theo and Eliza with great love, knowing that you are making and will make wonderful things of your own time.

Contents

Contents

List of Figures

List of Figures

Introduction

On 9 July 1931, the Mayor of Hackney, Frank Snewin, laid a cornerstone at 76 Shacklewell Lane, a street that curves eastward off the Kingsland Road in Dalston. The new building was a public baths, a single-storey red brick structure, dressed in Portland stone, with separate entrances for men and women. Since 2000, the Shacklewell Lane Baths has been home to a private childcare centre, the Bath House.

At first glance, the Shacklewell Lane Baths might seem to tell, in bricks and mortar, a familiar story of twentieth-century Britain, one that arcs between the collective provision of services in the mid-century to their delivery by the private market at the fin de siècle, a narrative about the decline of one political culture and the rise of another.[1] But there is a middle chapter to the story of this building that complicates such a history.

In June 1984, the Dalston Children's Centre successfully applied to the Women's Committee of the Greater London Council, the metropolitan authority for London, for £108,000 to convert the Shacklewell Lane Baths into a childcare facility.[2] The Dalston Children's Centre had been nomadic since its founding in 1980, moving between various terraced houses in Dalston. It provided childcare for up to forty children a day to local families, largely free of charge. The Dalston Children's Centre was a collective, whose aims were to provide childcare 'in an anti-racist, anti-sexist, anti-heterosexist and anti-authoritarian way'.[3] To do the renovations for the Baths, the Centre proposed using Matrix, the only

---

[1] See, for example, James Vernon, *Modern Britain 1750 to the Present* (Cambridge: Cambridge University Press, 2017), parts IV and V; Avner Offer, 'The Market Turn: from social democracy to market liberalism', *Economic History Review* 70/4 (November 2017): 1051–71, doi/10.1111/ehr.12537.

[2] GLC Women's Committee, 'Dalston Children's Centre', Funding Application, 22 June 1984, London Metropolitan Archives (LMA), GLC/DG/PRE/223/22.

[3] Dalston Children's Centre, *Annual Report*, Appendices (London: Dalston Children's Centre, 1983), https://hackneyhistory.wordpress.com/2017/08/09/dalston-childrens-centre-19823/.

feminist, all-female design collective in London. The body to which the Dalston Children's Centre had applied—the GLC Women's Committee—had explicitly feminist aims, to promote '[women's] welfare and interests in Greater London.'[4] This made it exceptional as a state agency in modern British history. The Women's Committee began in 1982 with a budget of £300,000 and a staff of four; by 1986, its budget was £16 million, and its staff numbered a hundred. Two weeks before the abolition of the GLC in 1986, the Women's Committee opened a large metropolitan women's centre at the old Kingsway Hall. The life of the Shacklewell Lane Baths in the 1980s was animated by the marriage between local feminism and municipal socialism.

In this respect, the Dalston Children's Centre was not atypical of the landscape of 1980s London. In 1991, Patrick Wright surveyed the 'rowdy exuberance' of Dalston:

> What comes after Voluntary Action on Dalston Lane is really still Ken Livingstone's GLC and the efflorescence of community organizations that thrived under its wing...Hackney Cooperative Developments is based here, proudly advertising the alternative shopping centre it has made of a battered Victorian row of shops in nearby Bradbury Street...Then...come the differentiated organizations of the rainbow coalition: the Asian Centre; Africa House with its special Advice and Community Centre...Hackney Women's Centre; Hackney Heatsavers; Hackney Pensioners...[5]

Wright evoked a distinct political landscape in late twentieth-century London, where a sometimes fractious but distinctive new politics was being worked out on the ground, often underwritten by local government.

While the bricks and mortar of the Shacklewell Lane Baths remain, many of the vestiges of this London have largely disappeared, as has its political context.[6] The GLC was abolished in 1986 by the Thatcher

---

[4] GLC, Report by Director-General, 10 June 1982, LMA, GLC/DG/PRE/223/01.

[5] Patrick Wright, *A Journey Through Ruins: The Last Days of London* (Oxford: Oxford University Press, 1991, 2009 edition), 18–19.

[6] Hilda Kean, 'The Transformation of Political and Cultural Space', in Joe Kerr and Andrew Gibson (eds.), *London from Punk to Blair* (London: Reaktion, 2012), 147.

government. With its demise, community organizations and spaces were starved of funds and hobbled both by the shrinking capacities of borough governments and the siren song of the free market. The women's centre at Kingsway Hall was sold off after abolition; it is now home to a hotel. In Dalston, the 'rowdy exuberance' of the 1980s was eclipsed by gentrification and hipsterdom, its elegy written in rising property prices, trendy bars, and high-end boutiques.[7] But the story of the Shacklewell Lane Baths testifies to a period in London's history when local social democracy and independent grass-roots initiatives created a different world, even at the moment when the city was being simultaneously transformed by thirteen years of Conservative government. Thatcher famously remarked, with respect to her reforming agenda, that 'there is no alternative', but 1980s London put the lie to that assertion.

This book is an excavation of one year, 1984, when alternative presents and contrasting futures lay before the city. It examines a collection of organizations, artefacts, places, and events. These include the Dalston Children's Centre, an anti-apartheid demonstration, a pop concert for the unemployed on the South Bank, protests against Docklands redevelopment staged on the Thames, a police raid on a gay bookshop in Bloomsbury, reports on the state of racial politics from housing estates in the East End and Tottenham, a parliamentary bill on police procedure, a major work of feminist architectural analysis, and controversial metropolitan initiatives on gay rights, race, and feminism.

London, 1984 explores, through the prism of a single year in the life of a city, the impact of radical political change upon London and ordinary Londoners, the experience of conflict that accompanied that change, and new understandings of society and politics that shaped late twentieth-century Britain. The disparate stories in this book are compelling in themselves, but they also hold a broader importance for understanding the 1980s, a critical decade in the shaping of modern Britain.

---

[7] For a broader view of such developments, see Roger Burrows and Caroline Knowles, 'The "Haves" and the "Have Yachts": Social-Spatial Struggles in London between the "Merely Wealthy" and the "Super-Rich", *Cultural Politics* 15/1 (2019): 72–87, https://doi.org/10.1215/17432197-7289528.

0.1

The 1980s crowned 'a great age of fracture' in global history at the end of the twentieth century.[8] In Britain, that break was between a post-war consensus built upon an interventionist state and the collective claims of society and an emerging political culture that emphasized the centrality of the free market, private property, and the individual. This new political culture was brought to life by three consecutive Conservative governments led by Margaret Thatcher between 1979 and 1990.

What these governments attempted has been given various labels: monetarism, market liberalism, Thatcherism, neoliberalism, and Thatcherite neoliberalism. This ideological approach was rooted in the reaction of particular economists like Friedrich von Hayek and Milton Friedman to the dominance of the Keynesian mixed economy and social democracy after the Second World War.[9] Such figures sought to reassert the primacy of the free market in social relations. For neoliberals, the principal role of the state was to restore and strengthen the market. This had a totalizing aspect, so that 'all domains and all activities' were to be governed by the market and individuals rendered as 'market actors'.[10] David Harvey has referred to this as the 'financialization of everything'.[11] And by this process, the social and political landscape changed: in the words of the critic Michael Bracewell, 'all the world [became] an office, all the world [became] a shop'.[12]

Neoliberalism entered the British Conservative Party in complex ways, but under the leadership of Margaret Thatcher it was increasingly the party's solution to what was perceived as the 'problem' of social democratic Britain and decline in the 1970s. Thatcherite neoliberalism also sought to reorient the ethos of twentieth-century Britain and the

[8] Daniel T. Rodgers, *Age of Fracture* (Cambridge, MA: Belknap Press/Harvard University Press, 2011), 3.

[9] See, among others, Quinn Slobodian, *Globalists: The End of Empire and the Birth of Neoliberalism* (Cambridge, MA: Harvard University Press, 2018).

[10] Wendy Brown, *Undoing the Demos: Neoliberalism's Stealth Revolution* (New York: Zone, 2015), 31.

[11] David Harvey, *A Brief History of Neoliberalism* (Oxford: Oxford University Press, 2005), 33.

[12] Michael Bracewell, *Souvenir* (London: White Rabbit, 2021), 41.

outlook of twentieth-century Britons.[13] Two well-known quotes from Thatcher underscore this point. On the second anniversary of coming to power, Thatcher remarked to *The Sunday Times* that '[e]conomics are the method: the object is to change the heart and soul'.[14] Privatizations of publicly owned industries and services, tax cuts, and deregulation were the means to this end. This also meant a radical dissembling of the balance between the collective and the individual. 'Who is society? There is no such thing!' Margaret Thatcher told the readers of *Women's Own* in 1987; '[t]here are individual men and women and there are families and no government can do anything except through people and people look to themselves first'.[15]

The paving stones of the road ventured upon by Thatcherite neo-liberalism after 1979 included the 1980 Housing Act, the deregulation of the financial markets in 1986, a wave of privatizations, and a series of tax- and government-expenditure-cutting budgets. These restored the primacy of the free market and transformed people's understanding of their own relationship to the state and the market.[16] The market was also introduced to areas of social provision such as council housing, health, and education. The Housing Act allowed tenants to purchase their council flats at a discount, a discount that was increased in 1984. This led to a steep drop in the building of public sector housing from 167,000 permanent dwellings in 1975 to 35,000 in 1990.[17] By 1982, 400,000 council homes had been sold. In 1980, private patients were afforded greater access to the National Health Service. Ten years later, the National Health Service and Community Care Act introduced an internal market to the provision of health care. The 1988 Education Act allowed opting out of the public system and undermined local control of schools.

---

[13] See E. H. H. Green, *Thatcher* (London: Edward Arnold, 2006); Ben Jackson, 'The think-tank archipelago: Thatcherism and neoliberalism', in Ben Jackson and Robert Saunders (eds.), *Making Thatcher's Britain* (Cambridge: Cambridge University Press, 2012), 43–61.

[14] Margaret Thatcher Foundation Archives, Margaret Thatcher, *Sunday Times*, 3 May 1981, https://www.margaretthatcher.org/document/104475.

[15] Margaret Thatcher Foundation Archives, Margaret Thatcher, *Women's Own*, 23 September 1987, https://www.margaretthatcher.org/document/106689.

[16] See Amy Edwards, *Are We Rich Yet?* (Berkeley: University of California Press, 2022).

[17] Figures from David Butler and Gareth Butler, *British Political Facts* (London: Macmillan, 1994), 333.

Restoring the market also meant increasing the importance of finance and services to the detriment of manufacturing. Controls to the money supply, cuts to manufacturing subsidies, higher interest rates, and a stronger pound all weakened industry. High unemployment was the immediate effect of such policies. By January 1982, there were three million people out of work; by September, the unemployed represented 14 per cent of the workforce. For the most part, the Conservative response to unemployment was negligible. The market was trusted to remedy the recession and to reshape workers for low-paid jobs.[18]

The resurgence of the right in the 1980s was complemented by the failure of the centre and left to mount an effective challenge to Thatcherite neoliberalism. The Labour Party was plagued by crisis and dissension throughout the decade. In 1981, a number of prominent right-wingers broke away to form the Social Democratic Party. Labour was also riven by tensions between its centre and the left. Neil Kinnock took the leadership in 1983 and made a concerted effort to root out left-wing influence within the party. Most famously, he confronted Liverpool Council in 1985, which was dominated by the Trotskyist Militant Tendency. After the 1987 election loss, Kinnock sought to 'modernize' the party through a policy review, an attempt to come to grips with the new political reality.[19] The wider labour movement was also thrown into disarray by Conservative governance. A series of trade union and employment acts undercut the power of unions, while the defeats suffered by the miners in 1985 and the printers in 1986 effectively blunted the strike weapon. Between 1979 and 1985, the total number of union members dropped from 13.4 million to 10.7 million.[20]

The new neoliberal consensus did not come without conflict, dissent, and, sometimes, violence. The decade began with disorders incited by racial tensions in Bristol, followed by a spring and summer of violence throughout the country in 1981. In London, the Brixton disorders of

---

[18] See Bernhard Rieger, 'Making Britain Work Again: Unemployment and the Remaking of British Social Policy in the Eighties', *English Historical Review* 133/568 (June 2018): 634–66, doi: 10.1093/ehr/cey087.

[19] See Colm Murphy, *Futures of Socialism* (Cambridge: Cambridge University Press, 2023).

[20] Chris Cook and John Stevenson, *The Longman Handbook of Modern British History 1714–1987*, 2nd edition (Harlow: Longman, 1988), 174–5.

April led to a major enquiry into the relations between ethnic minority communities and the police. The summer of 1981 also saw disturbances involving youth of South Asian descent in Southall. Four years later, Broadwater Farm in Tottenham was the scene of another serious disorder. Eight soldiers were killed in IRA bombings at Hyde Park and Regent's Park in 1982. In 1984, the Conservative conference held at Brighton was the target of another IRA bombing. The stationing of nuclear-tipped cruise missiles at American airbases prompted the renewal of the Campaign for Nuclear Disarmament and the establishment of a continual women's protest at the Greenham Common airbase. In London, CND organized demonstrations in 1981 and 1982 that brought out hundreds of thousands of people.

Global events also evinced a sense of conflict. The Cold War had intensified, with the deployment of new nuclear weapons in Europe, such as cruise missiles. In 1984, the Soviet Union boycotted the Los Angeles Summer Olympics. Proxy wars were being fought in southern Africa, Afghanistan, and Central America. In South Africa itself, the racist apartheid regime was facing increasing opposition from anti-apartheid groups such as the African National Congress. November 1984 saw the re-election of the Republican Ronald Reagan.

Historical views of the 1980s have unsurprisingly been largely monopolized by the imposing figure of Margaret Thatcher. As Andy McSmith has suggested, Thatcher dominated 1980s politics 'in a way that no other decade is associated with one individual'.[21] There have been important contributions to our understanding of Thatcherite economic and social policy in the 1980s.[22] More recently, historians have attempted to widen our understanding of the eighties and of neoliberalism. This has included stressing the importance of other trajectories or legacies,

[21] Andy McSmith, *No Such Thing as Society* (London: Constable, 2011), 4; similar accounts include Richard Vinen, *Thatcher's Britain* (London: Pocket Books, 2009); Alwyn W. Turner, *Rejoice! Rejoice!* (London: Aurum, 2010); Graham Stewart, *Bang!* (London: Atlantic, 2013).
[22] See, among others, Jackson and Saunders, *Making Thatcher's Britain*; Matthew Francis, '"A Crusade to Enfranchise the Many": Thatcherism and the "Property-Owning Democracy"', *Twentieth Century British History* 23/2 (June 2012): 275–97, doi: 10.1093/tcbh/hwr032; Florence Sutcliffe-Braithwaite, 'Neo-Liberalism and Morality in the Making of Thatcherite Social Policy', *Historical Journal* 55/2 (June 2012): 497–520, doi: 10.1017/S0018246x12000118; Rieger, 'Making Britain Work Again'.

such as the decline in social deference or the rise of individualism, which, though intersecting with Thatcherism or neoliberalism, do not necessarily originate with those ideologies.[23] Other work has suggested that the left was hardly supine in its reaction to the rise of Thatcher or that social democracy and neoliberalism were, in some spheres, linked.[24] There have also been important recent contributions to the history of race in the 1980s.[25] What we have less of are accounts of how the social and political changes of the 1980s were experienced in ordinary life, though those histories are beginning to appear, as seen in work by Amy Edwards, Chris Moores, Sarah Stoller, and others.[26] Most recently, Lucy Robinson has contributed a major study of the decade which uses a montage of objects and events to explore the 'ways in which the big issues get worked out – around the meaning of motherhood and the military covenant, the family and childhood, the relationship between

[23] See James Vernon, 'Heathrow and the Making of Neoliberal Britain', *Past and Present* 252 (2021): 213–47, doi: 10.1093/pastj/gtaa022; Matthew Hilton, Chris Moores, and Florence Sutcliffe-Braithwaite, '*New Times* Revisited: Britain in the 1980s', *Contemporary British History* 31/2 (June 2017): 145–65, doi: 10.1080/13619462.2017.1306214; Emily Robinson, Camilla Schofield, Florence Sutcliffe-Braithwaite, and Natalie Thomlinson, 'Telling Stories about Post-war Britain: Popular Individualism and the "Crisis" of the 1970s', *Twentieth Century British History* 28/2 (June 2017): 268–304, doi: 10.1093/tcbh/hwx006; Florence Sutcliffe-Braithwaite, *Class, Politics and the Decline of Deference in England, 1968–2000* (Oxford: Oxford University Press, 2018); Jon Lawrence, *Me, Me, Me?* (Oxford: Oxford University Press, 2019).
[24] See James Curran, with Ivor Gaber and Julian Petley, *Culture Wars: The Media and the British Left* (Edinburgh: Edinburgh University Press, 2005); Daisy Payling, *Socialist Republic: Remaking the British Left in 1980s Sheffield* (Manchester: Manchester University Press, 2023); Murphy, *Futures of Socialism;* Alexandre Campsie, '"Socialism will never be the same again": Re-imagining British left-wing ideas for the "New Times"', *Contemporary British History* 31/2 (June 2017): 166–88, doi: 10.1080/13619462.2017.1306211; Jonathan David and Rohan McWilliam (eds.), *Labour and the Left in the 1980s* (Manchester: Manchester University Press, 2018); Karl Pike, 'Mere theology? Neil Kinnock and the Labour Party's aims and values, 1986–8', *Contemporary British History* 34/1 (January 2020): 95–117, doi: 10.1080/13619462.2019.1636650; Guy Ortolano, *Thatcher's Progress* (Cambridge: Cambridge University Press, 2019).
[25] See Kieran Connell, *Black Handsworth* (Berkeley: University of California Press, 2019); Rob Waters, *Thinking Black* (Berkeley: University of California Press, 2018); Simon Peplow, *Race and Riots in Thatcher's Britain* (Manchester: Manchester University Press, 2019).
[26] See Hilton, Moores, Sutcliffe Braithwaite, '*New Times* Revisited', 146; Edwards, *Are We Rich Yet?;* Aled Davies, Ben Jackson, and Florence Sutcliffe-Braithwaite (eds.), *The Neoliberal Age: Britain Since the 1970s* (London: UCL Press, 2021); Chris Moores, 'Opposition to the Greenham Peace Camps in 1980s Britain: RAGE Against the "Obscene"', *History Workshop Journal* 78/1 (August 2014): 204–27, doi: 10.1093/hwj/dbt038; Chris Moores, 'Thatcher's Troops? Neighbourhood Watch Schemes and the Search for "Ordinary" Thatcherism in 1980s Britain', *Contemporary British History* 31/2 (June 2017): 230–55, doi: 10.1080/13619462.2017.1306203; Sarah Stoller, *Inventing the Working Parent: Work, Gender, and Feminism in Neoliberal Britain* (Cambridge, MA: MIT Press, 2023).

the populous, public interest and public security, the judiciary and the parliamentary system, the medium and the message for example.[27]

The present book contributes to our understanding of the 1980s in several ways. In the first place, it examines how the competing political and social changes of that decade were experienced across a wide register in London that stretched from north London streets to the House of Commons. Secondly, the book explores the shifts between social democracy and neoliberalism in the last third of the twentieth century as an important narrative of twentieth-century British history. While the present work acknowledges the growing power of neoliberalism in shaping British life, it points to persistent strands of social democracy not easily accommodated within neoliberalism. Thatcherism established 'enterprise zones', but zones of social democracy also appeared, some old and some born of the 1980s. Finally, the book emphasizes the importance of London as a primary site of social and political change in the late twentieth century.

0.2

London was a symbol of the fracture of the 1980s and a critical site in the ascent of Thatcherite neoliberalism. This was reflected in the transformation of the capital's space as much as anything, with establishment of the London Docklands Development Corporation and the creation of an 'enterprise zone' in east London in 1981, followed by a commitment to the commercial development of the King's Cross area.[28] That change was very much led by the Conservative government in setting 'the key

[27] Lucy Robinson, *Now That's What I Call a History of the 1980s: Pop Culture and Politics in the Decade that Shaped Modern Britain* (Manchester: Manchester University Press, 2023), 25–6.
[28] See for example, Susan Fainstein and Ken Young, 'Politics and state policy in economic restructuring', in Susan Fainstein, Ian Gordon, and Michael Harloe (eds.), *Divided Cities* (Oxford: Blackwell, 1992), 215–24; see also Sam Wetherell, 'Freedom Planned: Enterprise Zones and Urban Non-planning in Post-War Britain', *Twentieth-Century British History* 27/2 (June 2016): 266–89, doi: 10.1093/tcbh/hww004; see also Sam Wetherell, *Foundations: How the Built Environment Made Twentieth-Century Britain* (Princeton: Princeton University Press, 2020).

parameters which have allowed market forces to operate more freely'.[29] In October 1986, the Thatcher government set off the 'Big Bang' in the City of London by deregulating financial trading, underscoring London's importance as a global centre for capital. London was remoulded, physically and economically, by factors such as the commercial redevelopment of the Docklands, the growing dominance in London's economy of the service and financial sectors, the rise of information technology in the workplace, and the increasing importance of the property market in local and national economies. London was at the centre of the shift towards Thatcherite neoliberalism in other ways. One of the Conservatives' victories was the reduction of trade union power. The defeat of the miners' union in the strike of 1984–5 remains the most important symbol of the Conservatives' fight against organized labour, but, in London, the Wapping dispute of 1986 was another important example. News International, Rupert Murdoch's media empire which included *The Times*, sought to bring new technology into the print industry at a new plant in Wapping. This led to a lengthy, unsuccessful strike in 1986, which, like the miners' strike, confirmed the diminished strength of organized labour in the 1980s.

But if Thatcherite neoliberalism was in the ascendant in the 1980s, it did not entirely dominate London's eighties. As the singer-songwriter and writer Tracey Thorn has remarked, the eighties 'may have been Thatcher's decade…but it didn't feel like that at the time'.[30] London in the 1980s was home to spaces and movements that either were explicitly opposed to the Thatcherite ascendancy or emerged from older trajectories. As John Davis has argued, contemporary London was also profoundly shaped by changes and developments unfolding in the 1960s and 1970s.[31] By the 1980s, there were 'resistance movements of various kinds' against the rise of Thatcherite neoliberalism, some rooted in the moment, some grounded in longer-term changes.[32] That unruly

---

[29] Chris Hamnett, *Unequal City: London in the Global Arena* (London: Routledge, 2003), 14–15.

[30] Tracey Thorn, *Bedsit Disco Queen* (London: Virago, 2014), 158.

[31] See John Davis, *Waterloo Sunrise* (New Haven: Yale University Press, 2022).

[32] Nik Theodore, Jamie Peck, and Neil Brennen, 'Neoliberal Urbanism: Cities and the Rule of Markets', in Gary Bridge and Sophie Watson (eds.), *The New Blackwell Companion to the City* (Oxford: Wiley-Blackwell, 2011), 21.

Figure 0.1 Fly Posters, Ridley Road Market, Dalston.
Credit: Andrew Holligan.

diversity can be seen in the riot of posters and handbills on a wall in Dalston in 1984 (Figure 0.1). In many respects, contemporary London was forged in this fracture, in the ambiguous space between the rise of neoliberalism and the alternative political and social culture that existed alongside it.

One centre of gravity for this alternative culture was the Greater London Council. In May 1981, a month after the Brixton disorders, Labour won the most seats in the GLC elections. Ken Livingstone, a noted left-winger, took control of the Labour group and became Leader of the GLC. This victory set the stage for a battle within London and between London and the Conservative government over the next five years. The subsequent six years of Labour government was ended by the abolition of the GLC on 1 April 1986.

The present book is not a history of the GLC between 1981 and 1986, but the GLC is an important recurring character in its pages, sometimes taking centre stage, sometimes waiting in the wings, and often helping to construct the stage itself. In particular, the book's first chapters examine the policies and frameworks the GLC established in London after 1981 and assesses their impact on the city and on the ground. In 1984, the GLC was fighting for its future, the Conservatives having introduced legislation in 1983 to abolish it. Like the city it governed, the Labour GLC was a symbol of the fractures of the 1980s. Alongside local governments in Liverpool, Sheffield, and Manchester, the GLC was that rare thing in the eighties: an oasis of Labour power in an otherwise hostile environment of Conservative dominance.[33] Between 1981 and 1986, County Hall, Lambeth, stood as a physical and political affront to Conservative governments across the river at Westminster, a stubborn outcrop of social democracy at the moment when the terrain of late twentieth-century Britain was being reshaped by Thatcherite neoliberalism. The GLC explored new kinds of local state planning and investment in the economy, through its Industry and Employment Committee and the Greater London Enterprise Board, just as the boundaries of the central state were being sharply pared back. Against a political ethos that favoured the individual, the GLC sought ways of both reinforcing old social bonds and fostering new kinds of community and democratic involvement. In the absence of a national Labour government, the GLC was determined to 'counteract the market forces which have led inexorably to decline'.[34]

The GLC's challenge to the Conservative government was delivered on other fronts. It supported radical causes on the local, national, and international level. This included articulating support for the anti-apartheid and nuclear disarmament movements by declaring London an anti-apartheid zone and an anti-nuclear zone. The council also put

[33] See, for example, Payling, *Socialist Republic*.
[34] London Labour Party, *A Socialist Policy for the GLC—Labour's London Manifesto 1981* (London, 1981), 13.

on two major rock concerts in 1984 and 1985, attracting between 100,000 and 500,000 people, to promote anti-unemployment policies. Particular years were dedicated to specific causes, such as Peace Year 1983 and Anti-Racism Year 1984.

But the GLC was not merely a defence of how social democracy had been practised since the Second World War; it was also an attempt to take social democracy into unfamiliar spheres.[35] According to the critic Kobena Mercer, it promoted 'new social actors and new political subjects', such as women, people of colour, and gay and lesbian people, exploring new frontiers of equality and new meanings of 'social' and 'democracy'.[36] Through a large grant budget, the GLC funded a dazzling array of community groups on the ground in London. Spending on grant aid increased dramatically, from £6 million in 1981 to £50 million in 1984.[37] These groups fought to shape the city in myriad ways, some that were fiercely local, dealing, for example, with the police presence on a north London estate, and some that encompassed global causes, such as the anti-apartheid movement. In the 1980s, London was, in this way, a spectacle of resurgent social democracy, not just ascendant Thatcherite neoliberalism, a city symbolized not only by plans for glittering steel and glass office blocks but by a local women's centre on a high street, a bookshop, a youth association on a housing estate, or a jobs' festival on the South Bank. New kinds of community made new forms of politics by asserting such space in the city. Doreen Massey has argued that London was reinvented 'on a tide of neoliberalization'; the 'social city' of the nineteenth century was superseded by a 'market city' in the late twentieth century.[38] The spaces that the GLC tried to nurture might be taken as an assertion of the social city against the market city. Whether it was a last rage against the dying of that light is more complicated.

[35] For the larger context of this on the left, see Geoff Eley, *Forging Democracy* (Oxford: Oxford University Press, 2002), chs. 24, 26, and 27.

[36] Kobena Mercer, 'Welcome to the Jungle: Identity and Diversity in Postmodern Politics', in Jonathan Rutherford (ed.), *Identity: Community, Culture, Difference* (London: Lawrence & Wishart, 1990), 44.

[37] Figures from Stewart Lansley, Sue Goss, and Christian Wolmar, *Councils in Conflict* (Houndmills: Macmillan, 1989), 55.

[38] Doreen Massey, *World City* (Cambridge: Polity, 2007), 40, 43.

The GLC represented a negative centre of gravity for both the Conservative and Labour parties. The Conservatives and the tabloid press demonized it as the epitome of a 'loony left'.[39] In 1984, Margaret Thatcher notoriously referred to striking miners as the 'enemy within', but the original version of that speech had lumped local government in with the miners as such domestic threats.[40] If the Tories despised the GLC, the Labour Party under Michael Foot and Neil Kinnock despaired of it. To the Labour Party at Westminster, the GLC across the river was a dark lodestar, threatening to lure the party towards electoral ruin.[41] Some Labour MPs complained that London under the GLC had become 'an adventure playground ... for a variety of zany leftwing causes'.[42] With the appearance of Kinnock's 'New Model' Labour and Tony Blair's 'New Labour', the Labour GLC became a chapter of disavowal in the 'narrative of the 1980s and 1990s'.[43]

London was thus not only an economic battleground in the 1980s but a political, social, and cultural one. The 1986 abolition of the GLC, cuts to local government expenditure, and the 1990 abolition of the Inner London Education Authority (ILEA) were critical victories in the rise of Thatcherite neoliberalism. These were part of a deliberate campaign by the Conservative government at 'policing the market order' by eliminating rival systems of economic activity or social provision.[44] This was, according to Anna Marie Smith, a 'strategic moment' in the assertion of centralized power—something, as David Harvey has remarked, 'Thatcher had to abolish in order to accomplish her broader goals'.[45]

---

[39] James Curran, 'The Boomerang Effect: the Press and the Battle for London, 1981–6', in James Curran, Anthony Smith, and Pauline Wingate (eds.), *Impacts and Influences* (London: Methuen, 1987), 112, 140.

[40] Margaret Thatcher Foundation Archives, Margaret Thatcher, Notes for 1922 speech, 19 July 1984, https://www.margaretthatcher.org/document/105563; see also *The Times* (London), 20 July 1984.

[41] See Colm Murphy, 'The "Rainbow Alliance" or the Focus Group? Sexuality and Race in the Labour Party's Electoral Strategy, 1985–7', *Twentieth Century British History* 31/2 (2020): 291–315, doi: 10.1093/tcbh/hwz015.

[42] Quoted in Curran, 'The Boomerang Effect', 122.

[43] William Davies, 'Reasons for Corbyn', *London Review of Books* 39/14 (13 July 2017).

[44] Andrew Gamble, *The Free Economy and the Strong State* (Durham, NC: Duke University Press, 1988), 33.

[45] Anna Marie Smith, *New Right Discourse on Race and Sexuality* (Cambridge: Cambridge University Press, 1994), 15; Harvey, *A Brief History of Neoliberalism*, 60.

0.3

The coil of this book's analysis comes from a collection of particular events, moments, and spaces in 1984. Choosing one year as a turning point in history is, to be sure, a conceit. I do not argue in this book that 1984 is the only critical year or the only turning point in the history of the 1980s. But my choice of such moments or artefacts from 1984 is not arbitrary, nor is it to suggest a tie-in with George Orwell. Rather, each of these illuminates larger social and political changes in 1980s London and helps reveal the meanings of late twentieth-century politics in Britain. There were moments, documented in this book, that did leave a legacy on the development of modern London, such as the development of the Docklands, the passing of the Police and Criminal Evidence Act, and the debates over the abolition of metropolitan democracy in London. But *London, 1984* also examines moments that were both transient—produced by a particular political culture in London in the 1980s—and illustrative of longer-term historical change in contemporary Britain. This is particularly true of racial politics, the position of women, and the progress of gay and lesbian rights in the late twentieth and early twenty-first century. The events described in the present book are rooted in the 1980s, but they have echoes in the present day.

The events examined in *London, 1984* include the GLC's launch of 'Anti-Racist Year', a police raid on Gay's the Word bookshop, a massive anti-apartheid rally, a demonstration on the Thames, the first People's Armada against the redevelopment of the Docklands, and the first Jobs for Change concert. In parliament, there were important initiatives to abolish the GLC begun in 1984 and the passing of a major act that profoundly defined the role of police in everyday life, the Police and Criminal Evidence Act. All these moments in a single year afford an understanding of wider questions of race, sexuality, policing, global politics, the economy, and democratic governance, all of which shaped both London and the nation in the late twentieth century and into the twenty-first century. They also show how the political changes of the late twentieth century, in particular the tension between neoliberalism and social democracy, played out on the ground. I have also used other moments or artefacts from 1984 to explore these questions, some of which arise from the archives of the GLC and other groups in 1984. These include publications, such as Matrix Design Collective's *Making Space: Women and the Man-Made Environment*, a GLC report on racial harassment on East End housing estates, applications for funding from the GLC, notably from community organizations such as the Dalston Children's Centre and the Broadwater Farm Youth Association. These sources afford a glimpse of a different register of social and political change at this time, revealing sometimes overlooked spheres of urban life. They also throw light on important questions around identity, community, and politics.

Of course, this is not a comprehensive survey of urban radicalism in 1984. There are other moments or issues that might have been used, such as green politics, nuclear disarmament, the AIDS crisis, or the miners' strike, some of which have been ably covered in other work.[46] But the subjects covered in the present book nonetheless address critical issues in late twentieth-century British history.

In these different ways, *London, 1984* maps, if not a turning point, a series of moments that illuminate the ragged space between local social democracy, identity politics, and Thatcherite neoliberalism. The book also uses these moments to think about the experience of race, gender, class, and sexual orientation in late twentieth-century London, as well as the intersections among different registers of political culture. The present book does not offer a linear narrative of a single year, nor does it suggest that there were always direct connections between the issues, places, and artefacts described in the separate chapters. The context of race, gender, sexuality, and, indeed, Thatcherism did provide links, but there was also autonomy between events and artefacts. In his study of mid-eighteenth-century England, Nicholas Rogers offered a 'series of cascading, overlapping narratives', each of which, following Pierre Nora's view of event history, 'radiates out of itself to explore larger frames of reference'.[47] This has also been the intent of the present book.

[46] See, for example, Matt Cook, 'Archives of Feeling: The AIDS Crisis in Britain 1987', *History Workshop Journal* 83/1 (2017): 51–78, doi: 10.1093/hwj/dbx001; Diarmaid Kelliher, *Making Cultures of Solidarity: London and the 1984–5 Miners' Strike* (London: Routledge, 2021).
[47] Nicholas Rogers, *Mayhem* (New Haven: Yale University Press, 2012), 5; Pierre Nora, 'The Return of the Event', in Jacques Revel and Lynn Hunt (eds.), *Histories: French Constructions of the Past* (New York: New Press, 1995), 432.

Focusing on a particular year allows a perspective of the city that is sometimes panoramic (as in the political battle waged over the abolition of the GLC, the cultural campaigns around unemployment, and the activism in London against apartheid) and sometimes microscopic, as with the chapters on childcare in Dalston and the racial politics of housing estates in the East End and Tottenham. This is a way of thinking about how historical change in the 1980s was experienced in everyday life and how individual Londoners experienced that change in a variety of roles—as residents on a housing estate, as migrants, as parents, as workers, as consumers, and as political activists—and tried to shape their city in particular ways.

There are several themes that tie together the disparate stories, spaces, and people in this book and illuminate what Nora called 'larger frames of reference'. The first has already been noted: that London in 1984 was at the epicentre of a political fracture in the late twentieth century, between the decline of one dominant political culture, rooted in the post-war consensus, and the rise of another, driven by Thatcherite neo-liberalism. This book argues that London in the mid-1980s held the potential of an alternative political culture, though that future was foreclosed. In each of these moments can be discerned a profound challenge, to either what the city was or what it could become. This challenge was in the form of policy and ideology, in the consideration of racial, gendered, and sexual equality, for example, in democracy and governance (particularly in terms of popular participation in things like economic decision-making and the supervision of the Metropolitan Police), or simply in terms of how people might live differently in the city, what the design collective Matrix called 'new ways of organizing and living our own lives'.[48] These challenges were not always realized, though sometimes they took different, if more muted, forms in the late twentieth and early twenty-first centuries. What these challenges nonetheless underline is that there were worlds beyond Thatcherite neoliberalism in the 1980s. The present book is not intended as an archaeology of a lost London, but rather as a journey through an alternative London that

---

[48] Francis Bradshaw, 'Working with Women', in Matrix, *Making Space: Women and the Man-Made Environment* (London: Verso, 1984; 2022 edition), 90.

can still be glimpsed today, sometimes directly and sometimes out of the corner of an eye.

A central argument of the present book is that new means of social democracy were explored in 1980s London, as illustrated in detailed examinations of particular moments, spaces, and artefacts in 1984. These included new understandings of what the 'social' in democracy meant, particularly in terms of identity and how 'democracy' itself could be practised in the urban sphere. A principal ambition of the book is to historicize what Mercer called 'new social actors and new political subjects' through a history of the city that provided the landscape for those actors and subjects.

This book also argues that in this moment the connections among the local, the national, and the global in London were particularly acute. Such connections are most obvious over issues such as the anti-apartheid movement, but thinking about London in the mid-1980s also affords us the opportunity to understand how postcolonialism, the globalization of the economy, the deindustrialization of the British economy, and the transnational spread of ideas about race, gender, and sexual orientation were experienced on the ground in places such as the Docklands, Tower Hamlets, Hackney, and Tottenham.

A dominant motif of this book is conflict. In London, such conflict was political, between left and right and sometimes between left and left. Conflict was also about identity, in terms of class, race, gender, and sexual orientation. It was also about the nature of community in the city.

Conflict was played out in a variety of urban spaces: in the streets, in parks, within neighbourhoods and housing estates, over bookshops, and even on the Thames. Conflict and struggle took different forms. Some came in familiar guises—protests on the streets and local organizing— and some were products of the late twentieth century, notably the use of advertising and popular culture, as in the fight against abolition and the concerts and festivals organized against the economic policies of the Thatcher government. Such conflict was not simply metaphoric but also literal, particularly seen in racist violence and in the tensions between the police and Black communities.

Challenges and conflicts in 1980s London were not only situated in urban space but also often about urban space. The exploration of urban politics and society in this book is informed by thinking about space. The material environment of the city—its streets, housing estates, shops, parks, and buildings—was at the centre of political and social conflict and helped shape that conflict.[49] The redevelopment of the London Docklands, for instance, prompted a debate about the future shape of London's physical environment and the implications this had for community. The opening of women's centres, bookshops, centres for ethnic minority groups, and centres for gay and lesbian people were, similarly, physical testaments to a struggle over a new kind of urban politics and a new kind of city.[50] Sometimes the conflicts seen in 1984 were about what physical form London would take in the future—between, for example, the proposed glass and steel towers of the Docklands and humbler forms of community housing and enterprise, or, as shown in the example of the Dalston Children's Centre, the remaking of older structures to house new initiatives, a kind of radical retrofitting.

The present book is also concerned with how social and political change was perceived and experienced in 1980s London. In part, it argues that such change was rapid and immediate. This was obviously rooted in the rise of Thatcherism itself as a consciously dynamic and radical government of the right. Thatcherite change cascaded down to ordinary life in myriad forms: unemployment, housing, changes in immigration law, cuts to local government, and so on. But the present book also argues that the consciousness of change was also situated in trajectories other than that of Thatcherism. Among the mothers who established the Dalston Children's Centre, for example, a sense of change had its origins in long-term developments in women's lives, whether this meant reconciling work and childcare, single parenthood, the living of feminism or, for lesbian parents, the attempt to create spaces free from

[49] See, for example, Leif Jerram, *Streetlife* (Oxford: Oxford University Press, 2011); Karl Schlögel, *In Space We Read Time*, trans. Gerrit Jackson (New York: Bard Graduate Centre, 2016); Doreen Massey, *Space, Place and Gender* (Oxford: Polity, 1994); Suzanne Hall, *City, Street and Citizen* (New York: Routledge, 2012).

[50] On the importance of bookshops in this regard, see Colin A. Beckles, ' "We Shall Not Be Terrorized Out of Existence": The Political Legacy of England's Black Bookshops', *Journal of Black Studies* 29/1 (1998): 52–72, doi: 10.1177/002193479802900104; Lucy Delap, 'Feminist Bookstores, Reading Cultures and the Women's Liberation Movement, c. 1974–2000', *History Workshop Journal* 81/1 (2016): 171–96, doi: 10.1093/hwj/dbw002.

discrimination. The struggle over the Gay's the Word bookshop in 1984 was similarly about a moment in the development of gay and lesbian rights, building over many years but culminating in an attempt to assert the rights of gay and lesbian people in London. In this way change was linked to opportunity, often facilitated by local or metropolitan governments. In other spheres the consciousness of change was more painful. In the East End, for example, a white working class perceived the new presence of a growing Bangladeshi community with fear and resentment, while seeing its own communities under threat from offices and gentrification. The consciousness of change heightened the rhetoric around conflict in the 1980s. Whether in politics, in the newspapers, or on the street, there was, as there is today, a polarized discourse, often extreme in its portrayal of difference.

London, 1984 explores these tensions around identity and community in London. Within larger fields of conflict and change, there were particular struggles to assert both older and newer forms of community. Again, some of this was painful. In the Docklands, 'community' described a largely working-class area attempting to forestall what was perceived as an inimical economic development that would destroy community. On East End estates, 'community' meant the conflict between an older, white working-class community, shaped by a sense of grievance, loss, and fear, and a newer, ethnic minority community, shaped by racial violence and harassment. New kinds of communities were based in gender and sexual identity, the struggle for the rights of ethnic minorities, or simply in a sense of an alternative. Identity was clearly central to both conflict and community in London in the 1980s. The post-1968 period is often discussed as characterized by the rise of identity politics. The GLC Leader at this time, Ken Livingstone, wanted democratic socialist politics to slip the older moorings of class and move toward race, gender, and sexual orientation. Attacks upon the new identity politics were often launched from the older identity politics based upon whiteness and class.

Understandings of community and belonging were, similarly, often thought through in relationship to particular spaces. Patrick Wright suggested that the GLC and local community organizations and activists had created, in tandem, a new landscape of the city. This made visible a new politics. Just as gay and lesbian communities on both sides of the Atlantic, according to Manuel Castells and Karen Murphy, sought to 'become visible, without danger' in the 1970s and 1980s through acquiring a 'territorial basis', a new politics based on race, gender, and sexuality also sought to find a political home in the city in 1980s London.[51] In the Docklands in 1984, this also meant retaining visibility for working-class communities against what was perceived as the obliterating force of neoliberal economic development. The subtitle to Anna Minton's 2017 *Big Capital* was 'Who is London For?'[52] That was a central question to newer and older urban communities in 1984.

Identity politics has sometimes been characterized as 'post-material', but in the 1980s many of the things sought by new social actors were very material: a physical space in the city; childcare; improved employment prospects; freedom to walk around the city without what was perceived as harassment by the police; freedom to be in the city without physical or sexual threat; better housing; legal protection in the workplace and in public.[53] The new identity politics was as rooted in the material world as much as an older politics had been.[54]

There are many resonances between London in 1984 and the present day. We can see in 1984, for example, a presaging of some of the cultural conflicts and tensions of the present day, around questions of identity, not only struggles between progress and reaction but struggles within ideas of progress. What is also clear between the two eras is the increasing importance of race in British society, whether in terms of the experience of racial minorities, the form of racism, or attempts to articulate anti-racism. With regard to race and sexuality, we can also see the continuing importance of policing in a literal sense. The actions and attitudes of the

[51] Manuel Castells and Karen Murphy, 'Organization of San Francisco's Gay Community', in Norman I. Fainstein and Susan S. Fainstein (eds.), *Urban Policy Under Capitalism* (Beverly Hills: Sage, 1982), 238.

[52] Anna Minton, *Big Capital: Who is London For?* (London: Penguin Random House, 2017).

[53] On the 'post-material' in social movements, see Ronald Inglehart, *The Silent Revolution* (Princeton: Princeton University Press, 1977); Adam Lent, *British Social Movements since 1945* (London: Palgrave Macmillan, 2001); Matthew Hilton, 'Politics is Ordinary: Non-Governmental Organisations and Political Participation in Contemporary Britain', *Twentieth Century British History* 22/2 (2011): 230–68, doi: 10.1093/tcbh/hwr002.

[54] On this, see Stephen Brooke, 'Sexual Rights, Human Rights, the Material and the Post-Material in Britain, 1970 to 2010', *Revue Française de Civilisation Britannique* 14/3 (2015): 114–28.

Metropolitan Police and other state agencies (such as Customs and Excise) played a critical role in shaping the experience of minorities in the city in the 1980s and continue to do so today. The year 1984 demonstrated something that remains important today: the increasing visibility and power of minority groups and of what has been called identity politics around race, gender, and sexuality, and the tensions and reactions that are provoked by that new visibility and power.

Finally, a study of 1984 perhaps illuminates a tension that is more difficult to articulate precisely. In 1984, there were two Londons that vied for attention, one shaped by the neoliberalism of the Thatcher government, another facilitated by the social democracy of the GLC. It could be argued that both remain in contemporary London. Clearly, London is a markedly neoliberal city, shaped by finance and capital. But it also has vestiges of that other London, in the city's progressiveness, its diversity, and its cosmopolitanism. This was not really an accommodation between one London and another and not really the capitulation of one London to another, but rather, in the early 1980s, as this account of 1984 suggests, the beginning of an often uneasy coexistence.

This book comprises nine chapters. Chapter 1 explores the fight over abolition in 1984 as a way of introducing the background to the work of the Labour GLC and of exploring its political meanings and impacts. 'Anti-Racist Year', launched in January 1984, is the subject of Chapter 2, which lays out an example of the new equality initiatives that the GLC encouraged, both at the centre in County Hall, and in the grass roots among community organizations. Chapter 3 begins with three events in the spring of 1984—a protest staged on the Thames by local communities against Docklands development, a large rock concert organized by the GLC to promote an alternative to Thatcherite neoliberalism, and the purchase of a site on the South Bank by a community organization for development. All three throw into sharp relief the economic conflicts provoked by neoliberal change.

Chapters 4, 5, and 6 move to studies of particular artefacts, spaces, and organizations, which illuminate issues around identity, sexuality, and politics in the 1980s. Structured around the publication of *Making Space* by feminist design collective Matrix in 1984, Chapter 4 examines the impact of feminism upon London, both through the prism of a particular organization and through the work of the GLC's Women's Committee at County Hall, both of which sought to create a city for women. Chapter 5 revisits the police raid on the Gay's the Word bookshop in 1984, a controversy which threw into sharp relief the growth of gay and lesbian politics in the 1980s and the constraints faced by that movement. Chapter 6 begins with the funding application made in 1984 by the Dalston Children's Centre, the history of which in the 1980s demonstrated both the possibilities of the alternative politics of that decade and its tensions.

The question of race links the final three chapters of the book. Chapter 7 moves back to a more panoramic vision of London with an account of the anti-apartheid demonstration in June 1984; this was an event which linked the local and the global in London's radical politics in the eighties. The book concludes with two chapters rooted in studies of particular housing estates, one in east London, the other in north London. Both chapters highlight the dominant role played by race in the 1980s. Chapter 8 uses a report on racial harassment on East End estates in September 1984 to offer a focused picture of everyday life on one, the Lincoln Estate, where racial harassment and violence shaped the lives of white and ethnic minority people. The final chapter of the book explores two contrasting approaches to race and policing—the passing of the Police and Criminal Evidence bill in October 1984 and the tensions on a north London estate, Broadwater Farm, which erupted into violence a year later.

London, 1984: Conflict and Change in the Radical City. Stephen Brooke, Oxford University Press.
© Stephen Brooke 2024. DOI: 10.1093/9780191895395.003.0001

1

GLC London, 1981–4

In September 1984, the Leader of the GLC, Ken Livingstone, and three of his Labour colleagues resigned their council seats, prompting by-elections. This was an act of political theatre, designed to demonstrate public support for the GLC at a moment when the Conservative government at Westminster was trying to abolish it. What became the 1985 Local Government Act made good on a promise set out by the Conservatives during the 1983 general election to do away with six metropolitan authorities, including the GLC, that were deemed 'wasteful...unnecessary' and 'grossly extravagant'.[1]

The September 1984 by-elections provoked two contrasting responses from across the political spectrum. On 20 September, *The Sun* told its readers:

> In nine months, the [GLC] has distributed £31 million to voluntary organizations. *Here are just some of the 2,073 groups which have received amounts ranging from £111 to £77,835.*
>
> Babies Against the Bomb; English Collective of Prostitutes; Lesbian Line; Rights of Women (ROW); Cypriot Community Workers Act Group and Joint Council for the Welfare of Immigrants; I Drum; Migrants Action Group; London Region CND; London Region Trade Union Campaign for Nuclear Disarmament; National Peace Council....

The litany went on and on. Once *The Sun* had exhausted itself and possibly its readers, it asked, '[d]o *you think this is the way rate-payers money should be spent?* **If so, then Red Ken is your man. You deserve him!**'[2]

---

[1] Conservative Party General Election Manifesto, 1983, http://www.conservativemanifesto.com/1983/1983-conservative-manifesto.shtml.

[2] *The Sun* (London), 20 September 1984.

That same month, in an article entitled 'Face the Future' for the *New Socialist,* a publication with an admittedly much smaller pool of readers than *The Sun,* the critic and academic Stuart Hall stated:

> My favourite GLC slogan, plastered across a most unprepossessing corner of a sliproad onto the Brent Cross roundabout, is 'GLC WASTE DISPOSAL UNIT WORKING FOR YOU'. And a good thing, too, or the rubbish would be up to our ears.[3]

That sign was a humble example of what Hall thought the Labour-led GLC had been doing in London since 1981, making '*visible*' the 'thousand other collective needs' of ordinary people and grounding politics in 'the everyday experiences of popular urban life and culture'.[4] Hall's influence as a cultural theorist in the 1970s and 1980s is unrivalled, particularly in the thought he gave to the question of race in British society, established by his work with the Birmingham-based Centre for Contemporary Cultural Studies and the impact he obtained through television programmes such as *It Ain't Half Racist Mum* (1979) and other contributions to the public discussion of race. But the life of the GLC particularly engaged Hall in how he thought about post-war social democracy, neoliberalism, identity, and, not least, the city itself. If the GLC is a recurring force in the pages of the present book, Stuart Hall is a recurring presence as one of the most incisive observers of London in the 1980s.[5] To Hall, the GLC had become, since 1981, 'the most important front in the struggle against Thatcherism'. The abolition battle in 1984 represented a 'direct confrontation' between the 'two essential conflicting principles of English political life...the camp of the profit motive and possessive liberalism...and the camp of collective social need and the public interest'.[6]

What made Hall and *The Sun* unlikely bedfellows in 1984 was their shared conviction that the battle over the GLC was not only about rates

---

[3] Stuart Hall, 'Face the Future', *New Socialist* 19 (September 1984): 37.

[4] Hall, 'Face the Future', 37, 39.

[5] See Michael Keith, 'Urbanism and City Spaces in the Work of Stuart Hall', *Cultural Studies* 23/4 (2009): 538–58, doi: 10.1080/09502380902950989.

[6] Hall, 'Face the Future', 37.

and local democracy but also about deep-seated fault lines in British society. For Hall, the struggle was about what fundamentally animated political life in Britain. The GLC was a breakwater against the rising tide of neoliberalism. In giving life to a politics that reflected the landscape of ordinary life, the GLC was also a welcome disruption of what Hall perceived as the deadening tendencies of post-war social democracy, represented by the Labour Party. The GLC represented an alternative future against the failures of the past and the threats of the present.

The Sun shared Hall's view of the GLC as a profoundly disruptive force, but its reaction was one of revulsion. To *The Sun*, the GLC was a cipher for a new kind of identity politics, focused on race, gender, and sexual orientation. This menaced more traditional forms of social identity, such as class and the family, an affront to accepted norms, perpetrated by what the Conservative minister Norman Tebbit termed 'Livingstone and his weird friends'.[7] The fight between the Conservatives and the GLC was an early version of the culture wars of the early twenty-first century. *The Sun* and other newspapers similarly portrayed the GLC in the terms of a moral panic, something first to be demonized, and then effaced.[8] This was itself a kind of identity politics, a cultural struggle born of fear and grievance, shaped into a conservative populism based on white, heterosexual outrage at the usual suspects: ethnic minorities, feminists, and gays and lesbians, with pacifists, socialists, environmentalists, and, apparently, Cypriot community workers thrown in for good measure.

Both Hall and *The Sun* suggested, in very different ways, that what was at stake with the debate over the GLC in September 1984 was fundamental to an understanding of British society and politics in the 1980s, one of the fractures that opened up in that decade. The particular nature of the GLC after 1981 not only suggested a new way forward for left politics in Britain, but also provoked the Conservative government

---

[7] See Anna Marie Smith, *New Right Discourse on Race and Sexuality* (Cambridge: Cambridge University Press, 1994); Tebbit quoted in Ken Livingstone, *You Can't Say That* (London: Faber & Faber, 2011), 204.

[8] James Curran, 'The Boomerang Effect: The Press and the Battle for London, 1981–6', in James Curran, Anthony Smith, and Pauline Wingate (eds.), *Impacts and Influences: Essays on Media Power in the Twentieth Century* (London: Methuen, 1987), 113.

into foreclosing that alternative through abolition. This chapter reviews the work of the GLC between 1981 and 1984. This is not to overidentify the GLC with the 1980s or suggest it was the only agent of change in that decade, but to stress that its programme between 1981 and 1984 made visible, as Hall argued, critical changes in British society in the 1970s and 1980s.

1.1

In his recollection of 1980s London, the writer Michael Bracewell evoked a city on the cusp of change, 'unaware, as yet, of the approaching lights and construction sites', whose 'Deep Space Industrial Style' was emerging as 'Armani meets *Alien*'.[9] A sense of contrast tempered this London, between sleek new workplaces and worn dole offices, desolation and development, gloss and grit. Laura Oldfield Ford's graphic novel *Savage Messiah* (2011), set in the aftermath of the Thatcher era, portrayed the urban dissonance left in Thatcher's wake, 'gleaming obelisks overseeing dilapidated streets'.[10]

That duality emerged from the atmosphere of crisis and challenge hanging over London at the dawn of the 1980s. The city's population was in decline. Inner London had 2.5 million people, the least since the mid-nineteenth century. Greater London stood at 6.7 million, the lowest it had been since 1901. One urban planner described this as a 'frightening scale of population loss'.[11] London's economy was also at a turning point. Perhaps more than at any point since the 1870s, economic decline was keenly felt in the capital. The London Docks closed for good in 1981, ending an important source of employment in the East End. In September 1982, there were nearly 400,000 unemployed in London, one-eighth of the London workforce. In Stepney alone, one-third of the workforce was unemployed. Between 1978 and 1989, 336,000 jobs were lost in manufacturing in greater London.

---

[9] Michael Bracewell, *Souvenir* (London: White Rabbit, 2021), 63.
[10] Laura Oldfield Ford, *Savage Messiah* (London: Verso, 2011), No 1 (2005), unpaginated.
[11] Drew Stevenson, 'Taking Liberties at Coin Street', *Town and Country Planning* 51 (September–October 1982): 206.

Economic deprivation was a recurring motif in studies of eighties London. Between 1985 and 1987, the social scientist Peter Townsend conducted a survey of poverty and labour in the capital, a conscious return to Charles Booth's enquiry of a century before. Townsend argued that London's economy was 'in deeper crisis than it has been for a hundred years...[i]n certain respects it is worse than the 1930s'.[12] Townsend and his colleagues estimated that at least 500,000 people were unemployed in the spring of 1984. The main causes were the shedding of jobs associated with the Docklands and the collapse of manufacturing, even in formerly buoyant areas such as west London with the rundown of industrial estates in Park Royal and on the Great West Road. In some boroughs, such as Hackney and Tower Hamlets, there were unemployment rates of over 20 per cent. High unemployment was particularly pronounced among ethnic minority youth. Factors such as unemployment, old age, low pay, and gender resulted in 300,000 people below the poverty line, 600,000 on supplementary benefit, and 900,000 with 'incomes on the margins', a total of 1.8 million people out of a population of about 6.7 million.[13]

Deprivation was written on the landscape. David Thomson's portrait of Camden in 1981 showed an area steeped in decay: 'beautiful Regency houses falling to bits, scabby stucco, a broken window with a curtain flapping out, another mended with cardboard which had come loose, some doors and ground floor windows sealed with corrugated iron'. The human cost of this landscape was high: Thomson commented that he had 'never seen so many destitute people sitting for warmth in Cam. Tn. Tube station'.[14] This coincided with concern about the state of the inner city across Britain, a concern which prompted enquiries from official and non-official institutions.[15] The vision of the inner city was often

---

[12] Peter Townsend, with Paul Corrigan and Ute Kowarzik, *Poverty and Labour in London* (London: Low Pay Unit/Poverty Research London, 1987), 12.

[13] Townsend et al., *Poverty and Labour in London*, 57.

[14] David Thomson, *In Camden Town* (London: Hutchinson, 1983), 158.

[15] See Otto Saumarez Smith, 'The Inner City Crisis and the End of Urban Modernism in 1970s Britain', *Twentieth Century British History* 27/4 (December 2016): 578–98, doi: 10.1093/tcbh/hww032; Aaron Andrews, Alistair Kefford, and Daniel Warner, 'Community, Culture, Crisis: the Inner City in England, c. 1960–90', *Urban History* 20/2 (June 2023): 202–13, doi: 10.1017/S0963926821000729.

bleak. One contribution to the Church of England's Commission on Urban Priority Areas, which resulted in *Faith in the City* (1985), spoke of the 'human pain, misery and despair which is all too easily found among those living in the inner city'.[16]

But decline was not the only characteristic of London's economy in the 1980s. Over the decade, London's finance and service sectors gained 257,000 jobs.[17] Outer London's unemployment rate was half that of inner London. In his portrait of London poverty, Townsend could also point to "conspicuous wealth and rising prosperity" on the other side of the social spectrum as some Londoners enjoyed the benefits produced increasingly by unregulated financial markets and the lower taxes that came with a Conservative government.[18] *The Spectator* recorded a 28-year-old stockbroker's boast: 'I got another bonus last week. Third month running. So should make £127,000 this year in all.'[19] The photographer Anna Fox visually documented this world in *Work Stations* (1988), furnished with sleek offices, microcomputers, and briefcase-sized mobile phones.[20] The affluence of the decade was also reflected in parochial and international archetypes such as Sloane Rangers and yuppies. In eighties London, to co-opt the title of a 1987 Caryl Churchill play, *Serious Money* and serious poverty were side by side.

Multiracialism was also a profound change marking late twentieth-century London. The patterns of migration to the capital since the arrival of the HMT *Empire Windrush* at Tilbury Docks in 1948 'changed the face of the Londoner more significantly than any event since the Norman Conquest', in the words of Jerry White.[21] By the 1980s, about a fifth of the London population was of Black or Asian descent. Areas such as Southall and Spitalfields saw high levels of settlement from the Indian subcontinent, while Brixton and Notting Hill were home to large

[16] Archbishop of Canterbury's Commission on Urban Priority Areas, 'Submission by the Urban Ministry Project on Training for Ministry', 20 March 1984, ACUPA/R/1/2/18, ACUPA (84) 18, Lambeth Palace Archives, London.

[17] Figures from Nick Buck, Matthew Drennan, and Kenneth Newton, 'Dynamics of the Metropolitan Economy', in Fainstein, Gordon, and Harloe (eds.), *Divided Cities*, 83.

[18] Townsend et al., *Poverty and Labour in London*, 71.

[19] Nicholas Coleridge, 'The New Club of Rich Young Men', *Spectator* (London), 15 March 1986.

[20] See Anna Fox, 'Work Stations', https://annafox.co.uk/photography/work-stations-2/.

[21] Jerry White, *London in the Twentieth Century* (London: Bodley Head, 2017 edition), 131.

Afro-Caribbean communities. Other waves of settlement also affected London's demography, such as the migration of Kenyan and Ugandan Asians in 1968 and 1972 and Vietnamese, Iranian, and Kurdish refugees in the 1970s and 1980s. Inner London boroughs were markedly diverse and cosmopolitan by the 1980s, leaving outer boroughs such as Bromley and Barking as the remaining bastions of monoracial London. The emergence of multiracial London was not without pain. The clashes in Notting Hill between white and Black Britons of Caribbean and African origin in the 1950s were followed in the 1960s and 1970s by violence meted out to South Asians, particularly in the East End. The rise of fascist and racist organizations such as the National Front in the seventies led to the formation of Rock Against Racism, which held a huge demonstration involving 100,000 people at a concert in Victoria Park in 1978 as a defence of multiracial London.

Cities have always, of course, been viewed as problems to be solved. London had long been such a problem.[22] But this seemed particularly true in the late twentieth century. In part, this had to do with what was called the 'rediscovery' of poverty in the 1960s; in part, it had to do with national economic decline in the 1970s; in part it had to do with a perception of increased racial discord in the cities. All factors contributed to a picture of what James Callaghan, as Home Secretary, called 'severe social deprivation in a number of our cities and towns'.[23] In 1968, the Labour government began an Urban Programme which, by the 1980s, had a budget of £165 million.[24] Before 1979 the problem of the city was met largely by central government relying upon the public sector (and, in particular, local government) to provide services and stimulus.

Immediately after her June 1987 victory, Margaret Thatcher told party workers that 'we've got a big job to do in some of those inner cities'.[25] Her governments took a radical approach to urban policy. In the first place, they displaced the power and relevance of local government,

---

[22] See, for example, John Davis, *Reforming London* (Oxford: Oxford University Press, 1988).
[23] *Parliamentary Debates,* Commons, Fifth Series, 22 July 1968, vol. 769, c. 40.
[24] See Camilla Schofield and Ben Jones, ' "Whatever Community Is, This is Not It": Notting Hill and the Reconstruction of "Race" in Postwar Britain', *Journal of British Studies* 58/1 (January 2019): 149, doi: 10.1017/jbr.2018.174.
[25] Margaret Thatcher, Speech, 12 June 1987, https://www.margaretthatcher.org/document/106653.

most spectacularly with the abolition of six metropolitan councils in 1986 and the introduction of the poll tax in 1990, which undercut local power of taxation. Central government steadily reduced its financial support to local authorities, privatized council housing (with the 1980 Housing Act) and began the private outsourcing of what had been council services. Just as importantly, the Thatcher government sought to remove the public sector from the solution of urban problems. Regeneration—a term much in vogue in the latter stages of the Thatcher government—would be effected through the private sector. Of course, the state would help the market in this regard, with the establishment of low-taxed and lightly regulated enterprise zones, urban development, and regeneration grants targeted at the private sector, and, most importantly for London, the establishment of the London Docklands Development Corporation (LDDC) in 1981. The derelict acres of the Docklands would be brought to life through the LDDC and the private sector. This change represented a profound 'urban entrepreneurialism'.[26] The deregulation of the City in 1986, the so-called 'Big Bang', cemented the triumph of a neoliberal, globalized London driven by finance.[27] David Edgerton has argued that '[t] he City rebuilt the city'.[28]

1.2

On 7 May 1981, the Labour Party won the most seats in the GLC elections. After the victory, the left-winger Ken Livingstone deposed the moderate Andrew McIntosh as leader of the majority Labour group in the GLC. The subsequent six years of Labour government in London, ended by the abolition of the GLC on 1 April 1986, was a radical experiment in local democracy. The character of this government owed much to contemporary events, but it was also the result of several different developments at the local level in London beginning in the 1960s.

---

[26] Michael Parkinson, 'The Thatcher Government's Urban Policy, 1979–89: A Review', *Town Planning Review* 60/4 (November 1989): 429; see also A. Thornley, *Urban Planning under Thatcher* (London: Routledge, 1993).

[27] See, for example, Doreen Massey, *World City* (London: Polity, 2007).

[28] David Edgerton, *The Rise and Fall of the British Nation* (London: Penguin, 2019), 471.

Local government had been an important vehicle for social democracy in London between the wars, most famously under the stewardship of Herbert Morrison, but by the time the Greater London Council replaced the old London County Council as the metropolitan authority in 1963, Labour politics in the capital had become anaemic.[29] In the late sixties, a new energy was brought to local politics by a younger and more radical generation of activists. Some came from the new social movements of the 1960s, some from community organizing. They were disillusioned with national Labour politics.[30] There was a desire to move beyond the long-standing basis of support for Labour at the local level—established, 'traditional' working-class communities—towards new communities and interest groups. Groups born of the social movements in the 1960s contributed a new dynamism to politics at the local level, whether from the Women's Liberation Movement, gay and lesbian rights groups, or organizations representing ethnic minorities.[31]

In the 1970s, bolstered by disillusion with the 1974–9 Labour governments, the new urban left grew in London. It flourished in organizations such as the Campaign for Labour Democracy, the Labour Co-ordinating Committee, and the Socialist Campaign for Labour Victory. The left also grew in power within local constituency parties. A more radical generation of Labour politicians controlled borough councils, most notably in Islington, Wandsworth, Lambeth, and Lewisham, reasserting the local state as a lodestone of democratic socialism. One important aspect

[29] See Stewart Lansley, Sue Goss, and Christian Wolmar, *Councils in Conflict: The Rise and Fall of the Municipal Left* (London: Macmillan, 1989), 3.

[30] See Hilary Wainwright, *A Tale of Two Parties* (London: Hogarth Press, 1987); Patrick Seyd, *The Rise and Fall of the Labour Left* (London: Macmillan, 1987).

[31] On women's liberation, see Eve Setch, 'The Face of Metropolitan Feminism: The London Women's Liberation Workshop, 1969–79', *Twentieth-Century British History* 13/2 (June 2002): 171–90, doi: 10.1093/tcbh/13.2.171; Sheila Rowbotham, Lynne Segal, and Hilary Wainwright, *Beyond the Fragments* (London: Merlin, 1979); on gay and lesbian issues, see Lucy Robinson, *Gay Men and the Left in Britain* (Manchester: Manchester University Press, 2007), Rebecca Jennings, *Tom Boys and Bachelor Girls: A Lesbian History of Postwar Britain* (Manchester: Manchester University Press, 2013), Matt Cook, *Queer Domesticities* (Basingstoke: Palgrave Macmillan, 2014); on ethnic minorities, see Kennetta Hammond Perry, *London is the Place for Me* (Oxford: Oxford University Press, 2016), David G. Pearson, *Race, Class and Political Activism: A Study of West Indians in Britain* (Farnborough: Gower, 1981), Gideon Ben-Tovim, John Gabriel, Ian Law, and Kathleen Stredder, *The Local Politics of Race* (London: Macmillan, 1986), A. Sivanandan, 'From Resistance to Rebellion', in *A Different Hunger* (London: Pluto, 1982), 3–55, Sarah Glynn, *Class, Ethnicity and Religion in the Bengali East End* (Manchester: Manchester University Press, 2014).

of this was the belief that the local state could also be a force of decentralization and the devolution of power, as an exercise in a new kind of democratic socialism, 'in and against the state' as the writer Cynthia Cockburn described it.[32] In 1977, the left gained control of the London Labour Party.[33]

Ken Livingstone was very much a standard-bearer for this new Labour politics in London. Livingstone was 36 when he deposed Andrew McIntosh as leader of the GLC Labour group. He had joined the party in 1968 and gravitated to its left. With Lambeth borough leader Ted Knight and Jeremy Corbyn, then a Haringey council member, he helped establish *London Labour Briefing*, a forum for the left at the local level. Livingstone also distinguished himself by speaking out on gay and lesbian rights and anti-racism. He was not, ideologically, a strict Marxist, unlike many emerging from the New Left; rather, his radicalism fell within a tradition of radical, ethical socialism.[34]

Once in power, Livingstone had strong allies on the left within the GLC Labour group. These included John McDonnell, who assumed the role of Chair of Finance, Valerie Wise, the youngest woman to have won a London council seat, Paul Boateng, a Black lawyer who later helped run the Ethnic Minorities Committee, Andy Harris, who became Chair of the Planning Committee, Frances Morrell (who went on to head the Inner London Education Authority), Tony Banks, who chaired the Arts and Recreation Committee, and Michael Ward, Chair of the Industry and Employment Committee. Illtyd Harrington, a figure from the centre who had worked with Andrew McIntosh as Deputy Leader, stayed on. It is important to note two things about the years of Labour rule in London in the 1980s. In the first place, its popularity with voters was not strong until it was threatened with abolition.[35] Secondly, even within inner

---

[32] See Cynthia Cockburn, *The Local State* (London: Pluto Press, 1977).

[33] See Franco Bianchini, 'Cultural Policy and Political Strategy: The British Labour Party's Approach to Arts Policy, with Particular Reference to the 1981–86 GLC Experiment', PhD dissertation, University of Manchester, 1996, 184, https://eprints.soton.ac.uk/414571/1/17._Final_submission_of_thesis.pdf.

[34] See John Carvel, *Citizen Ken* (London: Chatto & Windus/Hogarth Press, 1984), 13; Curran, 'The Boomerang Effect', 114.

[35] See Christopher T. Husbands, 'Attitudes to Local Government in London: Evidence from Opinion Surveys and the GLC By-Elections of 20 September 1984', *London Journal* 11/1 (1985): 59–74, doi: 10.1179/ldn.1985.11.1.59.

London, there remained Tory borough councils, such as Westminster, Wandsworth, and Kensington and Chelsea, that were sites of varying degrees of resistance to the Labour GLC just as the GLC was a site of resistance to Westminster.

The new Labour GLC brought into power a belief that London was in crisis. The party's doorstopper of a manifesto for the 1981 municipal elections, *A Socialist Policy for the GLC*, argued that 'London's economy is in serious difficulty', characterized by 'industrial decline, worsening living standards and conditions for work for many Londoners, and the threats of technological unemployment and cuts in the public sector' and a devastated city: '[r]ows of empty buildings and stretches of vacant land, abandoned by industry'.[36] This picture of crisis in London was sharpened by a sense of political challenge and conflict. The Conservative government and the forces of capital posed 'an alarming–and unholy– mixture of blind prejudice and far-fetched gimmickry', according to the 1981 manifesto, with the government relying upon the 'forces of the market' and 'private greed'.[37]

Though the Labour GLC was perhaps best remembered as being in the vanguard of identity politics, its 1981 manifesto did not emphasize questions of race, gender, or sexuality, though it did commit a Labour GLC to 'counter the discrimination' against women, ethnic minorities, and gays.[38] Rather, the focus of the manifesto was on the economy and transport. The most radical proposal was to cut fares on London Transport by 25 per cent. In terms of the economy, the London Labour Party was determined to solve the crisis of London by 'counteracting the market forces which have led inexorably to decline'.[39] The public sector, not the free market, was the agent to deal with 'London's economic problems'.[40] Planning to solve unemployment would be taken up by the GLC's Industry and Employment Committee and a new body, the Greater London Enterprise Board. But the manifesto promised that this would not be an old, top-down state *dirigisme*. Rather, drawing upon the critique of centralism developed in the 1970s, there was a commitment

---

[36] *A Socialist Policy for the GLC* (London: London Labour Party, 1980), 6, 7, 8.
[37] *A Socialist Policy for the GLC*, 5.   [38] *A Socialist Policy for the GLC*, 12.
[39] *A Socialist Policy for the GLC*, 13.
[40] *A Socialist Policy for the GLC*, 7.

to revive the deadened relationship between the state and citizen. State-led planning would be 'democratic planning in conjunction with London's working people', guided by 'the extension of democratic control, over decision about new investment'.[41] The 1981 GLC manifesto emphasized the importance of popular planning, meaning the involvement of local groups and stakeholders in economic decision-making, something that was illustrated in its approach to the regeneration of the Docklands.[42]

The commitment to widening local democracy was reflected in other spheres. It would be realized by aiding 'appropriate neighbourhood, community and other interest groups', even while respecting 'the independence of these groups'.[43] The most controversial proposal in the manifesto was to make the Metropolitan Police more accountable to the GLC. A Police Committee would monitor the police and handle complaints, towards the end of 'democratic control' of the police force.[44] This policy was a direct response to what was perceived as the racist policing of Black communities in the 1970s.

An important element of the GLC's approach and the influence of Livingstone and other members of the urban New Left was an ambivalent approach to class as a structuring identity in politics. Through the 1970s there had been a desire to move Labour's base beyond the working classes towards other social groups. In part, this developed from an interest in anti-racism, anti-sexism, and anti-heterosexism, and in part it was an electoral calculation that such groups showed growth and dynamism, while the working classes, particularly with the decline of manufacturing in London, were losing strength. Ken Livingstone consistently advocated that Labour shift its focus. In 1983, he told the radical activist and writer Tariq Ali:

I have always felt that the Labour Party's almost exclusive concentration on the employed male white working class was a weakness ... you can't

---

[41] A Socialist Policy for the GLC, 5, 6.
[42] On the Alternative Economic Strategy, see Mark Wickham-Jones, *Economic Strategy and the Labour Party* (New York: St. Martin's Press, 1996), ch. 3; John Callaghan, 'The Rise and Fall of the Alternative Economic Strategy: From Internationalization of Capital to Globalization', *Contemporary British History* 14/3 (2000): 105–30, doi: 10.1080/13619460008581596.
[43] A Socialist Policy for the GLC, 5, 121.   [44] A Socialist Policy for the GLC, 78.

transform society solely on that basis. You need a coalition which includes skilled and unskilled workers, unemployed, women and black people as well as the sexually oppressed minorities. A socialist political party must act broadly for and with all the oppressed in our society.[45]

In 1984, he acknowledged the tensions of this approach: he had met people who told him, 'I've voted Labour all my life but I'm not voting for you because of your grants to those lesbians and queers.'[46] After the GLC's abolition, Beatrix Campbell and Martin Jacques, writing in *Marxism Today*, argued that the attempt to 'identify new constituencies previously unrecognized and buried by Labour's politics' was also rooted in the GLC's 'preparedness to see and profile London as it is'. These constituencies, not class, would be the foundation of future Labour support.[47]

The flagship policy of the new Labour GLC was 'Fares Fair', launched in October 1981, which reduced fares on London Transport by nearly a third, funded by a 5p increase in the rates. It was the failure of this policy that most profoundly shaped what the GLC did between 1981 and 1986. Fares Fair irritated a Conservative central government intent upon shredding local government expenditure, but the immediate challenge came from the leafy Conservative borough of Bromley. Its Tory council objected to ratepayers paying for subsidies to services that the outer suburbs would not use, and it took the GLC to court. The Appeals Court and the Law Lords declared Fares Fair illegal, on the grounds that the GLC had a fiduciary duty to provide a transport service that was economical, not for commuters, but for ratepayers.

It is a pleasing irony that, by wrecking Fares Fair, the burghers of Bromley simply enabled a more radical direction for the GLC. The frustration of the GLC's initiative left a huge social democratic surplus in the GLC budget, 'a full purse to finance a wide range of alternative projects'.[48] One GLC officer recalled, 'the rest of the GLC was left with all

[45]   Ken Livingstone and Tariq Ali, 'Why Labour Lost', *New Left Review* 140 (1983): 37–8.
[46]   Ken Livingstone, 'Renaissance Labour Style', *Marxism Today* (December 1984): 22.
[47]   Beatrix Campbell and Martin Jacques, 'Goodbye to the GLC', *Marxism Today* (April 1986): 8–9.
[48]   Lansley, Goss, and Wolmar, *Councils in Conflict*, 50.

this money and didn't know what to do with it. We were able to spend, spend, spend'.[49] The immediate beneficiary was the GLC's grants programme. The Council had the statutory ability to make grants to voluntary organizations which might provide 'a wide range of recreational facilities and assistance' to Londoners, or to activities that it deemed in the interests of Londoners, or that might help with the 'provision of certain health, welfare or child-care services'.[50] This helped the GLC's alternative initiatives both in economic policy and in the cultivation of and support for new constituencies based upon gender, sexual orientation, and race. After assuming office, the Labour GLC established several new committees: the Ethnic Minorities Committee (July 1981), the Police Committee (July 1981), the Gay Working Party (January 1982), and the Women's Committee (June 1982). The Gay Working Party had initially included lesbians, but a separate Lesbian Working Party was eventually set up within the structure of the Women's Committee. In concert with established GLC committees, such as the Arts and Recreation Committee, these new bodies were given the responsibility of dispensing grant aid to a variety of local groups. Part of the work of the new committees was to fund a variety of feminist, gay and lesbian, and ethnic minority organizations. There were those, on the left, who lamented a 'surrender' to the 'capitalist establishment', leaving only 'the small print, tiny grants to the publishers of feminist and gay magazines and the establishment of committees on the rights of women and ethnic minorities', but this was, conversely, also a 'window of opportunity for Labour's "rainbow coalition"'.[51] Spending on grant aid increased dramatically, from £6 million in 1981 to £50 million in 1984, with a particularly large increase coming in 1984.[52] In overall budgetary terms, that year external legal counsel recognized the 'prudence' of the GLC, while acknowledging that the main increase had come in the number of

---

[49] Quoted in Daniel Egan, *The Politics of Economic Restructuring in London, 1981–6* (Lewiston: Edwin Mellen, 2001), 109.

[50] GLC, Report by the Director-General, 17 February 1982, LMA, GLC/DG/PRE/223/01.

[51] Quoted in Livingstone, *You Can't Say That*, 208; Lansley, Goss, and Wolmar, *Councils in Conflict*, 50.

[52] Figures from Lansley, Goss, and Wolmar, *Councils in Conflict*, 55.

grants made to voluntary organizations, particularly with respect to ethnic minorities and women.[53]

There was certainly a political opportunity here for the GLC to nurture new constituencies. But it should also be noted that many of the grants made over the life of the GLC went to largely uncontroversial programmes, such as childcare, and much went to programmes of general economic development which helped older constituencies as well, such as the working classes. Nonetheless, it remains clear that the defeat of Fares Fair meant that what had been muted in the 1981 manifesto— identity politics—became a dominant leitmotif of the GLC's governance between 1981 and 1986.

1.3

The work of the Labour GLC was quickly read by the Conservatives and the right-wing media as extremist. Soon after the 1981 election, the GLC was being slated for making local government in London a 'haven for political loons and crackpots.'[54] In the midst of the arguments over Fares Fair early in 1982, Margaret Thatcher had written, in the margins of a memo on the situation, 'this is getting into a mess and we must take a firm hold quickly.'[55] Several months later, a member of her policy unit referred to the GLC as 'a continuous nuisance.'[56] By 1984, Norman Tebbit, then Trade and Industry Secretary, damned the GLC as a 'new, modern, divisive form of socialism', which had to be 'defeated'.[57] After the failure of Fares Fair, with the consequence of increased support for groups associated with the new identity politics, the GLC was castigated

[53] GLC, Lord Gifford, 'The Budget of the Greater London Council for the Financial Year, 1984–5', 7 October 1983, LMA, GLC/DG/PRE/223/17.

[54] Daily Mail (London), 20 August 1981.

[55] Margaret Thatcher Foundation Archives, marginal notes in Thatcher Archives, PREM19/0832 f175, Howell to Thatcher, 29 January 1982, https://www.margaretthatcher.org/document/141024.

[56] Margaret Thatcher Foundation Archives, PREM19/0835 f122, Policy Unit, 'The Local Government Impasse', Ferdinand Mount to Prime Minister, 19 July 1982, https://www.margaretthatcher.org/document/140992.

[57] Quoted in Lansley, Goss, and Wolmar, Councils in Conflict, 47.

by the tabloid press for supporting a 'lunatic fringe' and 'Queers' Lib'.[58] The media painted a picture of the GLC as a threat on a number of fronts: to the nation; to the ratepayer; to the family; and, perhaps most broadly, to what was construed as 'common sense' or 'normal values'. Grants to minorities, feminists, and gay and lesbian groups seemed, to such critics, to undermine 'traditional' values in especially sensitive areas, such as education. The GLC and the Inner London Education Authority were both targets for the criticism that they were radicalizing children in the classroom. Indeed, it was later claimed by a Labour MP that 'the Sun, Mail and News of the World are currently offering up to £200 for any tip off on a story which bashes London Labour Councils... All a freelance has to do is scrutinise copies of council minutes or school governors reports or any documents merely throwing up ideas for discussion and if just one sentence touches on race, sex or kids, they distort it out of all recognition.'[59] One of the most telling statements of this point of view came from Thatcher herself at the 1987 Conservative Party conference:

... in the inner cities—where youngsters must have a decent education if they are to have a better future—that opportunity is all too often snatched from them by hard left education authorities and extremist teachers. And children who need to be able to count and multiply are learning anti-racist mathematics—whatever that may be. Children who need to be able to express themselves in clear English are being taught political slogans. Children who need to be taught to respect traditional moral values are being taught that they have an inalienable right to be gay.[60]

The GLC thus became a lightning rod for right-wing anxieties and indignation after 1981. And, again, this was a portent of the culture wars of the early twenty-first century. In terms of the importance of local

[58] *The Sun*, 20 September 1984; *Daily Mail,* 16 February 1983.
[59] Bernie Grant Papers, BG/P/4/6/4, Part 2, Joe Ashton to Bernie Grant, 16 March 1987, Bishopsgate Institute Archives, London.
[60] Margaret Thatcher Foundation Archives, Margaret Thatcher Speech to Conservative Party Conference, 9 October 1987, https://www.margaretthatcher.org/document/106941.

politics to the national scene, this had an uncommon intensity in the 1980s. James Curran argues that there were two main reasons for the ferocity of the attack. In the first place, particularly after the 1981 Brixton disorders, Labour's support for police monitoring and for ethnic minority communities was perceived as a dangerous challenge to law and order. Secondly, the right-wing media feared that the GLC victory was the confirmation of a leftward swing within the national Labour Party. In 1980, the veteran left-winger Michael Foot had assumed the leadership. In January 1981, four leading members of Labour's right wing exited the party, eventually leading to the formation of the Social Democratic Party. Nineteen eighty-one saw the left-winger Tony Benn run a close second in the race for the deputy leadership. The Conservative government was also in a vulnerable position in 1981, with unemployment deepening and the shadow of Brixton hanging over the question of law and order. And, to be fair, Livingstone served this purpose well, soon enraging the media with his support for Irish republicanism and gay rights. In August 1981, for example, he remarked that 'everyone is bisexual'.[61] While condemning an IRA attack on Chelsea barracks which killed two, Livingstone nonetheless argued that Britain should get out of Northern Ireland. These comments earned him the title 'the most odious man in Britain' from *The Sun*.[62] To some tabloids he was 'The IRA-loving, poof-loving Marxist'.[63] Adding to this opprobrium was the GLC's decision to decline an invitation to the wedding of Prince Charles and Diana Spencer.[64] The funding given community groups incited a backlash against radicalism on the rates, fuelled by the tabloids' ferocious demonization of the GLC. The violence of the reaction was not always rhetorical: in March 1985, for example, an unnamed extremist group firebombed the offices of the Ethnic Minorities Unit (part of the GLC bureaucracy supporting the anti-racist initiatives), fortunately hurting no one.[65]

---

[61] *Guardian* (London), 19 August 1981.

[62] Quoted in John Carvel, *Citizen Ken* (London: Chatto & Windus, 1984), 95–6.

[63] *Sunday Express*, 27 September 1981, quoted in Curran, 'The Boomerang Effect', 118.

[64] See Carvel, *Citizen Ken*, 86.

[65] See Hazel A. Atashroo, 'Beyond the "Campaign for a Popular Culture": Community Art, Activism and Cultural Democracy in 1980s London', PhD thesis, University of Southampton, Faculty of Business, Law and Art, Winchester School of Art (2017), 173, https://eprints.soton.

It should not, however, be thought that the distaste for the GLC was a sole prerogative of the political right. Some, possibly many, within the Labour Party held similar views. The electricians' leader, Eric Hammond, warned the 1983 TUC conference of the 'terrorist groupies, lesbians and other queer folk in inner London Labour parties'.[66] Divisive parliamentary by-elections in Bermondsey in 1983 and Greenwich in 1987 prompted figures within the Labour Party to distance themselves from the kind of municipal socialism pursued by the GLC. In 1987, for example, Patricia Hewitt, Neil Kinnock's media adviser, argued that '[t]he gays and lesbians issue is costing us dear among the pensioners, and fear of extremism and higher taxes is particularly prominent in the GLC area'.[67]

Against the white noise of such controversy, it is sometimes difficult to assess accurately what the GLC was and what it did. What complicates this is that, in some ways, the GLC welcomed and mobilized the controversies it generated. During the 1983 election, the Conservatives had used the term 'extravagant' as a term of abuse about the GLC and other metropolitan authorities. 'Flamboyant' might be a more accurate, if less pejorative, description. Between 1981 and 1986, the GLC assumed a more ostentatious presence in the life of the city than previous administrations. This could be seen on a number of levels. At the most quotidian, the GLC used publicity widely, about its services, policies, and causes. The brands 'GLC Working for London' or 'London Against Racism' (underneath an image of the city's skyline with St Paul's predominant) were stamped on virtually all official GLC material, insinuating themselves on hoardings, bus shelters, tube advertisements, and tea mugs. This might be dismissed, in the words of Billy Bragg, as thinking that the revolution could be 'a t-shirt away', but, as a number of 1970s and 1980s political campaigns attest, from Rock Against Racism to the anti-apartheid movement, the material culture of some 1980s politics— ephemera such as badges, buttons, posters, zines, and, yes, T-shirts—was

ac.uk/414571/1/17._Final_submission_of_thesis.pdf; see also Kwesi Owusu, *The Struggle for Black Arts in Britain* (London: Comedia, 1986), 104.

[66] Quoted in Livingstone, *You Can't Say That*, 238.

[67] Quoted in Colin Hughes and Patrick Wintour, *Labour Rebuilt* (London: Fourth Estate, 1990), 19.

striking in its ubiquity and its imagery.[68] The GLC used branding to market its own radicalism with the same ubiquity, working a new political subjectivity into everyday ordinary life, so that, indeed, the revolution, or at least a new world, might well be a tea mug away.

The extroverted character of the GLC could also be seen in a more episodic and spectacular fashion. High-profile and well-funded metropolitan campaigns were dedicated to particular groups and issues in particular years. The year 1984 was, for example, Anti-Racism Year; 1985 was Women's Year and Jobs Year. Other issues were given similar attention. In 1982, the GLC declared London a nuclear-free zone and made the following year Peace Year. Spectacular occasions were organized to commemorate these issues. In 1982, for example, the declaration of an anti-nuclear zone was launched by a ceremony at County Hall. As Hazel Atashroo has shown, the GLC followed this up with a series of events that used urban space in different ways, including funding a peace festival at Brockwell Park (at which the bands Madness and the Style Council performed), and, for the more refined and delicate lot, a 'Proms for Peace', as well as putting anti-nuke billboards featuring the work of Peter Kennard across London.[69] There were two 'Jobs for a Change' concerts, in 1984 and 1985, the first on the South Bank, the second in Battersea Park during Jobs Year, with acts such as the Smiths, Billy Bragg, the Pogues, Aswad, and Orchestral Manoeuvres in the Dark. The Battersea Park concert saw upwards of 250,000 people in attendance.[70]

In a variety of ways, the GLC made a spectacle of government between 1981 and 1986, an example of what has been called a theatre state.[71] Urban spectacles and celebrations have a long historical lineage with governments of left and right.[72] The 1951 Festival of Britain, as has been

[68] Billy Bragg, 'Waiting for the Great Leap Forwards', *Workers' Playtime*, Go! Discs (1988).

[69] Hazel A. Atashroo, 'Weaponising Peace: The Greater London Council, Cultural Policy and "GLC Peace Year 1983"', *Contemporary British History* 33 (2019): 173, doi: 10.1080/13619462.2018.1519420.

[70] Susanne Schregel, 'Nuclear War and the City: Perspectives on Municipal Interventions in Defence (Great Britain, New Zealand, West Germany, USA, 1980–1985)', *Urban History* 42/4 (November 2015): 569, doi: 10.1017/S0963926815000565.

[71] On the idea of the theatre state, see Murray Edelman, *Constructing the Political Spectacle* (Chicago: University of Chicago Press, 1988).

[72] Among others, see Nadine Rossol, *Performing the Nation in Interwar Germany* (London: Palgrave, 2010); Vanessa Schwartz, *Spectacular Realities: Early Mass Culture in Fin de Siècle Paris* (Berkeley: University of California Press, 1998).

argued by Becky Conekin, was, for example, a spectacle designed by the Labour government with the 'goal of constituting a more enlightened citizenry'.[73] Thirty years later, with its various 'years', 'zones', and concerts, the GLC attempted a similar exercise. And just as the Festival of Britain had its educative and its entertaining forms (with its Pleasure Gardens), the GLC's staged political spectacles could be seen as both entertaining and celebrative, critical and educative, a mix of the political and the non-political. So, in many ways, the GLC was exactly what its detractors thought it was: a flamboyant, if not necessarily extravagant, disruption.

Such disruption and spectacle demanded a high level of political energy and commitment. And between 1981 and 1986, the GLC was a hugely energetic political body, even in the last years of its life: it did not go gently into that bittersweet night. Such dynamism not only was about staging political spectacle but also represented a profound, if short-lived, administrative disruption of how local democracy had been done in London. After 1981, County Hall brought in a significant cohort of activists unused to the corridors of power. Maureen Mackintosh and Hilary Wainwright's *A Taste of Power* (1987), the definitive inside history of the GLC, was in many respects an account of how outsiders such as Wainwright, Ansel Wong, Michael Ward, Sheila Rowbotham, and others came into County Hall after 1981 and saw this as an opportunity to revitalize and reorient local democracy. That cohort was in part responsible for the exceptional work, done over a short period, in presenting and publishing important surveys of London life in the 1980s, surveys that attempted to comprehensively map questions such as the state of industry, labour, women's lives, the problems of racism, and gay and lesbian rights, policing, among a number of other issues. In other words, the energy and intent of a new cohort of local government workers were reflected in critical governing work. *The London Industrial Strategy* (1985) was, for example, a 600-page survey of economic activity in London, from the cleaning industries to domestic work, from retail to

---

[73] Becky Conekin, '"Here is the Modern World Itself": The Festival of Britain's Representations of the Future', in Becky Conekin, Frank Mort, and Chris Waters (eds.), *Moments of Modernity* (London: Rivers Oram, 1999), 234.

furniture manufacturing, from the arms industry to Heathrow Airport. The same could be said of *The London Women's Handbook* (1986) published by the Women's Committee. The energy dedicated by the Arts and Recreation Committee and its Chair, Tony Banks, to promoting culture in London seemed endless. Whatever was thought of what the GLC did, the Labour administration was at least serious about the 'working' in its slogan 'Working for London'.

Through governance, policy, and spectacle, the GLC sought to create a different London and different Londoners. It sought to transform both space and political subjectivity. It also sought to offer a different sense of the political 'ordinary' than that simultaneously promoted by the Conservatives. Recent work has stressed how Thatcherism was an attempt to reorient post-war society around the individual, the family, and the market.[74] Historians have noted how the Conservatives of the 1970s and 1980s attempted to claim 'ordinariness' as a 'central – but contested– discursive theme', with the 'ordinary' meaning 'belonging to a large group of "normal" people in the middle of society'.[75] This recent work has resonances with historical and political work done in the immediate aftermath of the GLC's abolition. With respect to the former, in 1988 Ross McKibbin set out the Conservatives' ability, in a period of perceived crisis during the interwar period, to construct themselves as the party of an 'ordinary' public, positioned against the sectional claims of the organized working classes.[76] The same year, Stuart Hall argued that Thatcherism was attempting to 'become the "common sense of the age"', to become so embedded as to 'naturalize itself...to become invisible, to operate unconsciously'.[77]

[74] A good survey can be found in Florence Sutcliffe-Braithwaite, Aled Davies, and Ben Jackson, 'Introduction: The Neoliberal Age', in Aled Davies, Ben Jackson, and Florence Sutcliffe-Braithwaite (eds.), *The Neoliberal Age? Britain since the 1970s* (London: UCL Press, 2021), 20–3.
[75] Quotes from, respectively, Hilton, Moores, and Sutcliffe-Braithwaite, 'New Times Revisited: Britain in the 1980s'; Florence Sutcliffe-Braithwaite, 'Discourses of "Class" in "New Times"', *Contemporary British History* 31 (2017): 304, doi: 10.1080/13619462.2017.1306199. See also Claire Langhamer, '"Who the Hell are Ordinary People?" Ordinariness as a Category of Historical Analysis', *Transactions of the Royal Historical Society* 28 (2018): 175–95, doi: 10.1017/S0080440118000099; Robinson, Schofield, Sutcliffe-Braithwaite, Thomlinson, 'Telling Stories About Post-War Britain'; Lawrence, *Me, Me, Me*.
[76] Ross McKibbin, 'Class and Conventional Wisdom', in *Ideologies of Class* (Oxford: Oxford University Press, 1988).
[77] Stuart Hall, 'Introduction', in *The Hard Road to Renewal* (London: Verso, 1988), 13.

In its short life, the GLC was a profound disruption of such projects. It sought to offer a very different sense of the ordinary. In the realm of culture and identity, its understanding of the ordinary was populated by what Mercer called 'new social actors and new political subjects'.[78] If Thatcherism was intent upon creating a new political 'ordinary' based upon the individual, the family, and the market, the GLC posed a different view of the 'ordinary', with its emphasis upon minority rights, particularly in terms of sexuality, and based upon an anti-racist, anti-sexist, and anti-heterosexist ethos beyond the framework of class. This was, in many ways, simply a reflection of 1980s London. Against the 'common sense' promulgated by Thatcherism, Stuart Hall argued that the left could offer an alternative 'common sense': 'to construct the social imaginary in ways which enable us to see ourselves transformed in the mirror of politics, and thus become its new subjects'.[79] This would be grounded in the 'everyday experience of popular urban life and culture'.[80] The challenge was that this approach did require politicizing the public and the ordinary in new ways, beyond existing frameworks such as the family or class. In other words, a new political ordinary would be situated in critical frameworks such as anti-racism, anti-sexism, and anti-heterosexism. Social democracy would weave race, gender, and sexual orientation into a progressive outlook. In this way, the GLC's political culture—its common sense—was innately critical.

It is not clear how successful this was. Indeed, the most popular policies of the GLC may have been the least radical: cheaper transport fares, childcare, and local democracy itself. But it is nonetheless important to acknowledge the ambition of the project. This was fundamentally about political subjectivity and space. If, in the nineteenth century, as several historians have argued, the emergence of liberalism was accompanied by the emergence of a new liberal subject, in the late twentieth century there were two competing ideas of political subjectivity, with two different states (one national, one local) promoting different visions of that

[78] Mercer, 'Welcome to the Jungle', 44.   [79] Hall, 'Introduction', 8, 13.
[80] Stuart Hall, 'Face the Future', New Socialist 19 (September 1984): 39.

subject.[81] The individual of the GLC's political culture was not rooted in the family or the market but, rather, in newly emerging identities of race, gender, and sexuality. As argued in the following chapters, these identities were not presented deferentially or cloaked in 'respectability' but, rather, loudly and unapologetically, and as a central part of social life enabled by the state. Making those communities and identities visible and making discrimination visible as a part of social democratic politics was at the heart of what the GLC did. The struggle was also, of course, about space as well as subjects. The deregulation of the financial markets and the redevelopment of the Docklands would make London a pre-eminent market city.[82] Again, the GLC was a direct challenge to this, with its promotion of public sector development schemes and radical spectacles using public space. Its support of community organizations and activism, particularly in their attempts secure space and visibility in the city, made this new political subjectivity material.

The 'market' was very much the heart of neoliberalism, but the kind of alternative society the GLC was attempting to create did not reject the market. Rather, what the GLC facilitated was a different kind of market, largely through its grants programme. In many ways, this was about helping groups not usually or equitably represented in the market, such as women, gay and lesbian people, ethnic minorities, and the working classes, with public funds. The end point was also to create a social market, in which the provision of goods or services was not left either to private capital or the state but, rather, to a more diffuse group of actors across different economic scales. The critical difference between this and Thatcherite neoliberalism was that this belief in choice, freedom, and decentralization was informed by a deep commitment to equality. The GLC was simultaneously a demonstration of what a state could do and an exercise in how the state could decentralize and devolve power to its citizens. 'The purpose of power', Nye Bevan once remarked, 'is to be able to give it away', a view echoed during the 2019 election by a veteran of the GLC, John McDonnell: 'with us, it is about the pursuit of power – but

---

[81]   See Patrick Joyce, *The Rule of Freedom* (London: Verso, 2003).
[82]   Massey, *World City*, 40, 43.

to give power away'.[83] From this perspective, the GLC gave away a great deal of power.

As already noted, Stuart Hall was an acute, if sympathetic, observer of what the GLC was attempting to do after 1981. This was particularly reflected in essays he published in late 1984, in the midst of the fight over abolition. In part, this was a critical reflection on the state of social democracy in Britain and the state of the Labour Party. Hall argued that socialism had to 'imagine the future... in ways which are in touch with the cultural categories the mass of ordinary people use to imagine theirs'.[84] This meant moving away from an alienating statism, not towards an untrammelled free market but, rather, towards 'an expansive popular system'.[85] Hall saw such a system in the GLC, which had pursued 'a new relationship between power and the people' and attempted socialism as a 'self-active, democratic popular force'.[86] The construction of that dynamic was based in the GLC's assumption that ordinary citizens were not passive. The struggle against abolition after 1983 was an attempt to cultivate an active, critical urban citizenry.[87] But Hall also believed that the GLC's dynamic socialism was grounded in an acknowledgement of the diversity or 'autonomy' of the public, as reflected, for example, in its cultivation of disparate social movements such as feminism, gay and lesbian rights, and ethnic minorities.[88] It was also in the way that the GLC made visible, as Hall had argued in 'Face the Future', different aspects of everyday life and the politics around them. This included something like urban transport, but also culture (in the series of concerts put on by the GLC, both for causes and indeed for themselves). This was, in his view, socialism as a way of life, 'politicizing sites of daily life' and the 'everyday experience of popular urban life and culture'.[89]

One of the ways in which the GLC was mounting a challenge to an older route of social democracy was around the relationship between state and citizen. Hall argued that what a libertarian left shared with the

---

[83] See Michael Foot, *Aneurin Bevan*, Vol. 1 (London: MacGibbon & Kee, 1962), 221; Patrick Maguire interview with John McDonnell, *New Statesman*, 4–11 December 2019.
[84] Hall, 'The Culture Gap', in *The Hard Road to Renewal*, 211.
[85] Hall, 'The Culture Gap', 214.   [86] Hall, 'The Culture Gap', 218.
[87] Hall, 'Face the Future', 37.   [88] Hall, 'Face the Future', 37.
[89] Hall, 'Face the Future', 39.

anti-state right was an emphasis upon choice and diversity against a centralist state. Challenging the idea of 'choice' as 'an essentially reactionary, right-wing capitalist idea', Hall pointed to the way the GLC conceived of the public as a more pluralistic, diverse body and that its funding of both grass-roots organizations and small enterprises was a manifestation of this.[90] A later essay, written two years after the abolition of the GLC, similarly took Fares Fair, a policy that emanated from a state, as something that facilitated individual freedom and the diversity of the public:

> a 'Fares fair' society, a conception of all sorts of ordinary people, with different tastes, purposes, destinations, desires...nevertheless enabled by a system of public intervention in the pricing, provision and consumption of a social need...to enlarge their freedoms to move about the city...to see and experience new things, to go into places hitherto barred to them...in safety and comfort....There is a lesson here somewhere for those who have turned their backs so decisively and dismissively on the whole GLC experience to learn. It has to do, in part, with how to construct the social imaginary in ways which enable us to see ourselves transformed in the mirror of politics, and thus to become its 'new subjects'.[91]

Thus, for Hall, what was at stake in 1984 was fundamental—the construction of a new politics and a new way of imagining society.

1.4

Stuart Hall had named one of his 1984 essays 'Face the Future', and in that year the future the GLC had to face was decidedly perilous. Following the Conservative electoral victory of 1983, the Department of Environment published a White Paper, *Streamlining the Cities*, which laid

---

[90] Hall, 'The State – Socialism's Old Caretaker', in *The Hard Road to Renewal*, 228.
[91] Hall, 'Introduction: Thatcherism and the Crisis of the Left', in *The Hard Road to Renewal*, 13.

the groundwork for legislation to abolish seven metropolitan authorities in Britain, including the GLC. The shadow of abolition was an existential threat to the GLC. But there were also challenges from within that were provoked by the Conservative government. In 1984, the government demanded that eighteen local councils—sixteen of which were Labour-controlled—cap their rates and accept spending cuts. Within London, this group included the GLC, Islington, Lambeth, Hackney, Haringey, Camden, and Southwark. Outside London, Sheffield Council and the metropolitan council of Liverpool were also targeted.

The demand posed a profound dilemma for those on the left. To refuse to set a rate was illegal. It could also lead to individual councillors being subject to surcharges and bankruptcies. To set a rate would be to capitulate to an antagonistic Conservative government. The Liverpool council, under the leadership of Derek Hatton and Militant Tendency, refused to set a rate. Within London, Ted Knight, the leader of Lambeth Council, and John McDonnell, the Deputy Leader of the GLC and its main economic adviser, were for taking the same stand. In April 1985, McDonnell wrote that rate-capping was 'an integral part of the government's overall attack on the standard of living of our people and also on our basic democratic rights'; refusing to set a rate would be a 'courageous act of solidarity with socialists in struggle throughout the country'.[92] Not all within the GLC agreed. In October 1984, the outlines of a major disagreement emerged within the higher echelons of the Labour GLC. Against a policy of setting no rate, Livingstone and his advisers believed that, even with setting a rate to the cap demanded by the government, the GLC could count on a growth of £25 million.[93] McDonnell perceived this as an unacceptable political compromise, writing to Livingstone in October 1984: '[t]he whole point of our administration is that we are a challenge to the central capitalist state. To accommodate at this crucial stage would be to accept without challenge our subservience to Tory class rule'.[94] The deadline for setting a rate was 10 March 1985. Between October 1984 and that date, the Labour group on the GLC

---

[92] John McDonnell, *New Statesman*, 5 April 1985.
[93] Ken Livingstone, *New Statesman*, 22 March 1985.
[94] Quoted in Lansley, Goss, and Wolmar, *Councils in Conflict*, 40.

failed to develop a unified position on rate-capping. On the eve of the deadline, the opposition parties at County Hall proposed an alternative budget, below the stipulated maximum. Enough Labour members peeled off from the Labour group to allow this budget to pass. The GLC was left with a rate below what it had hoped for and a deeply divided Labour group. The fallout from the rate-capping controversy was ambiguous. It split the Labour group on the GLC. Hard and soft left within the Labour group were more divided after the rate-capping issue was resolved, with the hard left declining in influence. But rate-capping did not particularly disable the economic power of the GLC in its last two years. As one account has it: 'most councils could get by without cuts...the GLC in particular, was found to be awash with even more money'.[95]

But, of course, rate-capping was just one episode in a larger drama about the very existence of the GLC. At the end of 1983, the Conservatives introduced legislation to fulfil their election promises. This legislation set out the abolition of the GLC and the distribution of its powers either to borough governments or to newly created non-elected authorities. The introduction of this legislation set off a major battle between County Hall and Westminster about abolition in 1984. Because the Conservatives had a large parliamentary majority coming out of the 1983 election, it was unlikely that abolition could be avoided, but that struggle was nonetheless a difficult one for the government.

The first of many complications on the road to abolition was what to do about the GLC elections scheduled for May 1985. The Conservative government was concerned that allowing the elections to go forward would lead to an uncomfortable plebiscite on both the GLC and the government. The alternatives were cancelling the elections, thus allowing the Labour GLC another year, or substituting the GLC council with representatives from London's boroughs, which might lead to a Conservative-dominated council. In the 'paving' bill introduced in March 1984, the Environment Secretary, Patrick Jenkin, plumped for cancelling the elections and replacing the GLC with an interim body. This provoked criticism not only from the left but also from some

---

[95] Lansley, Goss, and Wolmar, *Councils in Conflict*, 41.

Conservatives. Thatcher's bête noire, the former leader Edward Heath, called it a 'negation of democracy'.[96] Nonetheless, the bill passed by a slim majority in the Commons and was sent to the Lords. In an odd twist, it was a partly hereditary house that honoured the claims of local democracy. In late June 1984, the bill was defeated in the Lords, a mix of Conservative, Labour, and Liberal peers banding together to vote it down. Jenkin's response was to cancel the elections, abandon the idea of substitution, but transfer some of the GLC's powers (over property, for example) to the Department of the Environment.

The abolition campaign was a stark contrast between the power of central government and the claims of local democracy. Even supporters of the government expressed doubts about the point of abolition— whether because it was too costly, too complicated, or looked politically vindictive—and the person chosen to shepherd it through, Patrick Jenkin, was not the sharpest of political cards. By contrast, the GLC campaign was professional and smooth. The GLC spent £5 million on the anti-abolition campaign and coordinated a large series of events, rallies, and publicity, all in the mould of what it had done before. An early decision was to make the services provided to Londoners by the GLC visible through the conspicuous use of the GLC logo on posters, publications, and advertisements. It hired parliamentary lobbyists to court Liberal and Tory peers. The GLC toured all the major party conferences in the autumn of 1983. In a move very common in contemporary politics, but innovative for local politics at this time and an anathema to some left-wingers, the council engaged an advertising firm—Boase Massimi Pollitt—to shape the GLC's message.[97] Some members of the shadow communications agency under Tony Blair in the early 1990s came from this firm.[98] The anti-abolition campaign featured posters and ephemera, such as the button seen in Figure 1.1.

What the subsequent publicity emphasized was, first of all, a concern that the road to abolition was being paved with other anti-democratic

[96] Quoted in Andrew Forrester, Stewart Lansley, and Robin Pauley, *Beyond Our Ken* (London: Fourth Estate, 1985), 74.

[97] See Husbands, 'Attitudes to Local Government in London', 71–2.

[98] See Boase, Massimi, and Pollett, *How the Left Learned to Love Advertising* (London: BMP, 2000).

Figure 1.1 A button for the anti-abolition campaign.
Credit: Homer Sykes/Alamy Stock Photo.

steps. In particular, the campaign focused on the proposal to cancel the GLC elections of 1985. One poster featured a dustbin with the slogan 'Next Year All Londoners' Votes Go the Same Way'. In another, against a picture of the Houses of Parliament, the question was posed, 'What Kind of Place Is It That Takes Away Your Right to Vote and Leaves You With No Say?' The slogan 'Say No to No Say' became an important motif in the campaign. What this evoked was the idea of an engaged and active urban citizenry being threatened with the withdrawal of democratic rights. At the same time, the poster campaign promoted a negative view of the central state, with snails and a gentleman from Whitehall replete with a bowler hat and a brick wall for a face giving the sense of what was about to take over. The same message was pushed by Livingstone. He told the readers of *The Times*, for example, that the abolition of the GLC elections was a 'democratic outrage'.[99] These messages gained traction among London voters; the GLC won more popularity at the end of the abolition campaign than it had enjoyed at the beginning, with an important exception in terms of its policies on gay and lesbian rights.[100]

The campaign against abolition was not only waged in outrage; humour also had a role, and flamboyance remained a constant. In 1984,

[99] Ken Livingstone, 'Let Londoners Decide', *The Times*, 10 April 1984.
[100] See Curran, 'The Boomerang Effect', 111.

the theatrical state became literally theatrical with the sponsorship of *The Ratepayers' Iolanthe*, written by Ned Sherrin and Alistair Beaton. This was, as the title suggested, a Gilbert and Sullivan parody. The Queen of the Fairies (Margaret Thatcher) attempted to get rid of Red Strephon (Ken Livingstone) by getting him off the GLC. Cue comic anarchy. *The Ratepayers' Iolanthe* played for a few weeks at the South Bank Centre before shifting to the West End for a month-long stint in September 1984, at exactly the moment of the by-elections. In the play, Red Strephon offered a comic, though some right-wing figures might say not so fictional, portrait of the world which the GLC had attempted to create:

> I have a dream...I see Greater London as a land of milk and honey. A land with a gay adventure playground on every street corner. A land where the Special Patrol Group helps old black lesbian ladies to cross the street...a land of street festivals for one-parent families, a land of free classes in socialist aerobics, a land of reggae and salsa, a land of touring comedies in the Marxist–Leninist tradition, a land of discos for the disabled, a land of culture, a land where the National Theatre caters to the needs of the ordinary sociologist in the street, a land where any man or woman, whatever his or her colour, creed, race, sexual orientation or tastes in underwear can stand up proudly...[101]

The abolition campaign was ultimately in vain. The passage of the 1985 Local Government Act led to the demise of the GLC on 1 April 1986. Nineteen eighty-four proved a year in which the arguments for the GLC and its alternative politics were articulated with great force but no effect, given the Conservative majority in parliament. The following chapters will explore how the politics of 1980s London were experienced in disparate spheres.

London, 1984: Conflict and Change in the Radical City. Stephen Brooke, Oxford University Press.
© Stephen Brooke 2024. DOI: 10.1093/9780191895395.003.0002

---

[101] Quoted in Forrester, Lansley, and Pauley, *Beyond Our Ken*, 33.

2

Anti-Racist Year

4 January 1984: on a blustery winter afternoon, about two thousand people come to County Hall, taking in craft displays, bookstalls, and exhibitions. The occasion is the launch of the GLC's Anti-Racist Year. This is intended as a 'comprehensive attack on racism, through a programme of public awareness raising…aimed at dismantling racism from society'. The GLC hopes to secure 'anti-racist commitments from as many of London's inhabitants as possible', with 'a commitment to become anti-racist by being deeply aware of all forms of oppression and taking action personally and collectively to end all oppression'.[1]

Over the course of 1984, the GLC was involved directly or indirectly in dozens of anti-racist themed events across London, including, on 1 July 1984, a GLC 'London Against Racism' rally opened by Stevie Wonder with 35,000 in attendance, as seen in Figure 2.1. The GLC also launched an intensive advertising campaign educating Londoners in anti-racism. A logo with familiar London landmarks—St Paul's and Tower Bridge—was emblazoned with the banner 'London Against Racism' on posters, communiqués, and tea mugs.

Anti-Racist Year was a singular initiative. No previous government, local or national, had made racism or racial inequality the subject of an explicit public campaign. The initiative came from the GLC's Ethnic Minorities Committee, one of the new committees created by the Labour GLC after the election of May 1981. From that point on, the GLC committed in important ways to both racial equality and anti-racism, culminating in Anti-Racist Year in 1984. In a major statement to the GLC made in September 1984, John Wilson, acting Leader of the GLC, asserted that the GLC had 'taken on the most comprehensive and

[1] GLC, Ethnic Minorities Committee, Anti-Racist Year Programme of Initiatives, Progress Report Implementation, Report by Principal Race Relations Adviser, 17 October 1984, LMA, GLC/DG/PRE/49/36, ARP 56.

Figure 2.1 Paul Boateng and Stevie Wonder, 'London Against Racism' rally, 1 July 1984.
Credit: Trinity Mirror/Mirrorpix/Alamy Stock Photo.

coherent programme to dismantle racist structures from a large institution ever launched by any part of the state apparatus.'[2]

The present book explores the politics of race in 1980s London in three chapters, two dealing with racial violence and policing, and, in this chapter, exploring the intersection between a top-down initiative launched by the GLC in 1984, Anti-Racist Year, and the work of community organizations and activists on race. The chapter begins with a discussion of the work of the Ethnic Minorities Committee and then looks at particular community organizations involved with race and anti-racism. Finally, it explores the broader idea of anti-racist London in 1984 as an attempt to reimagine social democracy, political culture, and political subjects.

Anti-Racist Year remains a significant moment in the politics of race in post-war Britain. For the first time in British history, racism was identified as a major social problem that demanded redress in terms of both

[2] GLC, Ethnic Minorities Committee, Report by Director-General, 'Race Relations in London," 26 September 1984, LMA/GLC/DG/PRE/49/34.

popular attitudes and institutional practices. That redress would be found in active governance and policy practice, rather than only in the legal provisions of the 1976 Race Relations Act. Resisting racism moved from being a passive practice that waited upon court or tribunal decisions to an active practice animating government. In 1984, this could be seen at several levels: in equal opportunity policy in employment; in contract compliance; in the discussion of policing; and, most spectacularly, in Anti-Racist Year itself, which was designed to make London and Londoners anti-racist.

At the same time, in 1984 a different kind of city was being made, from the street to County Hall, through the issues of race and anti-racism. Grant aid from the GLC and other bodies did not create local Black activism, but it did, for a time, underwrite a claim to the city being made by Black Londoners, facilitating a visibility that was both meta-phorical and literal. Local organizations created distinctly Black spaces in London.[3]

In a recent article, Marc Matera, Radhika Natarajan, Kennetta Hammond-Perry, Camilla Schofield, and Rob Waters have suggested that we need to recover the 'race politics of social democracy' from the 'margins of historical analysis'. They argue that we should take 'greater account of the experiences of people of colour and the place of race in the making of postwar social democracy'.[4] The GLC initiatives on race, grant funding, and the growth of political organizations in the 1980s, symbolized by Anti-Racist Year, comprised a conscious attempt to rewrite the terms of post-war social democracy by making race explicit in that political culture. With this, there was no longer an invisible Black British subject or space, but rather a visible Blackness that provoked a discussion of the problem of racism. At the same time, the white subject and white space that had long underpinned post-war social democracy was made visible, but in a critical light, illuminated by the problem of

---

[3] For a recent discussion of Black urban space, see Agostino Pinnock, Stephen Lawrence Centre, 'Unsettled Multiculturalisms', https://www.youtube.com/watch?v=7K7s8-U5T3I&t=2010s. See also Keith, 'Urbanism and City Spaces in the Work of Stuart Hall'.

[4] Marc Matera, Radhika Natarajan, Kennetta Hammond-Perry, Camilla Schofield, and Rob Waters, 'Marking Race', *Twentieth-Century British History* 34/3 (2023), 407–14, doi: 10.1093/tcbh/hwad036.

anti-Black racism. Making race explicit in these two ways was a critical, controversial, but lasting change in contemporary political culture, putting race (whether Blackness or whiteness) at the centre of thinking about politics and political subjectivity.

In 1980s London, anti-racism appeared in several forms and spaces, such as employment, contracts, advertisements, policy, and culture, and on streets and in neighbourhoods themselves. It also made an explicit connection between the local and the global. Racism and anti-racism in London could not be spoken of without reference to transnational or global issues, whether it was in terms of the promotion of migrant histories and cultures, the reflection of cosmopolitan communities in the funding of grass-roots groups, or, perhaps most profoundly, the transnational or global connections that had to be made in any discussion of race. As Chapter 6 will argue, discussing apartheid in South Africa meant discussing race in London. Promoting Black culture in London meant thinking about the global and colonial and postcolonial connections between London, Africa, South Asia, and the Caribbean.

2.1

Well before the 1980s, race had become central to British politics. This was less about the patterns of post-war migration and more about whiteness; in particular, it was about the power of white fear and anxiety. Enoch Powell's infamous 'rivers of blood' speech in 1968 had given voice to such fears. That speech forced Powell out of the Conservative Party, but its sentiments nonetheless became central to Conservatism in the 1970s. Ten years after the 'rivers of blood' speech, Margaret Thatcher offered a Powellite vision that had hardly softened with the passage of time: 'by the end of the century there would be four million people of the new Commonwealth or Pakistan here. Now, that is an awful lot and I think it means that people are really rather afraid that this country might be rather swamped by people with a different culture.' Such fear might, Thatcher warned, make 'swamped people...rather hostile to those coming in'. In such ways, as Anna Marie Smith has argued, Conservatism in the 1970s took race as a 'nodal point' in the construction of its political approach, particularly in the validation of white fear and hostility.[5] One way that this worked, both in political Conservatism and in the media, came with using race as a language of the malaise afflicting Britain in the 1970s. Stuart Hall and others suggested that the media representation of street crime and the policing of Black communities identified Blackness and Black youth as a symbol of the crisis threatening the stability of British society.[6] Again, this was much more about whiteness and its discontents and anxieties than it was about Blackness.

In the decades that followed Windrush, British governments responded to the growth of the multiracial society by alternately restricting immigration and attempting to improve race relations and discourage racial discrimination. Before the advent of the Labour GLC, the latest iteration of this two-step dance comprised the 1971 Immigration Act and the 1976 Race Relations Act. The second had two aims: 'to work towards the elimination of discrimination' and 'to promote equality of opportunity and good relations.'[7] The first aim would be accomplished through complaints brought to bodies such as industrial tribunals or through civil proceedings, as well as empowering criminal prosecution of incitement to racial hatred. The promotion of 'equality of opportunity and good relations' came through the establishment of the Commission for Racial Equality (CRE) and through giving local governments the statutory right to use their resources to promote good race relations. This was a statutory door that the Labour GLC flung open after 1981. There were other initiatives in the 1970s and early 1980s that also focused attention on the challenges of a multiracial society. Both the Home Office and the parliamentary Home Affairs Committee launched enquiries into racial harassment and violence. In 1985, the Swann Report sought to mitigate the 'fear and insecurity' caused by racism with an argument for multicultural education.[8] The 1978 Inner Urban

[5] Anna Marie Smith, *New Right Discourse on Race and Sexuality: Britain 1968–1990* (Cambridge: Cambridge University Press, 1994), 8.

[6] See Stuart Hall et al., *Policing the Crisis: Mugging: The State, and Law and Order* (London: Macmillan, 1978); Centre for Contemporary Cultural Studies, *The Empire Strikes Back: Race and Racism in 70s Britain* (London: Routledge, 1982).

[7] *Race Relations Act 1976*, 41 (1) (a) and 41 (1) (b).

[8] *Swann Report: Education for All* (London: HMSO, 1985), 36.

Areas Act provided considerable funding for projects (whether from government or voluntary groups) to address questions of social deprivation in particular inner-city areas, such as Lambeth, Islington, and Hackney. This funding could also cover questions of race relations.

From the 1960s on, Black British communities were faced with increasing challenges, whether this was in higher levels of unemployment (particularly among Black youth), inequality in education, or rising levels of racial harassment and violence. In her recent work, Christine Grandy has written of the deeply rooted, intense, and quotidian racism that Black people had to navigate in the post-war era, using Chester M. Pierce's term a 'mundane extreme environment' to describe that landscape.[9] In areas such as the East End, organized racist politics reappeared in the form of the National Front. The Metropolitan Police's heavy-handed use of stop-under-suspicion policing (the 'sus' laws) made racial disadvantage a daily experience for many young Black people. As Rob Waters has pointed out, Black intellectuals and activists developed a distinctive sense of 'Blackness' as a response to these experiences.[10] This was accompanied by the growth in community organization and activism. Civil disorders in Bristol in 1980 and Brixton, Toxteth, Southall, and Moss Side in 1981 were the product of frustration and anger in Black communities at policing, deprivation, and racial discrimination. The report on Brixton by Lord Scarman, released in November 1981, denied the existence of institutional or structural racism but did underline that racial disadvantage in British cities was an issue of the greatest urgency. On the ground, there was also a sense of urgency, particularly in Black communities. At the end of 1981, for example, a Black community organization on the Stonebridge estate in Brent noted: 'unemployment, especially among young blacks, is high. Community tension is high. Crime is high. There are virtually no community facilities. Stonebridge is a timebomb ticking away.'[11]

---

[9] Chester M. Pierce, quoted in Christine Grandy, *What the Audience Wants: Film, Television, and Audience Racism in Twentieth-century Britain* (forthcoming); I am grateful to Christine Grandy for allowing me to read this manuscript.

[10] Waters, *Thinking Black*.

[11] GLC, Industry and Employment Committee, Stonebridge Bus Depot Project Report Prepared by the Stonebridge Bus Depot Steering Group, December 1981, LMA, GLC/PRE/DG/223/10.

2.2

By the 1980s, 'race was a central force in British politics, which mediated and organized social, economic, political and cultural relations'.[12] In the decade that followed, Michael Keith states, '[t]he very ground on which discussion of racism and racial equality had been consensually based in the preceding decade appeared to be shifting under everyone's feet'.[13] The Labour GLC thus came to power at a particularly critical moment in the history of race in Britain. The Ethnic Minorities Committee was established in June 1981 to pursue the question of racial equality. Paul Boateng had been recently elected as a GLC member for Walthamstow. He took over as vice chair and served as chair of the Police Committee. Change was swift. In December 1981, the Council adopted an equal opportunity policy in its employment practices and contract compliance. A month later, the Council required that ethnic minority considerations be worked into all its policy considerations and programmes, and, in December 1982, it was announced that London would be declared an 'Anti-Racist Zone' in 1984, with an expansive programme of anti-racist activities and events. The GLC's initiatives on racial equality were cast widely:

> The promotion of the welfare of ethnic minorities, and such other minorities as fall within the ambit of the Race Relations Act 1976, in Greater London. The implementation of policies to promote equal opportunity for such minorities and to increase the range and level of opportunities open to such minorities within the council's employment. The promotion of adoption by London borough councils and other employers in Greater London of equal opportunity policies. Advocacy of the repeal of repressive and racially-discriminatory immigration and nationality laws and practices in the United Kingdom.[14]

---

[12] Waters, *Thinking Black*, 199.

[13] Michael Keith, *Race, Riots and Policing: Lore and Disorder in a Multi-racist Society* (London: UCL Press, 1993), 2–3.

[14] GLC, Ethnic Minorities Committee, First Meeting, 19 June 1981, LMA, GLC/DG/PRE/49/1.

Five main areas of focus guided these objectives: employment and training; the provision of services by the Council; community development; communication and information; and the promotion of racial equality.[15]

A support unit, the Ethnic Minorities Unit, was also established, with staff headed by a Principal Race Relations Adviser (PRRA). The Ethnic Minorities Unit's brief was a broad one: it was a resource for consultation with ethnic minority communities as well as a body to develop new policies across a wide spectrum, from housing to arts and enterprise, to press for employment equity policies within and beyond the GLC itself, and, most significantly, to 'monitor GLC activities' in general.[16] The Ethnic Minorities Unit was also responsible for handling grant aid requests, which would then be approved by the Ethnic Minorities Committee. The volume of these was considerable and, as a result, the budget for the unit increased significantly, from £850,000 in 1982/3 to £2.5 million in 1983/4.

Two figures were central to the Ethnic Minorities Unit. Herman Ouseley was the first PRRA. Born in Guyana and raised in south London, Ouseley served as a local government officer before being made PRRA. Ansel Wong came from Trinidad and Tobago as a university student at Hull in the 1960s, then moved to London and became involved in Black rights politics, through the Black Liberation Front. He also worked with self-help groups such as Ujamaa, housing associations, and Black education initiatives such as Ahfiwe, which focused on Afrocentric learning.[17] Wong became Ouseley's assistant as Race Relations Adviser and by 1984 was playing a critical role in shaping policy and vetting funding applications.

Before looking at specific issues and policies, it is important to understand how the Ethnic Minorities Committee defined ethnic minorities

[15] GLC, Ethnic Minorities Committee, Report by the Director-General and Controller of Manpower, 'The Development of the Work of the Ethnic Minorities Committee', 20 October 1981, LMA, GLC/DG/PRE/49/5.

[16] GLC, Ethnic Minorities Committee, Staff Committee, Report by Director-General, 'Ethnic Minorities Committee: Objectives, Work Priorities and Staffing', 2 February 1982, LMA, GLC/DG/PRE/49/6.

[17] 'Interview with Ansel Wong', GLC Story Oral History Project, Interviewed by Zahra Dalilah, Goldsmiths University, London, 16 February 2017.

and how it defined racism. As to the first, 'the main thrust' of the Ethnic Minorities Committee's efforts was directed at 'the black ethnic groups whose ancestral origins can be traced to Africa, Asia and the Caribbean'.[18] But the Ethnic Minorities Committee nonetheless adopted a catholic definition of which groups counted as ethnic minorities. Herman Ouseley said that '[t]he starting point is the acknowledgement by the GLC of the multi-ethnic composition of the capital's population and the recognition of such cultural diversity as a major asset'.[19] That diversity was reflected in grant aid. In a single meeting in June 1984, for instance, funding was approved for Chile Democrático-GB, an organ-ization dedicated to the approximately 3,000 Chileans living in London (many of whom had arrived as refugees when the government of Salvador Allende was ousted in a military coup in 1973), the Iranian Community Centre, another organization dedicated to the interests of a small community made up predominantly of political refugees, and the Migrants Resource Centre in Pimlico, which helped migrants from Portugal, Spain, Colombia, and Morocco.[20] Both the Irish and the Jewish communities of London were also targeted for support by the Ethnic Minorities Committee, since they were being recognized as older ethnic minority communities within the city. The PRRA circulated a policy paper in June 1984 arguing that the Irish should be recognized as a distinct, often 'ignored', ethnic minority group, suffering 'areas of dis-advantage' affecting their lives in London including housing, employment, media representation, and the law, most notably with the operation of the Prevention of Terrorism Acts.[21] The Ethnic Minorities Committee also supported explicitly religious organizations of a variety of faiths, including Sikh, Rastafari, and Christian. In 1984, the Ethnic Minorities Committee defined Travellers as an oppressed group who had 'faced

[18] GLC, Ethnic Minorities Committee, Abstract from Council Agenda, Report of the Ethnic Minorities Committee, 6 December 1982, LMA, GLC/DG/PRE/49/6.
[19] GLC, Ethnic Minorities Committee, Consultative Conference with Ethnic Minorities, 18 November 1982 (conference held 24 April 1982), LMA, GLC/DG/PRE/111/17.
[20] GLC, Ethnic Minorities Committee, 'Migrants Community Centre', Funding Application, 18 June 1984, LMA, GLC/DG/PRE/49/29.
[21] GLC, Ethnic Minorities Committee, 'Irish in Islington Project', Funding Application, 27 July 1984, LMA, GLC/DG/PRE/49/31; GLC, Ethnic Minorities Committee, PRRA Report, 'Policy Report on the Irish Community', 15 June 1984, LMA, GLC, DG/PRE/49/28.

hostility and indifference to their needs for centuries'.[22] The Ethnic Minorities Committee thus reflected not only London's multiracial character but also its cosmopolitan character, shaped by recent and older migrations.

Racism was defined as 'prejudice plus power'. Power was characterized as 'the ability to make things happen or to prevent things from happening'. Two principal foci of anti-racist work were identified. The first was 'institutional structures', including the GLC itself. The second was more amorphous: 'people's behaviour which is conditioned by racially prejudiced attitudes'.[23]

The embrace of anti-racism and racial equality transformed governance at County Hall. The work of the Ethnic Minorities Committee was rooted in an acknowledgement, one uncommon in government then and indeed still a contested idea, of 'institutional, individual and cultural racism and the widespread racial discrimination that it sustains'.[24] This meant changing London and Londoners, but also looking at institutions, including the GLC itself. Ken Livingstone remarked in April 1982:

> What we face today in local government...is not finding out where the sort of conscious racist bigot sits and decides to discriminate. We have to look at how the normal structures of the Council and its priorities have been set up in a way that produces the same end result.[25]

In 1983, Ouseley likewise called attention to the 'racist nature of the GLC itself'.[26] The following December, the Council was told that the Ethnic Minorities Committee's 'central objective is that of tackling institutional and structural racism' and, towards that end, the GLC itself had

[22] GLC, Ethnic Minorities Committee, PRRA Report, 'Review of GLC Policy on Travellers', 6 April 1984, LMA, GLC, DG/PRE/49/28.
[23] GLC, Ethnic Minorities Committee, 'Anti-Racist Advertising Strategy', 30 July 1984, LMA, GLC/DG/PRE/49/31.
[24] GLC, Ethnic Minorities Committee, Report by the PRRA, 'Information Paper on Ethnic Minority Committee Achievements', 27 October 1983, LMA, GLC/DG/PRE/49/19.
[25] GLC, Ethnic Minorities Committee, Consultative Conference with Ethnic Minorities, 18 November 1982 (conference held 24 April 1982), LMA, GLC/DG/PRE/111/17.
[26] GLC, Ethnic Minorities Committee, Report by the PRRA, 'Challenging Racism in London – Conference Report', 7 July 1983, LMA, GLC/DG/PRE/47/10.

to address how, as an institution, it had 'historically discriminated indirectly in many ways against black people and other ethnic minorities'.[27]

In this respect, there were three key strands to the Ethnic Minorities Committee's work, addressing three aspects of the GLC's role: as a site of policy and governance; as an employer; and as a purchaser of goods and services. All were grounded in the GLC's recognition of racial inequality and discrimination as serious problems and in the attempt to make equality a primary lens through which to see other kinds of policy. In January 1982, prompted by the Ethnic Minorities Committee, the GLC committed to 'the adoption of more positive approaches on race and ethnic issues, especially through the decision-making processes of the Council'. '[A]ll future reports to all committees' had to include 'appropriate comments' dealing with 'Ethnic Minority and Race Equality Considerations'. This was intended to place 'an ethnic minority and race equality dimension within the decision-making processes of the Council'.[28] While it was acknowledged that not all policies and reports would have such a dimension, this was a hugely significant step: it meant that equality (in this case racial and ethnic equality) would be a prism through which Council policy and programmes were viewed. Racial equality became a reference point in the day-to-day administrative life of the GLC in a way that presaged contemporary controversies.

Incorporating a racial dimension to policy and governance involved economic policy at both a micro and macro level—first, in the formulation of a metropolitan economic policy between 1981 and 1986 and in the encouragement of Black economic activity at the community level. This will be discussed in the next chapter. Second, a change was attempted in the day-to-day running of GLC employment practices, in what was called 'positive action', an early iteration of affirmative action or equal opportunity policies in hiring and employment. Third, the GLC took a radical approach to applying equal opportunity and anti-racist policies to the purchase of goods and services, by insisting upon

---

[27] GLC, Ethnic Minorities Committee, Abstract from Council Agenda, '9. Report of the Ethnic Minorities', 6 December 1982, LMA, GLC/DG/PRE/49/6.

[28] GLC, Ethnic Minorities Committee, Report by the Director-General, 'Introducing a Race Equality Dimension to the Decision-Making Processes of Council', 28 January 1982, LMA, GLC/DG/PRE/49/1.

contract compliance with equal opportunity guidelines. The last two of these initiatives attracted a great deal of criticism and controversy.

The Ethnic Minorities Committee (and subsequently the entire Labour GLC) expressed the determination to go beyond 'formal legal equality' in its role as an employer and purchaser of services. The Ethnic Minorities Committee promoted 'positive action' to 'enable disadvantaged groups to develop their potential, to overcome the effects of past discrimination which result from the wider society's discriminatory practices and "catch up" with the experience of other applicants and employees'.[29] The aim was, in part, to extend equal opportunity in employment and to engage 'a workforce that reflects the multi-ethnic community being served'.[30] It was noted that while ethnic minorities comprised 18 per cent of London's population, they represented only 8 per cent of the GLC's workforce.[31] The London Fire Brigade was often singled out as an example of this imbalance; out of its six thousand uniformed staff, only seven were ethnic minorities. 'Positive action' meant being more assertive in recruiting ethnic minority candidates within the GLC. 'Equality targets' were set within departments to achieve more diversity. Advertisements for positions were circulated within the ethnic minority press and to community organizations.

This became a lightning rod of criticism. 'Positive action' in employment policy met with a negative reception from the staff unions working at County Hall. Within the GLC, the Staff Association felt that 'positive discrimination...could well give rise to resentments'.[32] A representative of senior officers of the GLC and ILEA also bristled at the suggestion, saying 'nothing should interfere with the principle of selection and promotion on merit'.[33]

---

[29] GLC, Ethnic Minorities Committee, Staff Committee, Report by Controller of Manpower, 'Equal Opportunities in GLC Employment', 3 November 1981, LMA, GLC/DG/PRE/49/5.

[30] GLC, Ethnic Minorities Committee, 'Report of the Ethnic Minorities Committee', 6 December 1982, LMA, GLC/DG/PRE/49/6.

[31] GLC, Ethnic Minorities and the Abolition of the GLC (London, 1984), 12.

[32] GLC, Ethnic Minorities Committee, P. T. Hollocks, GLC Staff Association, to B. Watson, Head of Personnel Services, 6 November 1981, LMA, GLC/DG/PRE/49/5.

[33] GLC, Ethnic Minorities Committee, Ethnic Minorities Committee, S. Cosset, GLC/ILEA JNC for Senior Officers (Staff Side), 'Observations on Equal Opportunities in GLC/ILEA Employment Report', no date [December 1981], LMA, GLC/DG/PRE/49/5.

The GLC's 'positive action' also meant contract compliance with those companies seeking work with the GLC to ensure that equal opportunity policies were being followed at workplaces outside the GLC. The Council developed a Code of Practice for Tenders and Contracts, including compliance with the Sex Discrimination and Race Relations Acts. This required having procedures to deal with discrimination and having strategies to promote opportunities for greater equality, particularly if women and ethnic minorities were under-represented. A Contract Compliance Equal Opportunities Unit was established to pursue these issues with particular firms. This unit would write to firms on the list of approved contractors for the GLC to enquire how they were fulfilling or intended to meet the new policies. If firms did not submit this information, they risked being 'excluded from the Council's Approved List of Contractors.'[34] The Ethnic Minorities Committee and the Industry and Employment Committee conceded that there would be higher costs involved, with contract compliance possibly reaching £300,000 a year, but they still thought that it would be 'a legitimate use of the Council's commercial power for it to consider the equal opportunities policies of its suppliers and contractors.'[35]

Reaction to these policies on contract compliance was overwhelmingly negative. '[C]onsiderable objection' emerged from trade unions in the building trades, rooted in the 'social and political objectives' of the policy, its potential costs, and the possibility of duplication of the work of the CRE and the Equal Opportunities Commission. Employers large and small also resisted the policy. The Confederation of British Industry was 'totally opposed', and the association representing small and medium-sized building firms argued that there was no need for a formal equal opportunities policy: 'the workforce on the normal site is probably more free from racial and sex distinction than in almost any other sector of industry and commerce.'[36] No evidence was offered to sustain this

[34] See, for example, GLC, Ethnic Minorities Committee, J. Mellor to J. Jones, 31 August 1984, LMA, GLC/DG/PRE/49/35.
[35] GLC, Industry and Employment Committee, Legal and General Committee, Report by Director-General, 'Contracts and Tenders', 24 March 1983, LMA, GLC/DG/PRE/49/18.
[36] GLC, Industry and Employment Committee, Legal and General Committee, Report by Director-General, 'Contracts and Tenders', 24 March 1983, LMA, GLC/DG/PRE/49/18.

view. Smaller firms loathed the policy. A snapshot of responses received by compliance officers in 1984 exudes the flavour of this antipathy:

> The Company Secretary said she was too busy to see an adviser and did not care about being removed from the approved list. She said [they] were equal opportunity employers anyway and could not understand what we wanted to discuss...The Company Executive stated that the company regarded the Council's contract compliance policy as 'a load of rubbish' and on which they totally disagreed with [sic]...It was also added that the Company would prefer not to be on the Council's Approved List...if these requirements were insisted upon.... I tried to explain our work. [The firm's director] became abusive and said 'We are not prepared to get involved with GLC politics – we don't want all this bloody nonsense. I object to you phoning yesterday and speaking to my typist. We have two coloured workers. We are just a sort of family firm doing our best for our customers, okay. Thank you very much'. He then slammed down the phone.[37]

Contract compliance officers undoubtedly got used to the slamming of phones in their ears. In these two areas of policy—'positive action' in hiring and contract compliance—one can see the resistance in everyday labour and employment practices to an equality agenda.

2.3

In April 1982, the Ethnic Minorities Committee organized a large consultative conference with about two hundred representatives of ethnic minority organizations. There was some concern from these representatives that this was merely a 'cosmetic' exercise. Livingstone and Ouseley stressed the sincerity of the GLC's commitment to anti-racism. Livingstone singled out, for example, a desire to 'put an end to racism in

---

[37] GLC, Ethnic Minorities Committee, Contract Compliance Equal Opportunities Unit, Exclusion from the Approved List of Contractors, '...Builders', 17 September 1984; '...Construction (South) Ltd', 14 September 1984; '...', 13 September 1984, LMA, GLC/DG/PRE/49/35. Please note that firm names have been deleted.

our own housing [and] our own job recruitment', while wanting to launch a 'public fight...to convince white Londoners that racism is prevalent in all aspects of life in London'. Livingstone also wished to be told which 'course of action' to 'follow in developing policies and pro-grammes to combat racism'. The participants at the conference responded by foregrounding the problems of greatest concern on the ground to ethnic minority people: the struggles faced by Black youth in finding jobs and dealing with the police; the problems besetting the South Asian community in terms of the law affecting citizenship and immigration and experiences of racial violence; and the need for legal assistance to fight against racial discrimination. The assurances given by the GLC representatives at the conference included greater access to the GLC both in terms of employment and 'positions of power', including 'black representation' on the Greater London Enterprise Board and other 'strategic committees of the GLC'.[38] That answer indicated a willingness, as also indicated above, to transform the centre of London governance. But the Ethnic Minorities Committee's work was also deeply involved in facilitating grass-roots initiatives on race. Most importantly, this came in the form of grant aid.

Of course, there was a tension between power at the centre and the autonomy of community organizations. Some critics among the Black activist community saw this as a corrupting relationship. Ambalavaner Sivanandan, Paul Gilroy, and Mike Phillips were notable voices in this regard. The first evoked a period of growth in ethnic minority commu-nity organizations in the 1960s and 1970s when Black people 'had to address themselves to creating a social and educational infrastructure for the second generation – in self-help groups and social centres, supplementary schools in neighbourhood schools, workshops and bookshops, hostels for the unemployed and the homeless, youth clubs and associations', a growth which he feared was threatened not by out-right enemies but by friends: 'the centre of gravity of the race relations industry has moved from the central government and the CRE to the local state – and with it, the black struggle, not for community and class

---

[38] GLC, Ethnic Minorities Committee, Consultative Conference with Ethnic Minorities, 18 November 1982 (conference held 24 April 1982), LMA, GLC/DG/PRE/111/17.

any more, but for handouts and position'.[39] Paul Gilroy's concerns partly focused on the nebulous quality of anti-racist campaigning by the GLC, which he believed distracted from the material, quotidian issues of Black life.[40] Mike Phillips saw grant aid to community groups in the Black community as something that corrupted their purpose, making them more about obtaining funds than about developing community-based politics. Phillips argued that the GLC was driven, in his estimation mistakenly, by a crude desire to 'get the money out of the building', particularly through its grant aid.[41]

But getting the money out of the building might also be seen as one way of transferring power from the (local) state to the community. This process did not necessarily distort grass-roots efforts but, rather, reflected the messy variety of the work done on the ground by disparate organizations. The work of the Ethnic Minorities Committee was more complex in its whole than suggested by Gilroy, Sivanandan, and Phillips largely because of the breadth of groups that it dealt with. In other words, the interests and issues of community organizations tended to define the work of the Ethnic Minorities Committee rather than the Ethnic Minorities Committee defining the work of community organ-izations. The hand of the state was not intended to be heavy or deadening. Rather, a great deal of emphasis was placed on organizations' autonomy and on values such as self-help and self-reliance. At the same time, much grant aid went to material questions rooted in the everyday—employment, housing, and the provision of education, for example—particularly as it related to young Black people. Indeed, this work was not simply rooted in the everyday, it was literally rooted in London streets, through the GLC-funded acquisition of local premises.

Looking at particular organizations in receipt of GLC funding in 1984 gives a sense of how race and anti-racism worked at the grass-roots level. I have focused on organizations that received funding during

---

[39] Ambalavaner Sivanandan, 'RAT and the Degradation of the Black Struggle', in *Communities of Resistance: Writing on Black Struggles for Socialism* (London: Verso, 1990), 81–2, 107.

[40] See Paul Gilroy, *'There Ain't No Black in the Union Jack'* (Chicago: University of Chicago Press, 1987, 1991).

[41] Mike Phillips, 'The State of London', in Kerr and Gibson (eds.), *London: From Punk to Blair*, 153.

Anti-Racist Year and had emerged from the Black community. A particular argument in this section is that such organizations tackled both material and cultural issues in Black life in 1980s London. These organizations were also concerned with creating and securing Black space in the city.

Before looking at particular organizations in detail, it is important to review the quantitative aspects of grant aid funding, to think about who got grant aid from the Ethnic Minorities Committee. A breakdown of one year of such funding gives a sense of how the GLC's money was distributed. In the financial year 1983/4, £2,393,051 was spent on grant aid by the Ethnic Minorities Committee. About 4.6 per cent of this was given to institutions or organizations such as the Institute of Race Relations, the Runnymede Trust, and the anti-fascist organization Searchlight. The first received, for example, a grant of £60,000. About 32 per cent of the funds were distributed to organizations which did not cater to specific or identifiable ethnic minority communities. The rest of the money was divided among a host of organizations that can be roughly associated with particular ethnic, religious, and national communities. The smallest grant was £40, given to the Haringey Black Pressure Group on Education; the largest grant was £77,000, given to the Rastafarian Advisory Centre. There was a considerable variety in the kinds of organizations applying for money, including ones pursuing education, culture, anti-racism, religions (including Muslim centres and Christian churches such as the Nigerian Eternal Sacred Order of Cherubim and Seraphim), and community centres. Among identifiable ethnic minority groups, Afro-Caribbean organizations received approximately 34.7 per cent of all grant aid, with South Asian groups obtaining 12.7 per cent, and East Asian (in this example, exclusively Chinese), Jewish, and Irish groups all getting between 3 and 4 per cent. The smallest slice was for a Moroccan group, and there were also grants made to organizations dealing with British Cypriots, the Turkish community, and Spanish migrant workers.

Redressing racial inequities was tackled by the substantive funding of community organizations through grant aid. There was a kaleidoscopic range to such funding between 1981 and 1986, including language classes and self-defence workshops, private legal prosecutions (often around cases of racial violence and discrimination), and community history projects, home care for the elderly, and recording studios. It is a mistake, in many ways, to tidy up the dazzling variety of projects the Ethnic Minorities Committee funded, because it is that variety that defined the GLC's grant aid, as if it were attempting to capture the infinite variety of the city through state funding. But some focus might be brought to thinking about this most important aspect of what the Ethnic Minorities Committee did. This can be better understood by looking at a range of Black organizations applying to the Ethnic Minorities Committee for funding in 1984.

The Ladywell Action Centre applied to the Ethnic Minorities Committee for £9,000 in funding in January 1984. It had been founded in 1969 by a multiracial group of individual volunteers who focused on a variety of problems facing people of West Indian descent in Lewisham. These included housing, education, employment, and, in particular, relations with the police. By the 1970s, there were 'very poor police-Black relationships in the Borough.'[42] The Centre began to work within the Lewisham Council for Community Relations subcommittee on the question of policing and itself took on individual cases. In 1983, for example, a man had intervened when he saw a young Black girl struggling with two men. The man, Samuel James, was immediately 'set upon by two uniform [sic] policemen', arrested for obstructing and assaulting police officers who 'wrongfully and brutally beat him up'. The Ladywell Action Centre organized community support for James and had the charges dismissed.[43] The Centre also initiated a number of programmes to help ethnic minority people, particularly youth. These included a 'Black Leadership Programme' to give skills in administration and management so that participants could 'take an active part in public life'.[44] It also offered employment skills workshops to Black youth and

[42] GLC, Ethnic Minorities Committee, 'Ladywell Action Centre', Funding Application, 28 March 1983, LMA, GLC/DG/PRE/EM/1/4.
[43] GLC, Ethnic Minorities Committee, 'Ladywell Action Centre', Case Notes, 1981–4, LMA, GLC/DG/PRE/EM/1/4.
[44] GLC, Ethnic Minorities Committee, 'Ladywell Action Centre', Funding Application, 20 September 1985, LMA, GLC/DG/PRE/EM/1/4.

established a Black Theatre Workshop.[45] By 1984, the Centre's volunteer membership was dominantly Black, reflecting a change from its founding in the late sixties. In January 1984, the Ladywell Action Centre sought GLC funding to secure a long-term physical presence in Lewisham. The Centre had recently obtained a long-term lease on a property on Loampit Vale from Lewisham Council. But its resources were very meagre. Most of its financial support came from raffles, sales, and individual sponsorships for the London Marathon. Reviewing the application, the Ethnic Minorities Unit noted that the Centre's office equipment included 'a sub-standard desk and two chairs'.[46] The Ethnic Minorities Committee granted the Centre £4,300.

The application made by the Ladywell Action Centre to the Ethnic Minorities Committee gives a sense, first of all, of the kinds of work done at the local level by voluntary organizations on racial equality work. This involved, in particular, a focus upon Black youth and— something that would be a common theme across race equality work in London in the 1980s—an engagement with the problem of policing. The application also gives us a sense that such organizations, at this point, were largely staffed by volunteers but sought funds to employ full-time administrative and managerial staff. With a need for such staffing came a need for permanent or at least more secure space in the city, through long-term leases on property.

In Camberwell, the African People's Movement sought the same kind of support from the GLC in June 1984 to secure its work within the community. The African People's Movement had been founded in 1975. Its focus was less on questions of policing or employment and rather on culture, 'to provide for Africans and people of African origins in particular and people of the world in general, opportunity for personal opportunity and pride'. Its goals were to put on programmes of 'literature, culture and politics' highlighting the 'aspirations and major struggle of black people through awareness and respect of Africa'. We can see in this an example of the connection between local and global politics,

[45] GLC, Ethnic Minorities Committee, 'Ladywell Action Centre', Funding Application, 30 January 1984, LMA, GLC/DG/PRE/EM/1/4.
[46] GLC, Ethnic Minorities Committee, 'Ladywell Action Centre', Funding Application, 20 September 1985, LMA, GLC/DG/PRE/EM/1/4.

particularly through the prism of race and anti-racism. The African People's Movement clearly linked the work it was doing in south London with a larger understanding of global Black identity. In June 1984, it was considering a series of talks by speakers such as the exiled Kenyan writer Ngugi wa Thiong'o on 'African Immigrants' and the historian and journalist Basil Davidson on 'African Culture and History' to make audiences 'aware of the rich African culture'. Other Black groups, such as Creation for Liberation, similarly sought to encourage Black culture in London and situate that culture in a more global context.[47] In 1983, Creation for Liberation organized the 'first open exhibition of contemporary Black art in Britain', which sought to bring together the 'rich and powerful Asian, African and Caribbean heritage' with 'British and European heritage'.[48] Culture was a particularly important aspect to the kinds of work that organizations such as the African People's Movement were doing. In March 1984, Ouseley and the Arts and Recreation Committee stressed that a critical part of encouraging Black culture in London and fighting racism was drawing out the connections with global culture: '[t]he concerns of contemporary black artists are to identify, redefine and consolidate as black people living in Britain. This involves new concepts and new traditions being forged which embrace both the Afro-Caribbean, Asian and other origins of the black experience and its present reality in 20th century Britain.'[49]

The Movement had played a role in the establishment of other Black organizations, such as the Hackney Black Women's Association and a Black Women's Action centre in Southwark. The funds would help pay the salaries of a coordinator and a part-time assistant, as well as the rent on premises on the Camberwell Road.[50] What clearly infused the African People's Movement's efforts was an explicit connection between local Black issues and a global Black identity. Speaking about race in 1984 London meant excavating a wider Black identity.

[47] On Creation for Liberation, see GLC, Ethnic Minorities Committee, 'Creation for Liberation', Funding Application, 6 February 1984, LMA, GLC/DG/PRE/49/21.
[48] See Creation for Liberation, *Catalogue* (London: Creation for Liberation, 1983).
[49] GLC, Ethnic Minorities Committee, Report by Director of Recreation and the Arts and the PRRA, 'London Against Racism in Mainstream Arts Policies Programming', 12 March 1984, LMA, GLC/DG/PRE/49/24.
[50] GLC, Ethnic Minorities Committee, 'African People's Movement', Funding Application, 15 June 1984, LMA, GLC/DG/PRE/49/29.

In contrast to the Ladywell Action Centre and the African People's Movement, the Brixton Action Youth Outreach Centre was born of the rising of 1981. It was 'founded by a group of individuals who had been working within the black community as a result of the Brixton uprisings of 1981'. Believing that 'unemployment, educational cuts and poor communication channels' had led to a 'high crime rate and tension among local youths', the Centre sought 'to provide temporary rehabilitation' for Black youth, particularly those who had been convicted of a crime, 'so that such young people may grow to full maturity as individuals and members of society and become better equipped to take a useful and responsible place in the community'. This would be effected through counselling, education and training, the provision of recreational facilities, and 'liaison and discussion' with police. It was notable that the Centre did not set itself against the police in this manner.[51] What is perhaps striking is how much this younger organization, the Brixton Action Youth Outreach Centre, had in common with an older organization, the Ladywell Action Centre.

What linked many of the disparate organizations funded in 1984 was their desire to create Black space in the city, both in terms of acquiring physical premises for their work and in terms of the kind of work that would be done in those spaces, which reflected an engagement with both material and cultural issues shaping urban Black life.

Like the Brixton Action Youth Outreach Centre, the Afro-Caribbean Community Association had been founded in 1981, 'in the wake of the disturbances in 1981 in central Brixton and the resulting strained relationship between the local community and the police'. In 1984, it was housed in three temporary huts on the north end of Mayall Road (now Bob Marley Way) and applied to the Ethnic Minorities Committee that year for funds to construct more permanent premises: 'a purpose-built community centre in Brixton that could be controlled by and for the young people of Brixton'.[52] Ujima, an organization founded in 1977 in Finsbury Park 'to provide temporary and permanent housing, employment,

---

[51] GLC, Ethnic Minorities Committee, 'Brixton Action Youth Outreach Centre', Funding Application, 14 May 1984, LMA, GLC/DG/PRE/49/27.

[52] GLC, Ethnic Minorities Committee, 'Afro-Caribbean Community Association', Funding Application, 16 January 1984, LMA/GLC/DG/PRE/49/20.

training and social support to young black people', was similarly explicit in its aim of creating a Black space:

> The Project is based on the 'storefront' concept which has operated successfully in many ghetto areas of the USA...The central idea behind the Project is to provide a place where unemployed young people could gather, not only for recreational purposes but also to have access to constructive sporting activities, or employment opportunities.[53]

The Afro-Caribbean Community Association and Ujima wanted those Black spaces to house activities and initiatives that would address the material needs of Black people in London, whether that was unemployment, education, or, as with the example of an organization such as Brixton Young Families Housing Aid, homelessness. Another group, the Waltham Forest Caribbean Council, wanted permanent premises for programmes of 'women's rights, domestic and welfare rights, education and employment', including workshops on job skills such as carpentry.[54] Other organizations focused on Black cultural issues. Both Carib Theatre and Ujima, for example, requested funds for supporting Black-focused plays, talks on African history and culture, and staging exhibitions and screening films on Black life.[55] And many, like the Afro-Caribbean Community Association, simply saw the acquisition of premises as a way of providing space to Black people for their own use and, notably, their own control. In these ways and through these organizations, a Black London was established in the 1980s in another example of the marriage between municipal social democracy and community activism.

[53] GLC, Ethnic Minorities Committee, 'Ujima Housing Association Finsbury Park Project', Funding Application, 9 July 1984, LMA, GLC/DG/PRE/49/30.
[54] GLC, Ethnic Minorities Committee, 'Waltham Forest Caribbean Council', Funding Application, 9 July 1984, LMA/GLC/DG/PRE/49/30.
[55] GLC, Ethnic Minorities Application, 'Black Theatre in Education', Funding Application, 9 July 1984, LMA/GLC/DG/PRE/49/30; GLC, Ethnic Minorities Committee, 'Ujima Housing Association Finsbury Park Project', Funding Application, 9 July 1984, LMA/GLC/DG/PRE/49/30.

2.4

One of the consequences of the consultative meeting with community organizations in 1982 was a commitment to have a year dedicated to anti-racism. As PRRA, Herman Ouseley argued that, against a backdrop of increasing racial discrimination and harassment, a hostile and biased media, and concerns around restrictive immigration and nationality legislation, there needed to be 'an extensive programme of anti-racist activities'. This would not only address immediate problems but, more broadly, help create a culture of 'racial tolerance, fairness, equality and justice' in London. In 1984, London would be declared an 'anti-racist zone', with a dedicated campaign to 'raise public awareness' through public events and publicity which would expose 'the evils of racism and the positive aspects of multi-ethnic, multi-cultural London'.[56] Anti-racism would be tackled on several fronts: top-down from the GLC itself, but also ground-up from grass-roots organizations. Policy and politics would be mobilized, but so too would culture and leisure. It was, indeed, important to find a means beyond politics, through 'entertainments in themselves', which would 'initially secure a captive audience for exposure to anti-racist initiatives'.[57] Though there would be specific foci for anti-racist work, there was also an overarching belief that anti-racism would fundamentally change political culture, making anti-racism a 'permanent feature of London life'.[58]

Once launched in January 1984, Anti-Racist Year was as much an act of coordination among many community and local bodies as it was a GLC-driven programme. Over the year, for example, there was a series of borough council events. These included 'Celebrating African People in Camden'; 'One Islington'; the showing of *It Ain't Half Racist Mum*, Stuart Hall's 1979 television discussion, by Haringey Council; and a Lambeth Council-sponsored event which featured, among other things,

---

[56] GLC, Ethnic Minorities Committee, Report by PRRA, 'Programme for a Special Programme of Anti-Racist Activities 1983–4', 29 September 1982, LMA, GLC/DG/PRE/223/2.
[57] GLC, Ethnic Minorities Committee, Report by PRRA, 'Anti-Racist Programme Proposed Key Events', 9 December 1983, LMA, GLC/DG/PRE/49/18.
[58] GLC, Ethnic Minorities Committee, Report by PRRA, 'Programme for a Special Programme of Anti-Racist Activities 1983–4', 29 September 1982, LMA, GLC/DG/PRE/223/2.

speakers from the African National Congress. A wide variety of pressure groups and community organizations were also involved in putting on activities during the year, including the Africa Centre, Southall Monitoring Group, Newham 8 Defence Campaign, the Bengali Cultural Association, and the Campaign Against Racism and Fascism.[59] Halfway through the year, the GLC itself put on a massive event, a London Against Racism rally at Jubilee Gardens. The event, which featured musical acts such as Ian Dury and the Music Students and the South African band Matunibi, saw an opening address by Stevie Wonder, as well as speeches by Livingstone and Darcus Howe. Thirty thousand people attended the rally.[60]

Though Anti-Racist Year comprised many disparate elements, it was also an attempt, by the GLC, to create an overarching anti-racist political culture in London. This was, of course, a huge and sometimes amorphous ambition. It is worth thinking about what underpinned that aim. In the first place, what was racism and what was the strategy to combat it in broad terms? What the GLC's efforts around Anti-Racist Year suggested was that racism and anti-racism were less about Blackness than whiteness. Racism was identified as an 'intrinsically white problem', centred particularly in two constituencies: 'white policy/decision makers' and 'white (particularly white working class) Londoners'. The latter had to 'assess their own racist attitudes'.[61] An anti-racist strategy was particularly focused upon the white working classes, who were, to a certain degree equated with the 'poor and powerless'; for the GLC, the challenge for the anti-racist programme would be to engage 'the poor, unemployed and working class communities who live and work in precisely those environments where racism has its most devastating effects'.[62] The GLC's initial strategy was to make (white)

[59] GLC, Ethnic Minorities Committee, Report by Senior Race Relations Adviser (SRRA), 'Anti-Racist Year Programme of Initiatives Press Report on Implementation', 29 November 1984, LMA, GLC/DG/PRE/49/37.
[60] GLC, Ethnic Minorities Committee, Report by PRRA, 'London Against Racism Rally: Additional Costs', 12 September 1984, LMA, GLC/DG/PRE/49/32.
[61] GLC, Ethnic Minorities Committee, 'Anti-Racist Advertising Strategy', 30 July 1984, LMA, GLC/DG/PRE/49/31.
[62] GLC, Ethnic Minorities Committee, Report by PRRA, 'Anti-Racist Programme: An Interim Assessment', 25 April 1984, LMA, GLC/DG/PRE/49/26.

institutions and (white) Londoners self-critical and self-regulating or self-reforming spaces and subjects. An advertising strategy was devised to encourage Londoners to 'question their own racism' and to educate themselves 'to the facts of racism' and thus 'analyse their own racism'. This would be followed up by an effort '[t]o isolate, embarrass, expose, racist practices'.[63]

Anti-racism thus rested upon the construction of a new kind of political subjectivity, one in which political subjects were aware and self-critical, particularly with respect to race. Through Anti-Racist Year and other equality initiatives, the GLC also sought to populate the city with a new kind of self-regulating and self-critical political subject. What the GLC was promoting in the 1980s through Anti-Racist Year and other equality initiatives was a subject that was self-regulated in a new way, based upon critical self-reflection on questions of race, gender, and sexual orientation. To adapt Patrick Joyce's argument from *The Rule of Freedom* (2003), the GLC (as a local state) was performing anti-racism, anti-sexism, and anti-heterosexism, with the intent of creating a reflective, critical, and self-regulating anti-racist, anti-sexist, and anti-heterosexist subject.[64] Going back to the statement made on the launch of Anti-Racist Year, the aim was to create a citizen that would be 'deeply aware of all forms of oppression' and take 'action personally and collectively to end all oppression'.

This might be illustrated by a brief examination of three posters produced as part of Anti-Racist Year. Each poster addressed a somewhat different audience, and the message was different in each, but all were grounded in the aspiration to create both an anti-racist London and anti-racist Londoners, ordinary spaces, and subjects. The first, 'London Against Racism: If You're Not Part of the Solution, You're Part of the Problem', showed four white pedestrians walking by the poster, shielding themselves from its message with their newspapers. The poster articulated the need for an awakening, an acknowledgement of the problem of racism, in the first place, and a recognition, in the second

---

[63] GLC, Ethnic Minorities Committee, 'Anti-Racist Advertising Strategy', 30 July 1984, LMA, GLC/DG/PRE/49/31.

[64] See Patrick Joyce, *The Rule of Freedom* (London: Verso, 2003).

place, that something (albeit undefined) needs to be done about it. Thus, the wellspring of race would lead to a more reflective political subject, for whom anti-racism would be an important aspect of self-regulation. The second poster, 'Which Slice of the Cake are You Getting?', with one dark slice in an otherwise white decorative cake of London, deliberately splits its spectators into thinking about their relationship to the 'share of the Capital's resources' through the lens of race. Again, the starting point is the creation of a critical and reflective political subject. In this case, it is for non-ethnic minority people to consider what disproportionate advantages accrue to them and for ethnic minority people to consider what they are being denied. That reflection would lead to a correction of the political culture in London, in part through self-regulation. But the poster also encouraged viewers to embrace the GLC's attempts to confront its own institutional racism. The final poster, 'Let's Beat Racism Together', is of a different character than the other two. The poster shows a group of six men and women of different races dancing. The subtitle is 'Share the Word'. It shares with the previous posters a prescriptive element—to 'beat' racism. But it also offered a vision of what might be gained with the acknowledgement and struggle against racism. This comprises a diverse, unified, and joyful community—and one that is about twenty years younger in its median age than the first poster. These, then, are the new political subjects. Their political subjectivity includes anti-racism, and that anti-racism is both self-reflective and naturalized—it has been made ordinary and normal; indeed, it is the animating aspect of political subjectivity and civic community as the poster visually suggests.

As Chapter 8 suggests, the GLC's anti-racist campaign first of all ran aground on the persistent racial tension, harassment, and violence meted out on the street and on housing estates.

But the GLC's anti-racist messaging has been the subject of other, less violent criticism. The most incisive criticism remains that offered by Paul Gilroy—that this municipal anti-racism was rendered empty, first, by its excision of the problem from everyday, material life—racism as a thing that floated above ordinary life—and second, by the vagaries of what an anti-racist London meant in terms of change. But, however flawed the strategy of municipal anti-racism might have been, this message was an attempt to disrupt complacency about racism and to throw a critical light on whiteness. It was also an attempt to think through social democracy with a strong reference to race, whether that was Blackness or whiteness. And, of course, other kinds of similar attempts remain in play in different forms in the present day.

2.5

In September 1984, standing in for Livingstone, who was fighting a by-election to protest abolition, the acting Leader of the GLC, John Wilson, a councillor from Newham, reported to the Council on 'Race Relations in London'. The report was in part a review of what the Council had done in 1984 as part of Anti-Racist Year and since 1981 as part of its long-standing commitment to fighting racism. This was linked to an attack upon the Thatcher government's record on race, particularly in a year when Margaret Thatcher had hosted the South African Prime Minister P. W. Botha and hastily extended citizenship to the white South African runner Zola Budd:

> It is exactly three years on since the street uprisings of 1981 and during the intervening period the Council has been spearheading a major drive against racism whereas the Government has been rolling back the aspirations of the black and other ethnic minority communities....The punishment being meted out to black people by Thatcherism has been unrelenting. For those who have been the butt of the repressive and racist immigration laws, the biased national legislation, unrelenting brutal policing, among the ageless and with no hope for employment ever, sub-human housing condi-tions, a continuous mass media attack, and racial harassment and attacks, the recent Zola Budd incident of acquiring citizenship in an unprecedented ten days and the lunch date with South African Prime Minister Botha have been particularly savage insults. Some black people have described it as 'slapping us in the face while cutting our throats'.

By contrast with the Thatcher government, through Anti-Racist Year the GLC had attempted to construct a new kind of anti-racist political culture:

> ...in spite of Mrs Thatcher's determination to take action against the 'aliens' who threaten to 'swamp' her and her kith and kin's indigenous culture, the Council has succeeded in winning support for its anti-racism programme and inspire confidence among the large sections of the black and other ethnic minority communities that race equality and justice can yet be achieved in racist Britain.[65]

The end of 1984 did not, of course, end efforts to promote anti-racism. Nor did the abolition of the GLC end such efforts. They were carried on by borough governments and by the community organizations given funds by the GLC. Of course, the end of the GLC cut off a critical source of financial support and a larger context of support.

The meanings of Anti-Racist Year are ambiguous and uneven. For its part, the GLC clearly did not succeed in its aim of making Londoners and London anti-racist. As Chapter 8 will attest, this failure was written in the intense racial tension and violence that existed in the 1980s. Nonetheless, its efforts at introducing anti-racism or the consciousness of race into policy and governance were early explorations of a landscape that has become familiar in the early twenty-first century: attempts to work equality concerns into everyday practices such as hiring and contracts and in the broader work of anti-racism. These efforts must also be seen in the context of a conservative counter-reaction to questions of identity, including race. The GLC's equality initiatives, including the example of Anti-Racist Year, were also early explorations of a much darker landscape of cultural wars around identity.

This chapter has illustrated two other themes. In the first place, it has examined the racial aspect of social democratic political culture. The GLC's commitment to anti-racism highlighted not only Blackness in

[65] GLC, Ethnic Minorities Committee, Report by Director-General, 'Race Relations in London', 26 September 1984, LMA, GLC/DG/PRE/49/34.

that political culture but the role of whiteness as well, whether as something that was threatened by an increasingly multiracial society or as something that had to be reformed in order to achieve an anti-racist society. Finally, it has emphasized that Anti-Racist Year is a way of understanding the creation of Black London, not in a top-down fashion, but rather through the efforts of the Black community itself.

London, 1984: Conflict and Change in the Radical City. Stephen Brooke, Oxford University Press.
© Stephen Brooke 2024. DOI: 10.1093/9780191895395.003.0003

3

Capital City? People's Armadas, Pop, and Planning

In the spring and summer of 1984, a struggle over the economic future of London was played out on the Thames. On 13 April, Margaret Thatcher lunched at the offices of the London Docklands Development Corporation (LDDC) at the West India Docks in Millwall. The LDDC was an institutional child of her government, tasked with regenerating the Docklands as a lightly regulated and taxed 'enterprise zone'.[1] Thatcher's speech after the meal was a paean to the virtues of 'business and development', 'cutting down officialdom and bureaucracy' in the recovery of the 'derelict' Docklands.[2]

Four days later, what was called the People's Armada sailed up the Thames from the Docklands—a flotilla of pleasure boats carrying nearly a thousand people, accompanied by music. The armada passed the Houses of Parliament on its way to docking at Jubilee Gardens on the South Bank, where it was met by Ken Livingstone. After disembarking, the Joint Docklands Action Group (JDAG), a community organization, presented a parliamentary petition against the LDDC from people in the Docklands as well as its *People's Charter for the Docklands* put together in 1984.[3] The *People's Charter* emphasized that local people's needs, particularly in terms of jobs and housing, had to be consulted in the formulation of economic policy and that the public sector, rather

---

[1] On the emergence of the enterprise zone, see Wetherell, 'Freedom Planned: Enterprise Zones and Urban Non-Planning in Post-War Britain'.

[2] Margaret Thatcher Foundation Archives, Speech Visiting London Docklands, 13 April 1984, https://www.margaretthatcher.org/document/105660 (accessed 17 June 2023).

[3] See Loraine Leeson, 'Our Land: Creative Approaches to the Redevelopment of London's Docklands', *International Journal of Heritage* 25/4 (2019): 370–2, doi: 10.1080/13527258. 2018.1485166.

Figure 3.1 People's Armada, 1985.
Credit: Mike Seaborne.

than the free market, was the only way forward. There were two People's Armadas; the second, in 1985, is illustrated in Figure 3.1.

Two months later, on Saturday, 9 June 1984, the world's leading economies—the G7—met at the Connaught Rooms, near Covent Garden. At the meeting, Margaret Thatcher asserted that the G7 had to do 'as much as we can for job creation', but that this could only occur within a strict monetarist policy, in which ' "unrealistic" expectations of social provision must be curbed'.[4] The next day, those expectations were anything but curbed when, a mile away across the river in Jubilee Gardens, tens of thousands of people gathered for the 'Jobs for a Change' festival organized by the GLC, featuring acts such as the Smiths, Aswad, and Billy Bragg. 'Jobs for a Change' was a music-driven broadside against the monetarist economic policy of the Thatcher government, as Michael Ward, one of the architects of the GLC's economic policy, wrote after the concert:

[4] Margaret Thatcher Foundation Archives, Press Conference at G7 Summit, Saturday, 9 June 1984, https://www.margaretthatcher.org/document/105694 (accessed 17 June 2023); *The Times*, 9 June 1984.

We aim to promote new forms of industrial ownership and controls, to use technology to enhance working lives rather than to deskill jobs, and to take positive action to support the rights of women and black people. We set out, through the encouragement of popular planning and industrial democracy, to make economic decisions more accountable.[5]

The Armada and the concert were largely symbolic salvos against neoliberalism, but a material victory came a month later, not with a city-wide public spectacle but with a local financial transaction. In July 1984, Coin Street, a long-derelict area on the South Bank stretching from Waterloo to the banks of the river, was sold by the GLC at a discounted rate to a community group planning to develop the 5-hectare site in the interest of local residents and the local economy. Coin Street Community Builders borrowed the money from the GLC itself, through a public sector investment body, the Greater London Enterprise Board. This victory came after years of struggle between private developers bent on building office towers on the site and local groups determined to protect the local area against the domination of the private market.

These three moments in the spring and summer of 1984 were illustrative of a larger conflict in 1980s London around the city's economic future. The starting point was the belief, held firmly across the political spectrum, that the crisis of the city demanded economic restructuring. Coming to power in 1979, the Thatcher government was intent upon a neoliberal regeneration of London. The establishment of the LDDC in 1981 and the deregulation of the financial markets in 1986, the so-called 'Big Bang', helped create a 'market city'.[6] Against this, the GLC and community organizations struggled to find new life for a 'social' city, in which the public sector remained an active force and in which the interests of labour, particularly in terms of employment, remained paramount.

[5] Michael Ward, 'You Can't Crush the Spirit of the GLC', *London Labour Briefing* 41 (July 1984), 1.
[6] Massey, *World City*, 40.

Of course, we know the end of this story: a new city of capital emerged in the 1980s. This chapter examines challenges to that change. This is, in part, a narrative about the role played by the GLC, but it was not confined to a political agenda emanating from County Hall. Once again, as shown in the work of the Ethnic Minorities Committee, what the history of London in 1984 suggests is an engagement between power at the centre, represented by County Hall, and agency on the ground by community organizations. Alternatives to the neoliberal city originated in community groups on the ground, as the stories of the People's Armada and Coin Street illustrate. As well, this was a narrative in which politics and economics were entwined with other spheres beyond the corridors of power, notably that of feminism, race, and popular culture.

The debate over the city's economic future involved, more broadly, the relationship of people to power and an engagement with the question of democracy. Hilary Wainwright was a key player in the formulation of the GLC's economic policy in the 1980s as Deputy Chief Economic Adviser and as a force within the Popular Planning Unit. In 1987, she and others similarly involved with the GLC published *A Taste of Power*, an account of their time in office. But she began the book, not with the first steps within the corridors of power but, rather, with the story of an activist from East London, Connie Hunt, whose initial reaction to the GLC was sceptical:

> I was suspicious, and so were the majority of people around here. It wasn't long since we had been fighting the GLC, over the tower blocks. I said, we don't want them, we don't want them down here, no way.

Wainwright went on to state:

> From early on, many people in the GLC came to see the working relationships which developed between the council and its constituents as a crucial – even *the* crucial element – of economic and industrial policy…the most important lessons to be learned from the GLC about future Labour economic policy making, at local and national level, are about the relationships between the state, and the majority of its

citizens – or in other words about the political *process* by which a state authority develops and implements alternative economic policies.[7]

This chapter argues that economic challenges to Thatcherite neoliberalism involved not only a social democratic alternative to that economic ideology but a democratic alternative as well. The economic challenge seen in these initiatives also emphasized questions of equality, particularly in terms of gender and race, and addressed local working-class needs. The economic alternatives to Thatcherism emerged both from County Hall and from the work of community organizations. The present chapter looks first at the economic policy emanating from the GLC, then examines the efforts on the ground in the Docklands and on the South Bank.

3.1

Labour came to power in London in 1981 determined to challenge the emerging neoliberal economic agenda. The ability of local government to influence the economy was limited, but the GLC could use a 2p levy in the rates for a wide range of economic development projects and grants, a power it used explicitly to construct an alternative economy. The GLC's economic agenda was institutionally supported by four bodies. There was an existing Industry and Employment Committee, to which was added a smaller Economic Policy Group, and two bodies which had specific economic briefs: the Popular Planning Unit, designed to liaise with grass-roots organizations, and the Greater London Enterprise Board, which was an independent body dispensing grants and financial aid. Three figures who had worked outside of local government before 1981 were the moving forces on these bodies: Michael Ward, the new GLC member for Haringey who served as the Chair of the Industry and Employment Committee and Deputy Leader of Council; the socialist economist Robin Murray, a co-author of the 1968

---

[7] Maureen Macintosh and Hilary Wainwright (eds.), *A Taste of Power* (London: Verso, 1987), 1, 2.

May Day manifesto, who became Chief Economic Adviser and Chair of the Economic Policy Group; and Hilary Wainwright, an influential feminist writer who served as Deputy Chief Economic Adviser, headed the Popular Planning Unit, and sat on the Economic Policy Group. Another leading feminist, Sheila Rowbotham, also worked on economic policy within the GLC after 1981.

Three main factors guided the GLC's economic policy after 1981. The first was an emphasis upon production. That emphasis shifted the focus of economic policy from capital to labour, which distinguished the alternative economic policy of the GLC from both monetarism and Keynesianism. A second undercurrent of GLC economic policy was the belief that economic policy was a vehicle for decentralization and the reinvigoration of democracy. In the 1970s, the new urban left had argued that local government could be a means of deconstructing the state, dissembling central power by either devolving power to community groups or involving popular participation in the framing of policy and governing. This was a contradictory dynamic—'in and against the state'.[8] Figures such as Hilary Wainwright at once carried a suspicion of state power into County Hall after 1981 and saw the GLC as an opportunity to revitalize democratic participation in government. She recalled that the Economic Policy Group 'could make sense of becoming simultaneously both GLC "officers" up against hostile administrative institutions and also socialist economic advisers employed to turn the GLC into an animator, resource and platform, supporting Londoners' struggles to defend and create decent jobs, resist inequalities, and build convivial, sustainable communities'.[9] An odd syncopation thus drove the GLC's economic policy: the GLC wanted to influence the city's economy from the top, while trying to involve local actors on the ground in the framing and carrying through of economic policy. The third theme in the GLC's economics was the interweaving

---

[8] See Cynthia Cockburn, *The Local State* (London: Pluto Press, 1977); Edinburgh Weekend Return Group, *In and Against the State* (London: Pluto Press, 1979).

[9] Hilary Wainwright, 'The Economics of Labour: Robin Murray, Industrial Strategy and the Popular Planning Unit', https://robinmurray.co.uk/glc-ppu.

of economic policy with new concerns about equality, most clearly in the case of feminism and race.

The GLC perceived itself as a primary site of opposition to neoliberalism, whether this was in terms of action or rhetoric. In October 1982, Livingstone submitted a memo to the Council on 'Monetarism in London', written by Robin Murray. This was an explicit attack upon Thatcher and her government, who had 'engineer[ed] the deepest economic crisis since the 1930s', while deliberately fomenting conflict, favouring 'the financier against the industrialist, the employer against labour, and the rich against the poor'.[10] The vehicle of this was monetarism, with 'money as an instrument of control' and London as the policy's 'main bridgehead'.[11] The result had been a 'roll call of the dead', with thousands unemployed in the capital amid the destruction of factories and businesses.[12]

The GLC's alternative policy rested upon emphasizing production, reasserting the strategy of 'direct intervention' in the economy, lending money to businesses, encouraging empty factories to be used for new manufacturing, and preserving apprenticeship schemes.[13] This would not be old-style centralist socialist planning. 'Popular planning' would involve ordinary people in economic decisions in London. The Industry and Employment Committee also promoted other policies that were a direct riposte to Thatcherite urban policies. Over the development of the Docklands, for example, the 'unfettered private enterprise' of the new 'enterprise zones' established by the LDDC was rejected.[14] The Greater London Enterprise Board was established in 1982 with the intention of creating jobs working in cooperation with both employers and unions. It had a three-year budget of £60 million, with money earmarked for buying properties and supporting over a hundred businesses.[15] An example was the £1.25 million used to help keep afloat

---

[10] GLC, Industry and Employment Committee, 'Monetarism in London', Memo by Leader of Council, 12 October 1982, LMA, GLC/DG/PRE/223/02.
[11] GLC, 'Monetarism in London'.   [12] GLC, 'Monetarism in London'.
[13] GLC, 'Monetarism in London'.
[14] GLC, Director of Industry and Employment, Chief Economic Adviser, 'Enterprise Zones', 9 September 1982, LMA, GLC/DG/PRE/115/15.
[15] See Lansley, Goss, and Wolmar, *Councils in Conflict*, 84.

Austin's, a furniture manufacturer in the East End. A smaller firm took over Austin's, with the cooperation of local workers and the Furniture, Timber and Allied Trades Union (FTAT), the national furniture-makers' union.[16] Though a great deal of support went to existing businesses, through the Greater London Enterprise Board, the GLC also sought to encourage alternative models of enterprise, notably cooperative enterprises. By 1984, the Greater London Enterprise Board had loaned about £1 million to twenty-nine co-ops that employed about 400 people in London.[17] A well-known example was the listings magazine *City Limits*. As Geoff Mulgan and Ken Worpole have shown, there was a great deal of support for cultural industries and ventures.[18] In such a manner, there were ways in which the GLC, like the Thatcher government, offered a vision of enterprise and entrepreneurialism as drivers in the economy, but with individuals and co-ops rather than individuals and corporations as the main protagonists, and the state providing not just tax breaks but subsidies.

Drafted in 1984 and published in the following year, the *London Industrial Strategy* was the first of three monumental GLC surveys of the city's economy, followed by the *London Financial Strategy* and the *London Labour Plan*. In his foreword to the *London Industrial Strategy*, Robin Murray summoned the past in a description of the present: 'an impoverished low-tech, or no-tech, economy, sharply divided into two nations, north and south, rich and poor, in work and out, black and white'.[19] London was 'at the eye of the storm', a storm created by deindustrialization, urban 'collapse', and the fall in living standards of ordinary people. A recurring reference point was a temporal one, the London of a century before: '[n]ot for a hundred years have want and waste stood so clearly facing each other in London as they do today'.[20] This chasm was represented physically in the environment of places such as Tower Hamlets:

[16]   See GLC, *Working for London* (London: GLC, 1986), 29.
[17]   See GLC, *There is an Alternative* (London: GLC, 1984), 30.
[18]   Geoff Mulgan and Ken Worpole, *Saturday Night or Sunday Morning* (London: Comedia, 1986), ch. 5.
[19]   GLC, *London Industrial Strategy* (London: GLC, 1985), ix.
[20]   GLC, *London Industrial Strategy*, 18, 1.54.

...the council tower blocks stand facing the commercial skyscrapers of the City; the one representing one of the most depressed areas in Britain, the other sited in one of the richest square miles in the world.[21]

A language of conflict coloured the representation of the Conservative government and its economic policy. Their strategy was 'militarised market production'.[22] The *London Industrial Strategy* referred to the public sector as a 'battleground', the focal point of an 'attack' by 'private finance and industry'.[23] The GLC adopted the word 'strategy' to reflect a more martial approach. It was, the *London Industrial Strategy* argued, about the 'choice of ground on which to engage the enemy':

> What it implied in practice was a view of the London economy as composed of innumerable battlegrounds, involving a struggle for jobs against the pressures of the market, of particular employers and in some cases the direct opposition of the government itself. Each case was fought over a particular terrain, with its specific balance of forces – of local communities, workforces, perhaps the support of a borough council in one case, of a local resource centre in another. Each case required its own strategy, geared at first to the immediate terrain, but then broadening out to the developing contours and prospects of the industry as a whole.[24]

The *London Industrial Strategy* spoke of acting for Londoners as 'working people', against whom were arrayed the forces of private capital.[25] The GLC wanted to frame economic policy 'from the capacities and needs of Londoners and consider[ing] what action is necessary to match the two'.[26]

In a wide-ranging report of March 1984, the Industry and Employment Committee recommended that all grant-funded projects from the GLC

---

[21] GLC, *London Industrial Strategy*, 8, 1.21.
[22] GLC, *London Industrial Strategy*, 18, 1.52.
[23] GLC, *London Industrial Strategy*, 26, 1.76–7.
[24] GLC, *London Industrial Strategy*, 2, 1.06.
[25] GLC, *London Industrial Strategy*, 3, 1.11.
[26] GLC, Report by Director of Industry and Employment Committee, 'Future Employment Opportunities in Greater London', 14 January 1983, GLC/DG/PRE/111/19.

had to have some equality component and, even more wide-ranging, that equal opportunity be 'explicitly integrated into the process of enterprise planning'.[27] In this respect feminism was a notable influence on the GLC's economic policy. The major GLC statements of economic and employment policy in the 1980s foregrounded women's inequality in the economy and work. There was an explicit commitment to realizing the first two of the women's liberation's original four demands: equal pay and equal employment opportunities. GLC policy statements emphasized problems specific to women, such as homeworking, unequal pay, unequal access to training, sexual discrimination, childcare, and domestic work, as central to the aims of economic policy. This was shaped by both immediate and historical contexts. In February 1984, an Industry and Employment Committee memo on 'Women and Employment' painted a bleak picture of monetarism's effect upon women, which had left them segregated, underpaid, or unemployed and labouring under a burden of unacknowledged work in the home.[28] But this was linked to a much wider vision of the economic, social, and political transformation that was needed to improve women's lives. The 1984 draft of the *London Labour Plan* stressed the need to redefine the relationship between work and gender:

> Breaking the vicious cycle requires that the working class is seen to consist of both men and women. The typical worker neither is nor should be a man with a financially dependent wife who ensures that he arrives at the workplace unconstrained by family demands on his time. It requires the recognition that both men and women have families, and that for women to achieve equality it will require not that women become more like men at the workplace, but that jobs are such that they can be taken by people whose family makes demands on their time. That is, if equality is to be a serious goal, all jobs should be

[27] GLC, Industry and Employment Committee, Report by the Director of Industry and Employment and Chief Economic Adviser and PRRA, 'Review of Policy on Ethnic Minority Enterprise and Employment', 20 March 1984, LMA, GLC/DG/PRE/49/25.
[28] GLC, Women's Committee, Industry and Employment Committee, Greater London Training Board, Report by Director General, 'Women and Employment', 10 February 1984, GLC/DG/PRE/223/14.

flexible enough so that women at present can do them. And the double shift of paid and unpaid labour that women take on at present will have to become common to all workers, albeit in reduced quantities if it be shared more equitably.

This was a long-standing theme in feminist discussions of class, particularly by socialist feminists, who, from the time of Juliet Mitchell's *Women: the Longest Revolution* (1966) and the 1970 Ruskin conference, had criticized the effacement of gender from considerations of class, particularly in terms of the identification of work with class. This also extended, of course, to feminist history and analysis written before or contemporaneously with the Labour GLC by people like Rowbotham and Sally Alexander, which challenged 'a labour history which silences' women's claims for equality or presence.[29]

On an immediate level, the aim of gender equality in employment could be pursued within the GLC itself in its role as employer. This demanded a rigorous policy of 'positive action' involving things such as the regarding and restructuring of Council jobs so that they would be more open to women.[30] Childcare and job training, particularly in what were considered 'traditional' skilled manual occupations, were also seen as critical areas for attention in economic policy. Expanding training opportunities and education in skills was also pursued through support for local or community organizations such as Lewisham Women Workers' Group, which held workshops for young women to introduce skills such as electronics and carpentry.[31] Collectives and cooperatives that promised to make inroads into industries largely dominated by men or with practices that seemed to work against equal opportunity were supported through grants from the Industry and Employment

[29] See, for example, Sheila Rowbotham, *Hidden from History* (London: Pluto Press, 1973); Sheila Rowbotham, *Dreams and Dilemmas* (London: Virago, 1983); Sally Alexander, 'Women, Class and Sexual Difference', *History Workshop Journal* 17/1 (Spring 1984): 128, doi: 10.1093/hwj/17.1.125.

[30] GLC, Women's Committee, Industry and Employment Committee, Greater London Training Board, Report by Director General, 'Women and Employment', 10 February 1984, GLC/DG/PRE/223/14.

[31] See, for example, GLC, Women's Committee, 'Lewisham Women Workers' Group', Funding Application, 14 December 1982, GLC/DG/PRE/223/3.

Committee or the Women's Committee. Women in Print, a women's cooperative that hoped to produce print materials for women's groups as well as train women in printing, was supported, for example, as was the Poco collective organized by women workers to save a Lee Cooper jeans factory in Romford.[32]

The Industry and Employment Committee approached racial equality similarly. It sought to strengthen the hand of Black workers, particularly in the efforts to combat racism, whether this was within firms or indeed within unions. Though the Industry and Employment Committee was suspicious of the Thatcher government's cultivation or 'pacification' of a 'black business class', it was nonetheless interested in supporting Black enterprises. This was particularly so if such enterprises were community or cooperative enterprises or dealt with groups such as the Black unemployed and Black women. It saw the acquisition of financing and premises as a particular challenge for Black businesses. By 1984, the number of such enterprises supported by the Industry and Employment Committee or Greater London Enterprise Board was substantial. This included grants to Brent Black Music Cooperative (£193,000) and Toys for Lambeth (£18,000), as well as support for specific businesses such as Asian Flour Milling (£2,600) and Rapid Injection Moulding (£15,000). The first was particularly interesting. The Ethnic Minorities Committee had asked the Industry and Employment Committee and the Greater London Enterprise Board to help develop 'black music industry in the London area' by giving priority 'in assisting Black enterprises wanting to break into the music industry'. Herman Ouseley told the Industry and Employment Committee that the music industry exemplified the way inequality and racism constrained opportunity:

Because of restricted opportunities Black people only operate within the margins of the music industry despite aspiring for a breakthrough as producers, promoters, engineers and performers. As a consequence

---

[32] GLC, Industry and Employment Committee, 'Financial Assistance to Cooperatives: Women in Print', 15 June 1982, LMA, GLC, DG/PRE/111/13; GLC, Industry and Employment Committee, Report by Chief Economic Adviser, 'Proposal for a Clothing Cooperative of Women for Lee Cooper Jeans', 5 May 1982, LMA, GLC/DG/PRE/111/13.

of racism Black people have been forced to find...their own way into the music industry...The Black Music Industry has been under-financed, under-cut and undermined by leading companies, starved of access to media promotions, and has lacked the power to challenge the leading mainstream companies for a part of that market or into mak-ing concessions so that Black people could have equal access and opportunities at all levels in the music industry both locally and overseas.[33]

This is an example of the GLC not turning its back on markets or indeed entrepreneurialism in an age of emerging neoliberalism but, rather, thinking about encouraging a social market which would facili-tate people whose access to the market was otherwise constrained by economic inequality, race, gender, or sexual orientation. As a conse-quence, in the example of supporting Black music, the Industry and Employment Committee provided support for the Brent Black Music Collective, Zion Music Workshop, Ravens Recording Studio, and the Simba Project. Similarly, within the realm of Black cultural production, the Industry and Employment Committee supported Sheba Feminist Publishers.[34]

'Popular planning' was a critical aspect of the GLC's economic inter-vention in the 1980s. Hilary Wainwright later spoke of the staff of the Popular Planning Unit consciously taking the position of outsiders:

The idea of being 'in and against the state' was the only way the five of us who joined Robin Murray in 1982 to form the GLC's Economic Policy Group could make sense of becoming simultaneously GLC 'officers' up against hostile administrative institutions and also socialist economic advisers employed to turn the GLC into an animator, resource and platform, supporting Londoners' struggles

---

[33] GLC, Ethnic Minorities Committee, Report by PRRA, 'The Black Music and Record Industry in London', 15 June 1984, LMA/GLC/DG/PRE/49/28.

[34] GLC, Industry and Employment Committee, 'Sheba Feminist Publishers', Funding Application, 30 September 1981, GLC/DG/PRE/111/08.

to defend and create decent jobs, resist inequalities, and build convivial, sustainable communities.[35]

The aim was 'extending democracy' in the making of economic policy. In part, this determination derived from a desire to acknowledge the 'tacit knowledge' of workers and the relevance of that knowledge to planning.[36] This would also give attention to factors that had not always figured in such policy—'physical and emotional care', for example—as much as the 'making of things'.[37] Wainwright thought that the term 'popular planning' would be more accurate than 'workers' planning' because 'it wouldn't always be about the workplace[;] it would be about communities that were under threat from speculation and office buildings'.[38] Wainwright recalled that the fifteen-person unit was housed in a 'glass walled building on Westminster Bridge and made numerous forays out to local organizations, such as those in Docklands, to try to build bridges with local groups. Assemblies were held of interested groups, such as cooperatives, women's groups and community organizations opposing development in the Docklands'.[39] As Wainwright recognized, this had the 'messy, unevenness of an experiment in progress – a move towards open, power-sharing and devolving forms of administration'.[40]

The GLC's economic plans were hugely ambitious. They were an attempt not only to meet the challenge of neoliberalism explicitly but also to move away from what were seen as the Keynesian compromises of previous generations of social democracy. Winding together considerations of democratic participation and new equality concerns was similarly ambitious, trying to bring together the means and ends of socialism through economics. However, as a number of contemporary

[35] Hilary Wainwright, 'The Economics of Labour: Robin Murray, Industrial Strategy and the Popular Planning Unit', https://robinmurray.co.uk/glc-ppu.
[36] Hilary Wainwright interviewed by Claire Perrault, 'The GLC Story Oral History Project', 2 April 2017, glc.story.org.uk.
[37] Wainwright, 'The Economics of Labour: Robin Murray, Industrial Strategy and the Popular Planning Unit'.
[38] Hilary Wainwright interviewed by Claire Perrault, 'The GLC Story Oral History Project', 2 April 2017, glc.story.org.uk.
[39] See, for example, GLC, Industry and Employment Committee, 'Report of the First Popular Planning Assembly', 17 January 1983, GLC/DG/PRE/111/19.
[40] Wainwright, 'The Economics of Labour: Robin Murray, Industrial Strategy and the Popular Planning Unit'.

critiques of the GLC (usually from the left or centre) made clear, there were also considerable, if understandable, weaknesses in the GLC's approach.[41] In the first place, it was not clear, even given the generous funding the GLC could afford in the 1980s, that this would be much more than a drop in the ocean given the scale of London's overall economy. Thirty million pounds worth of grants was, it is sad to say, not very much in the bigger picture. As well, the kinds of businesses the Greater London Enterprise Board focused on tended to be small-sized firms and cooperatives, often with no more than a hundred employees. Again, given the scale of London's economy and the number of larger firms, this could only be a minor alteration in the balance of employment, production, and service. The GLC gave little thought to the problem of multinational ownership and was at times naive about the potential benefits of the increasing use of high technology in the economy, thinking of it only as a force that might improve the situation of workers in the construction of a more high-skills economy, rather than as something that might lead to greater exploitation of the workforce. But perhaps the greatest lack of clarity was about the market itself. The GLC's economic policy did not make particularly clear whether the point was to replace the market as a means of allocating resources and goods, to make it more equitable, or to strike a very different balance between the free market and a social market. Of course, this was not a small question. In the GLC's defence, it seemed to be exploring (in a way that was never named), what was emerging as 'market socialism' from a different sector of social democratic thought.[42]

The 'Jobs for a Change' festival held on the South Bank on 10 June 1984 was born of a concern that the GLC's economic message was not 'getting through to people'.[43] Using a popular music concert to promote

---

[41] See, for example, Michael Rustin, 'Lessons of the London Industrial Strategy', *New Left Review* 155 (January 1986): 175–84; John Palmer, 'Municipal Enterprise and Popular Planning', *New Left Review* 159 (September 1989): 117–24; Peter Nolan and Kathy O'Donnell, 'Taming the Market Economy? A Critical Assessment of the GLC's Experiment in Restructuring for Labour', *Cambridge Journal of Economics* 11/3 (1987): 251–63, doi: 10.1093/oxfordjournals.cje. a035029.

[42] See, for example, Julian Le Grand and Saul Estrin (eds.), *Market Socialism* (Oxford: Oxford University Press, 1989).

[43] John Hoyland, 'Reggae on the Rates', in Mackintosh and Wainwright, *A Taste of Power*, 373.

an alternative economic policy was in line with the GLC's use of spectacle to make political points, as in Peace Year in 1983 and Anti-Racist
Year in 1984, as well as the declaration of London as a nuclear-free zone.
Wedding politics to pop also revealed the GLC's willingness to embrace
popular culture, and, indeed, culture more generally, as a political act.[44]
In 1983, for example, the GLC and Sheffield City Council collaborated
on an examination of community television, remarking that 'the organ-
isation of cultural events such as rock and pop music, theatre and so on'
might be 'an integral part of...political activity', as it was on the
Continent, and a way of forging 'everyday links', particularly with young
people in an era of high youth unemployment.[45]

By any measure, the two 'Jobs for a Change' festival concerts, on the
South Bank in 1984 and in Battersea Park in July 1985 (linked with Jobs
Year 1985), were major events. The first attracted up to 100,000 people,
the second anywhere between 250,000 and 500,000. Both involved
major acts such as the Smiths, Aswad, the Pogues, the Communards,
and Orchestral Manoeuvres in the Dark. Figure 3.2 shows pop meeting
politics in 1984, as Ken Livingstone and Michael Ward posed with
Morrissey from the Smiths, Winston Rose from Misty in Roots, Mari
Wilson, and Drummie Zeb from Aswad. Early in the planning, the GLC
acknowledged that it did not have the expertise or ability to organize a
large concert, so it brought in a number of outside advisers, including
Tony Hollingsworth, who had experience with the Glastonbury Festival
and later became involved in the seventieth birthday concert for Nelson
Mandela.[46] How did one mix pop and politics, as Billy Bragg, a head-
liner at both festivals, later asked?[47] The festivals were explicitly political
on the one hand: the poster for the festival, for example, set out 'Jobs for
a Change' and 'Meeting Needs and Making Jobs' as the themes of the
festival. During the festival itself, there were debates and workshops
on political themes. But on the stage the 'politics of the festivals was

---

[44]   See Simon Frith and John Street, 'Party Music', *Marxism Today* 31/6 (June 1986): 28–32.
[45]   *Cable and Community Programming* (London/Sheffield: GLC/Sheffield City Council,
1983), 54.
[46]   See Peter Elman, 'Tony Hollingsworth', at https://tonyhollingsworth.com/?q=content/
glc-festivals-and-concerts.
[47]   Billy Bragg, 'Waiting for the Great Leap Forwards', *Workers' Playtime*, Go! Discs (1988).

Figure 3.2 GLC 'Jobs for a Change' festival, 1984.
Credit: Marx Memorial Library/Mary Evans Picture Library.

low-key and muted, and intentionally so'.[48] Hollingsworth felt that the explicit political message should be underplayed: 'the music stages would not be used for political debate or anti-Thatcher slogans… campaigning must be positive and must show what the GLC was doing about unemployment, rather than attack Thatcher'.[49]

In the end, the economic intervention of the GLC was unable to provide a breakwater against the waves of neoliberalism in London. Once the GLC was abolished in 1986, there were no metropolitan funds to fuel an alternative, production-based, or community-based economy. By the 1990s, public–private initiatives were the new orthodoxy, and even if this was not full-blooded neoliberalism, it was certainly a compromise with neoliberalism rather than a challenge to it. 'Jobs for a Change' did not divert the course of employment policy after 1985. The concerts were a spectacle of resistance to Thatcherism, and, importantly, this was a state (albeit a local one) emphasizing the cause of the

---

[48] Hoyland, 'Reggae on the Rates', 394.   [49] Elman, 'Tony Hollingsworth'.

unemployed rather than leaving that cause to the unemployed themselves. There is a sense here, then, not of an alternative future being
developed but, rather, of it being foreclosed in the mid-1980s. The work
of the Industry and Employment Committee and the spectacle of the
'Jobs for a Change' concerts showed a challenge to neoliberalism at a
panoramic, metropolitan level. But there were other struggles against
neoliberalism that occurred at the local level, driven by the efforts of
grass-roots organizations, which had mixed results.

3.2

The name 'Docklands' was a child of the struggles in the 1980s over the
economic redevelopment of areas that included the Isle of Dogs,
Millwall, Newham, Bermondsey, and North Southwark. On the one
hand, 'Docklands' became a shorthand for neoliberal and post-industrial
development of East London; on the other hand, 'Docklands' was an
emotive evocation of an area and a community under threat.[50] For hundreds of years, the areas around the Docklands had provided the engine
for London's economy. The loading and unloading of the world's cargos
gave work to hundreds of thousands in the capital, whether directly as
dockers or indirectly in the manufacturing and clerical industries that
spun off from the docks. The centrality of the Docklands to London's
economy contrasted with its spatial isolation from the rest of the city.
Well into the late twentieth century, the Isle of Dogs, Rotherhithe, and
Deptford were worlds separate from the rest of London. Such isolation
had lent social homogeneity to the areas around the docks, dominated
by a white working class whose gender relations were structured around
traditional male manual labour.[51] In the mid-twentieth century, the
Docklands was profoundly affected by two events. The first was the Blitz,
which destroyed a third of the housing in the area. The second was the
cutting of the area's economic lifeblood. Changes in shipping, notably

---

[50] See Bill Schwarz, 'Where horses shit a hundred sparrows feed: Docklands and East
London during the Thatcher years', in John Corner and Sylvia Harvey (eds.), *Enterprise and
Heritage* (London: Routledge, 1991), 75–90.

[51] On this, see Sue Brownill, *Developing London's Docklands* (London: Chapman, 1990), 18.

the rise of container traffic, made London's docklands obsolescent as a major port after the war. Traffic shifted downriver to Tilbury or across the North Sea to Rotterdam. In 1967, the closure of the docks began, with the last finally shut down in 1981. This left thousands unemployed and acres of land derelict in the East End.

What was to be done with what was increasingly called the 'Docklands'? This question dogged London's planners in the 1970s. A major consultation process prompted the formation of local community groups advocating for a local say in change, such as the Joint Docklands Action Group and the North Southwark Community Development Group, and private developers seeing an irresistible opportunity to develop land close to the centre of London. By the end of the 1970s, there seemed to be one dominant plan that favoured public sector intervention which would prioritize the needs of local employment and housing.

Enter the Thatcher government. In 1981, Michael Heseltine, the Environment Secretary, announced the establishment of the LDDC and the creation of an 'enterprise zone' covering much of the Docklands. Both meant that redevelopment of the area would be through the private sector, aided by the lifting of local government planning restrictions, the abolition of business taxes, and a state commitment to the improvement of transport links, most obviously with the construction of a light rail network. According to the LDDC, such incentives provided 'red carpet treatment' to 'developers, investors and employers'.[52] Office development, rather than industrial production, luxury flats rather than social housing, and mega projects such as an airport in the Royal Docks for short take-off and landing (STOL) aircraft were the preferred routes for Docklands regeneration. This vision of the Docklands future was caught in an official LDDC photograph adorning one of its annual reports of jet skiers at play in front of an abandoned industrial landscape. As one observer noted, the '[g]eography' of the Docklands had become the 'ideology' of neoliberalism.[53]

[52] LDDC, *LDDC Annual Report and Accounts 1981/2* (London: LDDC, 1982), 11.
[53] James Anderson, quoted in Wetherell, 'Freedom Planned', 280.

Even the LDDC admitted that its vision of a 'brave new technological future' had not won over all local residents; there remained those who were 'unsure of their ability to take any part in [it]'.[54] Local opposition to the LDDC was immediate. There was, in particular, a strong objection by some local residents to their exclusion from planning and from decisions. The JDAG called the LDDC 'undemocratic'.[55] It launched a campaign 'to restore democracy in the Docklands'.[56] The GLC also emphasized its view that 'local democracy has to be crushed in order to impose the Monetarist Strategy on Docklands'.[57] Critics of the LDDC focused on the LDDC's failure to address what was seen as the real problem of the area: high unemployment and the loss of industry. If jobs were created in the Docklands, they either would go to people outside the area or local people would simply be 'porters and lavatory attendants for passing businessmen'.[58] This charge was not without foundation: a study from 1987 suggested that most of the new jobs in the Docklands were office workers or in service and retail, none of which recruited among local people; so much so that the area's male unemployment figure in 1986 was 32 per cent.[59] Similarly, critics of the LDDC believed that luxury housing effaced the needs of local housing.[60] In 1982, a JDAG activist claimed that, of 2,608 homes built, only three were public housing units.[61] Between 1981 and 1993, homelessness increased by 304 per cent in the Docklands area, with only 5 per cent of new housing in the area being council housing.[62] Even the cheapest new private housing available in 1984 was often beyond the financial means of local people;

[54] LDDC, *LDDC Annual Report and Accounts 1983/4* (London: LDDC, 1984), 17.

[55] JDAG, *Docklands in Danger* (London: JDAG, 1980).

[56] JDAG for the Campaign to Restore Democracy in Docklands, *Docklands Fights Back* (London: JDAG, 1983).

[57] GLC, *East London File* (London: GLC, 1983), 32.

[58] Newham Docklands Forum, *The People's Plan for the Royal Docks* (London: Newham Docklands Forum/GLC PPU, 1983), 4.

[59] A. Church, 'Urban Regeneration in London Docklands: A Five-Year Policy Review', *Environment and Planning C: Government and Policy* 6 (1988): 192, 198, doi: 10.1068/c060187.

[60] See Janet Foster, *Docklands: Cultures in Conflict, Worlds in Collision* (London: UCL Press, 1999), 104; see also Nicholas Deakin and John Edwards, *Enterprise Culture and the Inner City* (London: Routledge, 1993), 94.

[61] Bob Colenutt, letter to *Town and Country Planning*, 51/7 (July–August 1982), 194.

[62] Figures from Michael Keith and Steve Pile, 'Introduction Part 1: The Politics of Place', in Michael Keith and Steve Pile (eds.), *Place and the Politics of Identity* (London: Routledge, 1993), 14.

the inflation of such housing prices after 1985 made this even more difficult. That private housing was built in the Docklands so quickly, given the previous slowness of public housing provision, was also galling. In all, there was a fear of a kind of social cleansing of the area through redevelopment, whether this involved employment or housing, as one of the posters of local campaigners suggested: 'Big Money Is Moving In: Don't Let It Push Out Local People'.

The alternatives proposed by the opponents of the LDDC relied upon the public sector to resurrect industrial production in the docks. This took various forms. The repair and expansion of existing dock facilities represented one. There was also the suggestion to create a 'public sector market', through local and central government funding, which would establish new businesses in the form of cooperatives and employee-owned firms, the aim of which would be production and social utility rather than profit.[63] Alternative plans for the docks also paid attention to the specific problems of women in the area, such as childcare, lack of employment opportunities, and poor shopping facilities and transport. Public housing rather than luxury developments was a priority.

The campaign against the LDDC's development of the Docklands was a marriage between power at the centre, in the form of the GLC, and community organizations on the ground in the Docklands area. This was an example of the decentralized, democratic control of economic policy which the GLC Popular Planning Unit wanted to develop in London. The community organizations in the Docklands did represent a spectrum of local groups and individuals, including, for example, former trade union officials and labour organizers in the former industries of the Docklands and tenants' groups. Connie Hunt, a leading member of the campaign against the STOL airport in the Royal Docks had, for example, campaigned against the GLC in its role as a landlord in the 1970s as a member of a tenants' group. In the 1970s, groups like JDAG, fearing the prospect of uncontrolled development of the Docklands, had lobbied the London Labour Party and, partly because of these efforts, the 1981 Labour manifesto had featured a commitment to opposing the

---

[63] See *The People's Plan for the Royal Docks*, 9.

LDDC.[64] After gaining power, the Labour GLC was keen to show material support for the efforts of development opponents in the Docklands. It gave significant amounts of funding to the Docklands Forum and JDAG: £31,000 and £76,000 respectively in 1983 and 1984.[65] Popular planning was also realized through these campaigns. During the campaign against the STOLport, for example, Hilary Wainwright went down to listen to local groups: 'I just sat there and listened and then at a certain point said sounds like you've been thinking about alternatives to the airport as well[;] I'm just here to say the GLC's behind you and supports your campaign[;] [w]hat do you need? How do you want to do it?'[66] The GLC funded the establishment of a People's Plan Centre on Woolwich Pier, as well as the hiring of five staff (all local people) to canvass local opinion on Docklands redevelopment, on the doorstep, with businesses, and in bingo halls.[67]

Local groups succeeded in representing the conflict over the Docklands as one that involved, as Michael Keith and Steve Pile have argued, a politics of space and identity.[68] In 1982, Reg Ward of the LDDC referred to the Docklands as a 'blank canvas upon which we can paint the future'.[69] Groups like the JDAG and the Newham Docklands Forum gave the lie to this picture, showing that Docklands was not a blank canvas, but a deeply rooted community. That community was clearly identified with a working class and with a rich past of that working class. As *The People's Plan for the Royal Docks* argued, one point was to assert the presence of this community, against the feeling that it comprised a 'forgotten people' on a 'forgotten island'.[70] What was at stake for many in these community organizations was the survival of this community in the face of development, one that had been threatened forty

---

[64] See Mackintosh and Wainwright, *A Taste of Power*, 300.

[65] GLC, Industry and Employment Committee, 'The Voluntary Sector in Docklands: Paper by the Docklands Community Support Steering Group', 4 July 1983, GLC/DG/PRE/111/24.

[66] Hilary Wainwright interviewed by Claire Perrault, 'The GLC Story Oral History Project', 2 April 2017, http://glc.story.org.uk.

[67] See Mackintosh and Wainwright, *A Taste of Power*, 310; Hilary Wainwright interviewed by Claire Perrault, 'The GLC Story Oral History Project', 2 April 2017, http://glc.story.org.uk.

[68] See Keith and Pile, 'Introduction Part 1: The Politics of Place'.

[69] Quoted in Lesson, 'Our Land: Creative Approaches to the Redevelopment of London's Docklands', 367.

[70] *The People's Plan for the Royal Docks*, 5.

years before by the Blitz, as one activist stated: '[w]e survived Hitler's
bombs but we're not sure we'll survive the bulldozers'.[71] The LDDC
responded by portraying this conflict as one between a promising future
and an obsolescent and obstructionist past, questioning the 'ability of
existing unemployed residents to seize opportunities as and when they
come along'.[72] Keith and Pile have spoken of the Docklands conflict representing the battle between 'an imagined geography and a spatialized
political economy' of a particular area, and one could also argue that
this was the conflict between a historicized geography and political
economy, between past and future.[73]

Of course, the reality about the identity of the Docklands was more
complicated and problematic. The campaign against the LDDC was nei-
ther homogeneous nor necessarily unified. Groups such as the JDAG
were linked strongly to the London Labour Party, while other groups,
such as the Association of Island Communities, were apolitical. There
was some resentment at the GLC's and other Labour councils' refusal to
deal with the LDDC. One local remarked, for example, in criticism of
local Labour politics, 'you've gotta try and get what you can out of it and
you don't get that by not talking'.[74] An anthropological survey of the
area done in the 1980s also underlined a significant current of apathy
and fatalism in response to the LDDC's redevelopment.[75]

Perhaps more worrying were fissures around race and gender that
opened up in the Docklands. The campaign against Docklands development emphasized the saving of a working-class community, but this was
also a dominantly white working-class community and the evocation of
a working-class past was often that of a dominantly male working-class
past. The ethnic minority communities in the area, particularly people
of South Asian descent, were not considered by the Newham Docklands
Forum until 1989, for example.[76] A social anthropology of the area,
done in the late 1980s, underscored how the defence of a traditionally
white working-class area against gentrification could also become a

[71] Quoted in Schwarz, 'Where horses shit a hundred sparrows feed', 88.
[72] LDDC, *LDDC Annual Report and Accounts 1983/4*, 17.
[73] Keith and Pile, 'Introduction Part 1: The Politics of Place', 17.
[74] Quoted in Foster, *Docklands*, 94.   [75] See Foster, *Docklands*, 82.
[76] Brownill, *Developing London's Docklands*, 115.

defence not only of the working-class identity of that area but of the whiteness of that area.[77] In the 1990s, the British National Party made inroads on the Isle of Dogs, electing a local councillor in 1993, largely on the back of discontent over housing and what were perceived as ethnic minority outsiders. As well, the argument over Docklands development tended to foreground an older gender ideology, one based upon older ideas of male work, as one female activist suggested: 'it was dismissed really, a lot of the work we were doing. You got a pat on the head and told very good, but nobody wanted to know about it. It was what was going on in the docks – the macho stuff – they wanted to know about.'[78]

In 1984, with the Armada on the Thames, resistance to Docklands development was made more visible across London. Culture and spectacle had long figured in the Docklands campaign. The Docklands Community Poster Project (DCPP) was established in 1981, with visual artists Loraine Leeson and Peter Dunn as its guiding lights. The DCPP worked with other community organizations to produce posters and murals—often using photographic montage—promoting the idea of a historic community under threat from neoliberal development. In one, 'The Changing Picture of the Docklands', an array of ordinary people dominated the foreground and the message, quoting a local organizer, stressed the 'birthright' and 'heritage' of 'the people' in the Docklands area, against the interests of the private ownership of land.[79] Spectacle was an important aspect of this cultural work. Murals and posters used ordinary spaces to promote the anti-development message. Documenting the Docklands communities was another aspect of this work. In 1983, the photographer Mike Seaborne began a collaboration with the Island History Trust, founded in 1980 by Eve Hostettler, to document visually the changing shape of the Docklands.[80]

At a meeting of various Docklands organizations in 1984 discussing the need to present parliament with a petition, a delegate 'pointed out

---

[77] See Foster, *Docklands*, ch. 7.

[78] Quoted in Brownill, *Developing London's Docklands,* 129.

[79] See Lesson, 'Our Land: Creative Approaches to the Redevelopment of London's Docklands'.

[80] The photographs are collected in Mike Seaborne, *The Isle of Dogs: Before the Big Money* (London: Hoxton Mini Press, 2018).

that since both Docklands and parliament were situated on the river, that made it a potential route for delivery of the petition'.[81] There was a former lighterman from Wapping at the meeting, and he volunteered the use of his barge. Other delegates expressed support for the idea and approached the GLC for support, which it provided, for publicity and the renting of other pleasure boats to join the Armada. Jean Lowe of the JDAG and Stewart Luck of the North Southwark Community Development Group did much of the organizing. Arts groups were central to the planning, such as the Basement Arts Workshop that printed banners and Cultural Partnerships which helped organize people to paint the barges and provide music and other support. A striking image that emerged from this planning was that of the Docklands Dragon, a creature whose shape mirrored the curves of the Thames around the Isle of Dogs. It was conceived as a 'dragon of myth and legend, a force of the underworld, and the power of repressed emotion'.[82]

On 17 April 1984, the Armada set out from Docklands. We can reconstruct what that day was or might have been like from photographs of the first Armada in 1984 and Mike Seaborne's photographs of the Armada of 1985.[83] Seaborne's photographs of 1985 begin with groups of older people and young mothers and children gathered at the corner of Westferry Road and Cuba Street, waiting to be taken to the pleasure craft on the river. Some of the older women are smoking, while the young mothers wait with their children in pushchairs. The groups are mostly white and mostly women. Once on the boat, the younger women and children look off the stern at the Docklands slipping into the distance. In the cabin, older men and women drink pints and Coke, and wave to other boats in the Armada. The 1984 photographs show a bright red barge passing the Houses of Parliament, a huge banner displaying the Docklands Dragon with the slogan 'Docklands Fights Back' below it. Once disembarked at Jubilee Gardens, children carry a mock black

[81] 'The People's Armada to Parliament', http://cspace.org.uk/archive/docklands-community-poster-project/armada-2/.
[82] 'The People's Armada to Parliament', http://cspace.org.uk/archive/docklands-community-poster-project/armada-2/.
[83] 'The People's Armada to Parliament', http://cspace.org.uk/archive/docklands-community-poster-project/armada-2/; 'Docklands Armada, 1985', photographs by Mike Seaborne, http://www.80sislandphotos.org.uk/docklands-armada-1985/.

dragon on their shoulders in the forecourt of County Hall, while inside a tent a large crowd mills about, some people carrying plastic bags with the GLC logo. A group of speakers carrying the People's Charter gather behind microphones on a stage, including Tony Banks.

The People's Armada did not stop the redevelopment of the Docklands or the progress of neoliberalism in London. The Docklands was developed, the airport was built, and Thatcherite economic policy was not derailed by the economic policy adopted by the GLC.

But there was a victory, albeit on a smaller scale, on the South Bank of the Thames. Like the Docklands area, Coin Street, near Waterloo, was a largely derelict area by the 1970s. That emptiness, and its proximity to the West End, had excited much interest from commercial developers. Urban development abhors a vacuum, and the Coin Street area also prompted a long planning debate between developers and government. As with the Docklands, the potential for a full-throated commercial development of the area worried local residents, whose problems were, like in the Docklands, housing and jobs. In the late 1970s, those local organizations sought to insert an alternative plan that would favour the interest of local people's need for housing and the potential of smaller enterprises that would have jobs for locals. In 1979, concurrent with the accession of the Thatcher government, a new enquiry was launched, and the prospect was what a planning journal called a 'new battle of Waterloo'.[84] But this Battle of Waterloo was not over in a day. Rather, it became 'one of the longest, costliest and most important and most confused enquiries ever held'.[85] The Conservative Minister of the Environment, Michael Heseltine, wanted the matter 'to be determined by the market'.[86] And that market, represented by the developer Lord McAlpine among others, would determine the matter in favour of hotels, luxury housing, and retail. Against this, local organizations rallied, just as they did in the Docklands. These organizations included the Association of Waterloo Action Groups and the Coin Street Action

[84] *Town and Country Planning* 48 (1979), 7.
[85] *The Times*, quoted in Nick Jeffrey, 'Coin Street Yields a High Return', *New Statesman*, 20 June 1997.
[86] Iain Tuckett, 'Pigs Now Flying Above Coin Street', *Town and Country Planning* 55 (July–August 1985): 198.

Group, which settled on a plan that emphasized affordable housing, workshops, and cultural spaces designed for the community. Unlike in the Docklands, the grass-roots activism was accompanied by minor clashes between activists and the police.

After coming to power in 1981, the GLC made a dramatic intervention in this issue. Following its faith in grass-roots organizations and campaigns that resisted neoliberal development, the GLC put a very heavy finger on the scales in favour of the community organizations. The Council rezoned the land for mixed use, which reduced its value. The land was then offered to Coin Street Community Builders, who bought it freehold using a loan, conveniently enough from the Greater London Enterprise Board, for £1 million, on the agreement that the site could only be developed along socially useful lines, without profit.

Coin Street later developed its own compromises with the new culture and economy. In the late nineties, for example, Coin Street Community Builders redeveloped the 1920s art deco Oxo Tower, which had been part of the original Coin Street purchase. The redevelopment included seventy-eight affordable flats, some priced at £77 rent a week, with residents coming from housing cooperatives and council waiting lists. But the top of the tower now featured a Harvey Nichols restaurant, transplanted from Kensington. Conflicts were soon reported between 'angry Oxo Tower residents and noisy, well-oiled revellers leaving Harvey Nicks'. As one account suggested, Coin Street perhaps symbolized the uneasy compromises and ironies of a new age and a new London:

> It is an audacious blend of nineties chic and seventies social purpose, wholly apt for the dawning of a another new age, that of New Labour...Coin Street captures the paradoxes of New Labour – socially concerned, yet willing to collaborate across a wide coalition of interests....[87]

With the Armada, the 'Jobs for a Change' concert, and the purchase of Coin Street, an economic alternative or resistance to the growth of neoliberalism can be seen in the spring of 1984. The economic vision that

---

[87] Jeffrey, 'Coin Street Yields a High Return'.

these moments emphasized clashed with the policies of the Thatcher government: stressing employment and production; putting the needs of local communities above the potential dividends of corporate development; and, not least, emphasizing a connection between political democracy and economic planning. As we can also see in the work of the Industry and Employment Committee, new strands were worked into economic policy, particularly in terms of the claims of women and racial minorities and the way that culture could promote economic policy. Of course, this is not a story of success, of a social democratic David taking down, or even particularly slowing down, a neoliberal Goliath. Neoliberalism won. The Docklands was redeveloped, possibly far beyond the dreams of even the LDDC. Full employment as a government policy did not return. Coin Street was an oasis of local control in a desert of corporate development on the South Bank. But these moments in the spring of 1984 nonetheless showed that there were some challenges on the journey towards a new city of capital in the 1980s.

London, 1984: Conflict and Change in the Radical City. Stephen Brooke, Oxford University Press.
© Stephen Brooke 2024. DOI: 10.1093/9780191895395.003.0004

4

A City for Women?

In November 1984, at a small gallery near Covent Garden, Pluto Press and the feminist design collective Matrix launched the book *Making Space: Women and the Man-Made Environment*.[1] The cover of the book had a photograph showing a woman struggling to get an infant in a pushchair up some concrete stairs. Graffiti on the wall behind her read 'Rat Race Recs [*sic*]'. Within its covers, there were other images of women and the challenges that the city posed to them: crossing a busy intersection; navigating long tunnels and ramps with children, again with the dreaded pushchair; dealing with the threat of violence in a blind alley. But the book was also illustrated with other visions, of buildings and urban environments that were potentially less alienating to women, seen in plans for a health centre specially designed to be open and warm, or a childcare centre that would allow carers and parents to watch their children from a distance, or a training workshop to give technical skills to women. These designs would create a different space for women, one that was 'useful, comfortable [and] likeable'.[2]

Making Space was a pioneering study of women's relationship to the urban environment. It was based upon a simple premise: 'women play almost no part in making decisions about or in creating the environment. It is a man-made environment.'[3] Buildings and the urban environment, *Making Space* argued, had been and continued to be planned and created by men, based upon traditional gender stereotypes. Separate spheres for men and women, for example, continued to be marked out spatially in the late twentieth-century city.[4] The book evoked an affective

---

[1] Katie Lloyd Thomas, 'Foreword to the 2022 Edition', Matrix, *Making Space: Women and the Man-Made Environment* (London: Verso, 1984, 2022), xix.

[2] Francis Bradshaw, 'Working with Women', in Matrix, *Making Space*, 90.

[3] Matrix, *Making Space*, 3.   [4] Matrix, *Making Space*, 4.

ecology of alienation, isolation, discomfort, oppression, and fear in which women existed:

> Women's independence is severely restricted outside the home. If we walk on the streets after dark, we are accused of inviting violent sexual attack from men. If we do not have cheap and convenient public transport, we are physically restricted since most of us cannot afford a private alternative. If we are with our children we are made unwelcome in pubs, shops, restaurants and public buildings.[5]

Making Space took inspiration from second-wave feminism to argue for a new approach to the built environment, to overcome 'the invisibility of women's lives', to make 'challenges to men's power', and to find 'new ways of organizing and living our lives' by making buildings and cities that would be for women.[6] That project had emerged, one of its contributors argued, from a collective consciousness rooted in feminist collaboration:

> During the time we have been working together as Matrix we have continued to feel that more and more women are exploring the same ideas, wanting to learn how we can mould the physical environment around us... It is a process of unravelling all the ways we are conditioned to think about the places around us, and then creating our own ways, our own spaces.... If we can become more aware of how the buildings we live and work in relate to how we live, then we can create buildings that work with women's struggle for liberation rather than against it.[7]

The contributors to *Making Space* were members of the feminist design collective Matrix. A year before the publication of *Making Space*, Matrix had applied for funding to the GLC Women's Committee as a 'feminist architectural practice working with women's and community groups'.[8]

---

[5] Matrix, *Making Space*, 4.   [6] Bradshaw, 'Working with Women', *Making Space*, 90.
[7] Bradshaw, 'Working with Women', *Making Space,* 105.
[8] GLC, Women's Committee, 'Matrix', Funding Application, 31 March 1983, LMA, GLC/DG/PRE/223/13.

It sought funding for projects such as the Dalston Children's Centre, Acton Women's Aid, and Hackney Women's Centre.

Nineteen eighty-four also saw Matrix take on probably its most important project—the design for the Jagonari Women's Educational Centre in the East End.[9] In 1982, a group of British Bangladeshi women sought to establish a women's centre that would provide support and education to the Bangladeshi community in the East End. They formed a group called 'Jagonari', meaning 'women awake'. A space on the Whitechapel Road, the Davenant School, was chosen, a grant of £600,000 was obtained from the GLC, and Matrix was engaged to do the work.[10] The work began in 1984, was completed in 1987, and the Jagonari Centre existed until 2018.

For Matrix and Jagonari, the GLC and, in particular, its Women's Committee were critically important. Matrix applied to the Women's Committee for funding, arguing that its work was central to the larger cause of improving the lives of women in London:

> ...the quality of our environment in London is very much part of the wellbeing and health of every person living in London. Women's needs are important, the way buildings have been designed with the assumptions based on the needs of white middle-class males, has put certain groups at a disadvantage including women and ethnic minorities... [Our proposal] is a vision of future life-styles of people living in London, the future share women will have of resources, and future roles of women.[11]

The Women's Committee had become a major source of funds for feminist organizations in London since its inception in 1982. It was also a driver of feminist change in terms of governance and policy. In 1983, the Women's Committee published 'a Programme of Action for Women in

---

[9] See http://www.matrixfeministarchitecturearchive.co.uk/jagonari/ (accessed 4 May 2023).
[10] See https://eastendwomensmuseum.org/blog/2020/9/2/jago-nari-jago-banhishikha-a-short-history-of-the-jagonari-centre-in-whitechapel; https://c20society.org.uk/building-of-the-month/jagonari-asian-womens-education-centre-whitechapel-london.
[11] Matrix, 'Notes for GLC Application', 1983, from Matrix Feminist Architecture Archive, http://www.matrixfeministarchitecturearchive.co.uk/wp-content/uploads/2021/08/M02329.jpg.

London'. This was a collection of statements from a variety of working groups drawn from feminist and community organizations, which dealt with housing, Black and ethnic minority women, transport, lesbians, women's centres, and pregnancy and motherhood.[12] The programme was a kaleidoscope of views united by the underlying belief that women were 'living in a man's world', a world shaped by sexism. One passage underlined the difficulties of that world for women: '[w]omen are poor… [w]omen need childcare and work…. [W]omen are abused… [w]omen are isolated… [w]omen are under-represented'.[13] The aim of 'A Programme of Action' was to 'change the way London is run so that the interests and welfare of women are equally important'.[14]

The work of the Women's Committee and the many organizations it supported thus addressed the same fundamental problem set out by *Making Space*: to remedy the lack of agency and power women had in 'creating the environment'. The Women's Committee's interests were not limited to the problem of architecture and planning, but to every aspect of women's lives in the 'man-made environment' of the city: safety, work, the home, sex, culture, and health. *Making Space* and the Women's Committee shared the belief that a city that oppressed women had to be made into a city for women. In 1984, the historian Sally Alexander wrote that '[f]eminism looks outward at the social forms of sexual division and the uneven destinies that claim the two sexes'.[15] Both Matrix and the Women's Committee, and many other women's organizations, worked to think through how sexual division existed within London and the uneven destinies that women and men followed. Both thought about how to challenge and disrupt those divisions and destinies.

This chapter tells two stories. The first is a focused examination of *Making Space* as an artefact from 1984. The book was a groundbreaking intervention in thinking about the relationship between gender, feminism, and the city. It was also an example of a wider trend, that of feminist

---

[12] GLC, Women's Committee, 'Programme of Action for Women of London: Additional Sections', 19 January 1984, LMA, GLC/DG/PRE/223/14.

[13] GLC, Women's Committee, 'A Programme for Women in London', February 1983, LMA, GLC/DG/PRE/223/3.

[14] GLC, 'A Programme for Women in London', February 1983.

[15] Alexander, 'Women, Class and Sexual Differences in the 1830s and 1840s', 130.

organization and critique shaped by particular social and political circumstances at the end of the twentieth century. A focused examination of *Making Space* also affords, in thinking about the city, a perspective that is both conceptual in considering the experience of women in the city and about the lived physicality of that experience from below.[16] As the title of its book suggested, Matrix stressed the critical relationship between gender and space.

A powerful factor in those circumstances is the core of the second story, about the work of the GLC Women's Committee, a body which helped fund Matrix and many other feminist organizations in London between 1982 and 1986. That story is more panoramic, an account of how London was briefly shaped by an explicitly feminist agenda. It is not a comprehensive history of the Women's Committee, which can be found in Mackintosh and Wainwright's work; rather, this chapter highlights the relationship between work on the ground on feminist issues and the work attempted from a different vantage point by the Women's Committee.

Both stories document the particular position of women in late twentieth-century London. That position was, by the 1980s, defined by possibility: greater educational opportunities; greater economic participation; greater reproductive control; divorce reform; and, with the emergence of second-wave feminism, the forceful articulation of women's rights. But women's position was also defined by challenges, such as continuing inequality, sexual violence, and the persistence of traditional gender stereotypes that shaped women's lives in private and in public. The challenges and possibilities facing women in the 1980s city mirror those challenges and possibilities. The histories of Matrix and the Women's Committee evoke the way that feminism attempted to transform London in the late twentieth century, to create a space for communities of women, to assert women's rights and equality, to make it a city for women.

---

[16] On this combination of perspectives, see Les Back and Michael Keith, 'Reflections: Writing Cities', in Hannah Jones and Emma Jackson (eds.), *Stories of Cosmopolitan Belonging* (Abingdon: Routledge, 2014), 15.

4.1

The work Matrix and the GLC Women's Committee did in the 1980s was rooted in the emergence of second-wave feminism, as well as the changes seen in women's lives at work and at home in the 1960s and 1970s. By the 1980s, more women were working, whether part-time or full-time, whether they were single or married. More women were also participating in higher education and entering the professions or white-collar work. The 1969 Equal Pay Act and the 1975 Sex Discrimination Act reflected this increasing presence in the public sphere. Both set out an idea of equality in the public sphere, but this equality proved elusive. Women's private lives were shaped by greater accessibility to both repro-ductive control and to divorce. In theory, by the 1970s women were enjoying a greater public presence and personal autonomy. But, of course, that was only part of a larger ambiguity around the persistence of older factors shaping the position of women. Women remained largely responsible for childcare and domestic work. Deep inequality in pay continued between men and women. Men's dominance was largely unchecked, whether this was in terms of structural or institutional power or in social and private life.

The development of second-wave feminism was a challenge to the existence and persistence of the oppression and inequality of women.[17] In February 1970, the Women's Liberation Movement was launched at Ruskin College, Oxford. It carried with it four demands: equal pay; equal educational and job opportunities; twenty-four-hour nurseries; and free contraception and abortion on demand. Between 1970 and 1978, there were national conferences for the Women's Liberation Movement as well as the establishment of local organizations. At the same time, the growth of women's liberation was accompanied by important actions by women workers over inequitable conditions, at

---

[17] For a survey of 1970s feminism, see Lynne Segal, 'Jam Today: Feminist Impacts and Transformations in the 1970s', in Lawrence Black, Hugh Pemberton, and Pat Thane (eds.), *Reassessing 1970s Britain* (Manchester: Manchester University Press, 2013), 149–66; for an examination of a particular issue and space in London, see Judith Walkowitz, 'Feminism and the Politics of Prostitution in King's Cross in the 1980s', *Twentieth Century British History* 30/2 (June 2019): 231–63, doi: 10.1093/tcbh/hwz011.

Ford's in Dagenham in 1968, among night cleaners in 1972, and at Grunwick film processing plant in 1976. There were also particular labour campaigns such as Wages for Housework and the Working Women's Charter which resonated with the agenda of second-wave feminism. The new attention given to women's history, particularly after a conference at Ruskin in 1969, and feminist approaches in other disciplines such as geography and sociology were also critical in framing and grounding a feminist view of the world.

London was an especially important sphere of feminist activity and organization. In 1969, the London Women's Liberation Workshop (LWLW) was established.[18] 'A Woman's Place' was the LWLW's centre in Earlham Street. By 1980, there were about 300 local women's liberation groups, in places like Clapham and Belsize Park. Consciousness-raising was central to the work of such groups, as was an emphasis upon new methods of organization based upon collective discussion and the deconstruction of hierarchy.[19] What feminism needed was a physical foothold in the city, in terms of the acquisition of space to break the 'cycle of insecurity' often plaguing feminist groups, who were forced to meet in private homes or rented accommodation.[20] The local and national state partially met this need through the establishment of feminist spaces like bookshops.[21]

Making Space emerged from this milieu of second-wave feminism. Its contributors—Jos Boys, Francis Bradshaw, Jane Darke, Benedicte Foo, Sue Francis, Barbara McFarlane, Marion Roberts, Anne Thorne, and Susan Wilkes—came from varied backgrounds in architecture, design, and building. Some had trained as architects or, like Fran Bradshaw, had moved from architecture to the building trade. That training was, in itself, a feminist education, whether this was in terms of male dominance in the profession or in the sense that 'public space wasn't for women'.[22]

[18] Setch, 'The Face of Metropolitan Feminism'.
[19] See Sue Bruley, 'Consciousness Raising in Clapham: Women's Liberation as "Lived Experience" in South London in the 1970s', *Women's History Review* 22/5 (2013): 717–38, doi: 10.1080/09612025.2013.769378.
[20] Setch, 'The Face of Metropolitan Feminism', 174.
[21] See Delap, 'Feminist Bookstores, Reading Cultures and the Women's Liberation Movement'.
[22] Anne Thorne, Interview, 20 February 2018.

Participation in housing co-ops, squatting, and short-life leases was also common among its contributors. Within 1970s architecture, radical groups emerged, such as the socialist New Architecture Movement, and the Feminist Design Collective had addressed questions of inequality, hierarchy, and discrimination in architecture. Other groups such as Solon Cooperative Housing, the Association of Community Technical Aid Centres, and Support, all of which were involved with issues like short-life housing, were also important.[23]

A conference on 'women and space' led to the founding of the Matrix collective in 1980. Matrix was intended to take 'a feminist approach to design through practical projects and theoretical analysis.'[24] The original intent of Matrix was not necessarily to be an architectural practice but, rather, to advise women in the building trades. A significant number of the women involved in Matrix worked as builders, and there was also a socialist determination to 'dissolve the class differences between themselves and the builders, especially women builders'.[25] Matrix was consciously 'located within' the women's liberation movement.[26] Its feminism was reflected in its all-women membership, a determination to challenge what was perceived as the sexism of the architectural profession and press, to recognize architecture as 'not neutral but expressive of social values and relations', and to have working practices that reflected the ideology of second-wave feminism.[27] The last was approached on several fronts. First, in terms of the organization of the thirty-person collective, its management structure stressed cooperation and a revolving group of managers. Those working at Matrix had to accept a 'commitment to working collectively in a mutually supportive way'.[28] In its operating practices, Matrix made a deliberate attempt to deconstruct and dissemble what it saw as the hierarchical practices of

---

[23] Suzy Nelson, Interview, 20 February 2018.

[24] Jos Boys et al., 'Introduction' to *Making Space*, viii.

[25] Julia Dwyer and Anne Thorne, 'Evaluating Matrix: Notes from Inside the Collective', in Doina Petrescu (ed.), *Altering Practices* (London: Routledge, 2007), 42–3.

[26] Janie Grote, 'Matrix: A Radical Approach to Architecture', *Journal of Architecture and Planning Research* 9/2 (1992): 159.

[27] Dwyer and Thorne, 'Evaluating Matrix', 45.

[28] Matrix, 'Job Description for Feminist Architectural Worker', n.d., from Matrix Feminist Architecture Archive, http://www.matrixfeministarchitecturearchive.co.uk/wp-content/uploads/2021/08/M02303.jpg.

previous generations of architects, placing great importance on consulting with its clients and the potential users of spaces as a way of 'changing who controls buildings'.[29] Matrix was particularly concerned with developing architectural and design practices and plans that would address the particular position of women. In its operation, for example, Matrix consciously thought about the problems of childcare and the need for flexible hours for the members of the collective. It also put considerable emphasis upon collaboration and discussion—'meetings all the time', as one member recalled.[30] Nonetheless, the work of Matrix was, from the beginning, driven by considerable energy, a 'no fear attitude...we were firing on all cylinders'.[31]

Making Space began with a two-fold intention—to offer an 'understanding of how we are "placed" as women in a man-made environment' and 'to use that knowledge to subvert it'.[32] The idea of 'placing' had different meanings in the book, all of which were consonant with feminism in the 1980s. 'Placing' had a literal meaning, about how women were physically situated in the city in terms of its landscape and buildings. But this also implied a cultural and indeed historical meaning, an analysis of women's ideological and historical situation in public and private spheres. Finally, it showed an understanding of how women were 'placed' structurally and institutionally, often without power, agency, or voice, whether this was in terms of architecture, planning, or building. They were excluded from 'making decisions' about women's place in the city and from the enactment of those decisions.[33]

Making Space located the placing of women in the environment in the historical development of gender and the way gender ideology shaped space and space shaped women. This drew upon the work of Leonore Davidoff and Catherine Hall (some of which became *Family Fortunes*, published in 1987) for Britain and Gwendolyn Wright and Dolores Hayden for the United States.[34] Grounding *Making Space* in a historical

---

[29] Bradshaw, 'Working with Women', Matrix, *Making Space,* 100.
[30] Suzy Nelson, Interview, 20 February 2018.
[31] Julia Dwyer, Interview, 22 February 2018.   [32] Matrix, *Making Space*, viii.
[33] Matrix, *Making Space*, 3.
[34] See Leonore Davidoff, 'The separation of work and home', in S. Berman (ed.), *Fit Work for Women* (London: Croom Helm, 1979); Gwendolyn Wright, *Moralism and the Model Home* (Chicago: University of Chicago Press, 1980); Dolores Hayden, *The Grand Domestic Revolution* (Cambridge, MA: MIT Press, 1981).

context occurred at a moment of considerable richness in women's history, of course, when critical works were being published and research being done. These included Sheila Rowbotham's *Hidden from History* (1977) and Sally Alexander's 'Women, Class and Sexual Differences' (1984), as well as research by Anna Davin, Judith Walkowitz, and Jane Lewis, among others.

Making Space offered a powerful interpretation of how that history could still be seen in the environment. What shaped the relationship between gender and architecture was, first of all, the way that architecture normalized and indeed spatialized particular gender and family roles, providing 'explicit models of how houses ought to be, and the way people should live.'[35] Surveying examples from the nineteenth century to the present day, such as model dwellings for working-class people, upper-middle-class housing plans, suburban houses, and post-war council housing, the contributors to *Making Space* argued that what united disparate plans was a shared gender ideology. In the first place, architecture upheld the 'proper segregation of home and work and women and men', in other words, the fact that the ideology of separate spheres found material form in the home.[36] Privacy was also a theme in architectural history—that the home was somewhere about marking off boundaries from other people, stressing the inviolability of the nuclear family. In both ways, the design of buildings placed women firmly in the private sphere and in the home. The architecture of buildings did not allow for innovative or public roles for women, even in periods such as the 1960s and 1970s in which those roles were clearly emerging. Indeed, because women were structurally absent from the design of buildings, even the maternal or familial roles accorded them in the private sphere were not well catered for. Few house designs thought through what was needed by women in terms of kitchens, for example, or space needed for childcare. *Making Space* did highlight those moments when women's involvement in the planning or design process or when broader social needs disrupted the traditional gender ideology shaping architecture. This was particularly clear in women's role in planning housing in the

[35] Jos Boys et al., 'House Design and Women's Roles', in Matrix, *Making Space*, 80.
[36] Matrix, *Making Space*, 44.

wake of the First World War and in the promotion of communal feeding with the establishment of British Restaurants in the 1940s.

Making Space also reflected upon the structural or institutional constraints that women continued to face. In the case of architecture, this centred on the monopoly enjoyed by 'middle-class males' in the profession.[37] The class aspect of this was important. Architecture demanded a long period of post-secondary training, and in the 1970s and 1980s this meant that those trained were 'overwhelmingly from middle-class backgrounds' and were dominantly 'white, middle-class men'.[38] This often separated them from understanding many of the clients serviced by their projects, particularly in the case of council housing. Jane Darke interviewed architects about the tenants of council housing and the replies were illuminating, ranging from the benignly patronizing to the blatantly offensive.[39] The class aspect was critical, because *Making Space* was trying to make the underlying point that 'architects are out of touch with those who use their buildings' and 'their professional training is part of the process that removes them from many of the people they design for'.[40] This was important for working-class people, and it was important for women; both were alienated from the designs and planning that placed them in the environment.

The experience of architectural training and its practice was also a source of alienation for women. In part, this was about the dearth of role models: '[o]nce in a school of architecture, many of us found it was extremely difficult to identify with a future role as an architect because we never came into contact with women practitioners'.[41] There was also prejudice from male architectural students and colleagues, 'who hope that the women they work with might change their behaviour or appearance to fit their own concept of how "girls" should act or look'.[42] Fran Bradshaw also remarked that there was a resistance to women's ideas in training: '[w]e have all been trained conventionally by and with men,

[37] Jane Darke, 'Women, Architects and Feminism', in Matrix, *Making Space*, 11.
[38] Darke, 'Women, Architects and Feminism', in Matrix, *Making Space*, 12, 13.
[39] Darke, 'Women, Architects and Feminism', in Matrix, *Making Space*, 14–15.
[40] Darke, 'Women, Architects and Feminism', in Matrix, *Making Space*, 11.
[41] Darke, 'Women, Architects and Feminism', in Matrix, *Making Space*, 22.
[42] Darke, 'Women, Architects and Feminism', in Matrix, *Making Space*, 22.

who have often devalued or ignored our work, describing it as "emotional" or "confused"'.[43] Once qualified, women architects could look forward to enduring a significant gap in earnings compared with their male colleagues. Reconciling motherhood with architectural practice was difficult and not well regarded. The route out of this was, in the first place, about the structure or the institution. More women had to be brought into the profession and encouraged in its practice. But a greater change had to happen—the working in of a 'feminist consciousness among architects'—as this would effect a 'change in their approach to design'.[44]

What set *Making Space* apart from other works of architectural criticism was that it dedicated attention to the inner landscape of women's lives within buildings, giving voice to the emotional effects of a man-made landscape and man-made buildings. It was a powerful example of how second-wave feminism explored the relationship between the personal and the political. One member recalled:

> the starting point was sometimes emotional but it's also very conditioned by what we were reading and by the women's movement beginning to put words into those feelings and those concepts that people had.[45]

In *Making Space*, this interest was particularly clear in a chapter by Benedicte Foo which explored the experiences mothers had of their houses and the city. Foo began by suggesting that such feelings were often treated as 'trivial, routine and unworthy of examination and they therefore become invisible and invalid', which was 'part of the way society ignores the situation of women with growing children – an extension of its lack of concern for the needs of women generally'.[46] '[T]alking about our homes and our feelings round the idea of "home" and "the family"' was, Foo stated, 'extremely personal', but that personal and often emotive view was critical to understanding the relationship of

---

[43] Bradshaw, 'Working with Women', in Matrix, *Making Space*, 89.
[44] Darke, 'Women, Architects and Feminism', in Matrix, *Making Space*, 24.
[45] Julia Dwyer, Interview, 22 February 2018.
[46] Benedicte Foo, 'House and Home', in Matrix, *Making Space*, 120.

women to society and how they were placed within society.[47] For the chapter she canvassed her friends, admitting that this was a highly selective survey and one that was limited to middle-class women. This limited testimony was nonetheless indicative, in the first place, of the absolutely critical relationship between private and public space and motherhood—the size of corridors, the arrangement and use of rooms, and access to public transport and private conveniences such as washing machines and driers were all of paramount importance in women's experience of bringing up children. There was, for example, a consistent reflection upon how houses and public spaces opened up or restricted movement for mothers. Central to this was the way that reproductive and domestic responsibilities continued to fall on individual women in a 'privatized society'.[48] This produced a range of emotional responses: 'loneliness and alienation', a sense of isolation, and 'psychological distance'.[49] Outside the home, public spaces showed a 'lack of tolerance of babies and toddlers', further frustrating and isolating women.[50] The solution to this was both long-term and immediate. In the long term, society had to become more sensitive to women's needs as mothers. As well, Foo argued for the socialization of childcare and domestic work. But in the immediate term, a solution could be found in listening to women talk about space from a personal or emotional perspective, in the 'thoughtful and sensitive production of safe houses'.[51]

Safety was also a theme brought up in *Making Space*. This connected to emotions in the sense of the fear that women could feel in the environment. That fear came from male violence. The book's introduction included the statement that a man-made environment not only was alienating to women but also could be frightening: '[i]f we walk on the streets after dark, we are accused of inviting violent sexual attack from men'.[52] It is significant, of course, that the book was written in the aftermath of the Yorkshire Ripper murders and with a conscious

---

[47] Foo, 'House and Home', in Matrix, *Making Space*, 120.
[48] Foo, 'House and Home', in Matrix, *Making Space*, 135.
[49] Foo, 'House and Home', in Matrix, *Making Space*, 135, 122.
[50] Foo, 'House and Home', in Matrix, *Making Space*, 135.
[51] Foo, 'House and Home', in Matrix, *Making Space*, 136.
[52] Matrix, *Making Space*, 4.

acknowledgement of campaigns to reclaim the streets. In her contribution, Jos Boys argued that 'most women feel they are not safe anywhere', particularly from 'male behaviour outside the home', and that the planning of things like housing estates created areas of danger for women, with dark passageways and blind alleys, a 'no-woman's land'.[53] Safety was, in this way, a fundamental element of accessibility in the city for women.

If *Making Space* gave attention to the way women were placed in a man-made environment, how did it suggest that should be subverted? In many ways it was not simply about what buildings would look like, but how they would be designed and built.

That attention to voices beyond the privileged position of the architect was key to the approach advocated by Matrix in *Making Space*, and it was one taken directly from the Women's Liberation Movement in terms of methods of community-building, an underlying theme of Fran Bradshaw's contribution, 'Working with Women'. This reflected a consciously feminist approach. What was critical in this regard was a process that involved women as clients from the beginning, developing 'a way of designing buildings together, which values women's involvement in all stages of the evolution of a building'.[54] The collaboration of women in the process would produce a different, and better, architecture: 'if women collectively organize, design and make buildings that suit their needs rather than having to fit into well it exists already (buildings created by patriarchal culture) then the buildings are bound to look and feel different'.[55] In this, it would not simply be a distinctively female space that would be created but also a distinctively feminist method would be tried. Jane Darke remarked that this reflected an explicitly feminist method: '[w]omen's groups, which have worked together using the methods developed in the women's movement – listening to each other, giving every woman space to express her feelings and developing theories from women's own experiences – will want to work with architects who understand and can use the same approach'.[56]

---

[53] Boys, 'Women and Public Space', in Matrix, *Making Space*, 52, 46, 49.
[54] Bradshaw, 'Working with Women', in Matrix, *Making Space*, 89.
[55] Bradshaw, 'Working with Women', in Matrix, *Making Space*, 90.
[56] Darke, 'Women and Feminism', in Matrix, *Making Space*, 24–5.

By 1984, Matrix had had several examples of such a method. All involved women's organizations, and Bradshaw argued that this was not designing for women's groups but, rather, 'designing with women's groups'.[57] One example was the Stockwell Health Centre, a project pursued by a local women's group—the Stockwell Health Group—as a way of persuading the local health authority. The Stockwell Health Group was looking for the recognition that 'the design of building affects women's lives in all sorts of ways' and that a particular environment should be nurtured in any new health centre:

> the centre should fulfil the needs of the community as a resource, and…it should feel open, inviting and easy to use. These principles should be demonstrated clearly and simply by a building.[58]

But the method of achieving this was important as well, in particular the process of 'working in groups' with an architectural practice, rather than with an individual, and to 'discover *with* the group how a health centre, democratically run and open to the community could be designed'.[59] This collaborative and consultative method was recognized to take more time than was usual in the designing process, 'trying out possibilities and finding ways women can become more confident about expressing their ideas about buildings'; and, in various projects, including the Stockwell Health Centre, but also the Dalston Children's Centre and the Lambeth Women's Workshop, this required new methods of discussing architecture, whether it was through models or new kinds of plans.[60] In its application to the Women's Committee, for example, Matrix set out what was needed in terms of consultation over the Dalston Children's Centre: 'to discuss the project with all the groups and individuals involved…childminders' group, mothers of under-fives, workers premises group, management committee'.[61] The point was to allow women's

---

[57] Bradshaw, 'Working with Women', in Matrix, *Making Space*, 90.
[58] Bradshaw, 'Working with Women', in Matrix, *Making Space*, 91.
[59] Bradshaw, 'Working with Women', in Matrix, *Making Space*, 91, 92.
[60] Bradshaw, 'Working with Women', in Matrix, *Making Space*, 96.
[61] GLC, Women's Committee, 'Matrix', Funding Application, 31 March 1983, LMA, GLC/DG/PRE/223/13.

'feelings about the spaces women know and their everyday experiences in them' to be heard.[62] This was also about an alteration in the power between architects and clients, and, to this end, Bradshaw argued that it was feminist politics itself that facilitated the dissembling of the usual power relationship: '[i]t is our shared politics and feminist intentions that make an equal relationship possible'.[63] And what was the result in the design of the buildings? Though Stockwell Health Centre was never built, the plans that Matrix and their clients came up with did reflect new values. In particular, there was a desire to make buildings less 'cold and institutional' and less 'intimidating', and instead to encourage warmth, connection, and friendliness.[64] In material ways, what this meant was a plan to have a cafe and meeting place at the heart of the Health Centre, as a physical expression of a new approach generated by collaboration and an attempt to nurture different values critical to the liberation of women.

And, of course, the subversion of the man-made environment came with what kinds of buildings were being worked on. As Matrix noted in its application to the Women's Committee, certain kinds of buildings were the product of new social and political needs: '[w]omen have been creating new kinds of buildings to respond to newly articulated needs'.[65] Those buildings included childcare centres, such as the Dalston Children's Centre, women's centres such as Hackney Women's Centre, refuges such as Acton Women's Aid, and centres to help train women in new skills or in areas where men had dominated, such as Lambeth Women's Workshop. The construction of such buildings that attended to women's needs was a critical way of changing the man-made environment of the city, making it a city for women, with buildings for women. In 1986, with funding from the Women's Committee, Matrix published two leaflets, one on the practicalities of establishing such new buildings,

[62] Bradshaw, 'Working with Women', in Matrix, *Making Space*, 94.
[63] Bradshaw, 'Working with Women', in Matrix, *Making Space*, 103.
[64] Bradshaw, 'Working with Women', in Matrix, *Making Space*, 100.
[65] GLC, Women's Committee, 'Matrix', Funding Application, 31 March 1983, LMA, GLC/DG/PRE/223/13.

specifically childcare centres, the other on how women could negotiate the architectural profession and building trades.[66]

The Jagonari Centre in Whitechapel was, perhaps, the most important project undertaken by Matrix, in the same year as the publication of *Making Space*. It demonstrated many of the distinct feminist qualities and aims advocated in *Making Space*. As one of the members of Jagonari explained, the building would not only be a critical resource for women in the East End but also represent materially the desire of women to have more power and autonomy:

> We were also some pioneering women too working in the communities in early 80s when men dominated the whole scene of community work and us women tagged along with them while they looked down on us. We knew that and decided us women of Bangladeshi origin need to take control of our destiny and do what we want, not what men tell us to do.[67]

Jagonari approached Matrix to do the design for the building. The process of design reflected many of the aspects set out in *Making Space* and in the work of Matrix up to this point. In particular, enormous emphasis was placed on consultation with Jagonari and British Bangladeshi women in the East End. The desire that Jagonari had for the project was to have 'a women only building which would enable them to carry out a variety of activities in a range of different spaces – from Asian dance/drama to computer studies'; it would also include a crèche. Solma Ahmed later remarked that what Jagonari sought in the building was 'safety, security, childcare, sensitive to women's cultural and religious needs while breaking some myths about Muslim women in particular'.[68] Balance was critical. On the one hand, Jagonari wanted the centre to have an Asian and Muslim character to it. On the other hand, there was

[66] See Matrix, *Building for Childcare* (London: Matrix/GLC, 1986); Matrix, *A Job Designing Buildings* (London: Matrix/GLC, 1986).
[67] Solma Ahmed, quoted in https://c20society.org.uk/building-of-the-month/jagonari-asian-womens-education-centre-whitechapel-london.
[68] Solma Ahmed to Anne Thorne, 24 August 2019, in Matrix Feminist Architecture Archive, http://www.matrixfeministarchitecturearchive.co.uk/wp-content/uploads/2021/07/M00066a.jpg.

Figure 4.1 Jagonari Women's Centre, Whitechapel.
Source: Martin Charles/RIBA Collections.

a concern that too overt an Asian quality would 'invite abuse from racists or from men affronted by the idea of a women-only institution'.[69] Indeed, many of the women from the area had experienced racial

[69] Dwyer and Thorne, 'Evaluating Matrix', 48.

violence and harassment.[70] The compromise was to have a courtyard influenced by South Asian and Islamic architecture, with a public front that was more restrained in its identity, though having South Asian-accented protective window grills (as can be seen in Figure 4.1).The building was also notable because of the thought it gave, singular at the time, to disabled access. The process of consultation included Jagonari showing Matrix examples of South Asian buildings and discussions of particular needs for a communal kitchen, and spaces for recreation and meetings.[71]

4.2

The kinds of projects that Matrix worked on were all supported by state funding. Some early women's centres had been funded by Urban Aid, but the coming to power of the Labour GLC took this support to new levels. Fran Bradshaw later recalled the importance of this change to the women's movement in London:

> These groups were used to meeting in basements...and then the GLC came along and said we can provide you with money and we will put this building in your name, and we will provide these things that give you a certain stability...that was really radical.[72]

The GLC Women's Committee was critical in this regard. In 1982, Valerie Wise, the GLC member for Wandsworth, Battersea South, and a member of the GLC Industry and Employment Committee, announced to a Labour Local Government Conference in Sheffield that the GLC was establishing a Women's Committee. The Women's Committee began with a budget of £300,000 and a staff of four; by the time of the GLC's abolition, its budget was £16 million and its staff numbered a hundred,

---

[70] See https://c20society.org.uk/building-of-the-month/jagonari-asian-womens-education-centre-whitechapel-london.

[71] See https://c20society.org.uk/building-of-the-month/jagonari-asian-womens-education-centre-whitechapel-london.

[72] Interview, Fran Bradshaw, 21 November 2017.

including a Women's Committee Support Unit. There were women's units and women's committees in places like Sheffield, Nottingham, and Stirling, but they did not approach the scale of what was attempted in London. Nor was the experiment repeated at the national level. The promise the national Labour Party made in the 1980s and early 1990s to have a Ministry of Women was not realized when Labour came to power in 1997. The experience of the Women's Committee under the GLC thus remains exceptional.

A key change leading to the establishment of the Women's Committee was the movement of feminists within the Labour Party in the 1970s, seeking to get 'hands on the resources'.[73] The antipathy and indifference often shown by the Labour Party and the trade union movement towards women's issues meant that socialist feminists did not take easily to the Labour Party.[74] But by the late 1970s some feminists 'believed that the old structure was breaking up', presenting an opportunity for feminists to enter the party and bend it towards feminist ideals.[75] Sheila Rowbotham saw this as a process of 'dismantling' older ways, replacing them with 'more open, harmonious alternatives' from the feminist movement.[76] In 1979, due to the efforts of 'a determined group of women community workers', Lewisham had established the first women's rights working party at the local government level.[77] The voice of the local Labour left in London, *London Labour Briefing*, became another platform for feminism within the party. The Labour manifesto for the GLC elections in May 1981 included a pledge to fight sex discrimination, alongside other areas of discrimination.[78]

This commitment has been referred to as 'a bit of an afterthought', but it found a critical sponsor in Ken Livingstone, the new leader of the

---

[73]   Marie Kane, in 'Making Waves', *Marxism Today* (July 1986), 16.

[74]   Stephen Brooke, *Sexual Politics* (Oxford: Oxford University Press, 2011).

[75]   Wainwright, *Labour: A Tale of Two Parties*, 165.

[76]   Sheila Rowbotham, 'Planning from Below' (1982) and 'Women, Power and Consciousness: Discussions in the Women's Liberation Movement in Britain, 1969–81' (1982), in *Dreams and Dilemmas* (London: Virago, 1988), 345, 145; see also Rowbotham, Segal, and Wainwright, *Beyond the Fragments*.

[77]   Lansley, Goss, and Wolmar, *Councils in Conflict*, 144.

[78]   *A Socialist Policy for the GLC*, 33.

GLC.[79] Livingstone saw feminism as a crucial part of the new politics Labour had to adopt. The creation of the Women's Committee in 1982 presented second-wave feminists with their first opportunity to 'gain access into a major political institution, thus giving them the chance – for the first time ever – to have a voice in the planning and provision of services'.[80]

It did not occur without resistance. 'Fleet Street went really bananas when we established a Women's Committee', Livingstone noted.[81] The tabloid reaction was predictable, perhaps, but even broadsheet characterization of Valerie Wise could be sexist. She was portrayed by *The Guardian* as the 'the feminist witch of Fleet Street and Red Ken's right-hand person'.[82] *The Times* called her both a 'wicked witch' and 'the most powerful woman in local government'.[83] The terms 'warlock' or 'wizard' were not applied to Wise's male colleagues. '[V]itriolic and inaccurate abuse' might have been expected from the media and political rivals, but what was also striking was the opposition closer to the GLC's political home.[84] When Valerie Wise originally announced the creation of the Women's Committee, it was 'treated...as a huge joke' by other Labour authorities, so much so that David Blunkett 'almost fell backwards off his chair' in apparently uncontrollable mirth.[85] Writing retrospectively, the Women's Committee stated that 'WCSU officers had to work under the pressure of considerable open hostility from other parts of the Council'.[86]

The Women's Committee was given a significant budget for grant aid. Its funding priorities included '[p]rojects increasing public awareness of, and campaigning against women...organizations campaigning on behalf of women's rights...projects enabling women with young children to go out to work and lead full and active public and social life

[79] Quoted in Lansley, Goss, and Wolmar, *Councils in Conflict*, 144; on Livingstone, see Wes Whitehorse, *GLC: The Inside Story* (London: James Lester, 2000), 142.
[80] GLC, *The GLC Women's Committee, 1982-6: A Record of Change and Achievement for Women in London* (London: GLC, 1986), 2.
[81] Livingstone, *You Can't Say That*, 212.
[82] Sue Pilkington, 'Wise before the event', *The Guardian*, 2 April 1986.
[83] Yvonne Roberts, 'Wicked witch or power for good?', *The Times*, 13 May 1985.
[84] *The GLC Women's Committee, 1982-6*, 9.
[85] Livingstone, *If Voting Changed Anything*, 238; Livingstone, *You Can't Say That*, 212.
[86] *The GLC Women's Committee, 1982-6*, 14.

[*sic*] ... organizations providing resources such as meeting rooms, librar-
ies, access to equipment'.[87] Grant aid was also a way of acknowledging
the 'self-help' that women had been forced to take up because of women's
lack of access to 'decision-making and resources'.[88]

The Women's Committee was also committed to changing the way
government worked. Early in its life, it held an Open Meeting at County
Hall in July 1982. Nearly three hundred women attended, representing
over fifty organizations, including the BBC, Lesbian Line, *Spare Rib*, the
Childcare Network Group, and the Women's Collective Photographic
Agency. Wise invited the members of the organizations attending to
form particular working groups—on a wide spectrum of issues including industrial and employment policy, lesbian issues, violence against
women, ethnic minority questions, and the anti-nuclear movement.
Childcare, lesbianism, and black women's rights were the three issues
that attracted particular interest. Open meetings became a quarterly fix-
ture of the Women's Committee; by 1984, there had been eight.

The establishment of the Women's Committee also complemented
other evidence of a greater feminist presence in the GLC. The GLC's
Industry and Employment Committee committed to looking at questions of gender equality in areas of employment, training, and domestic
work, as discussed in Chapter 3.

Believing 'every issue to be a women's issue', the Women's Committee
argued that its establishment had given women in London, for the first
time, 'a voice in the capital's strategic authority'.[89] During its four-year
existence, the Women's Committee fulfilled a variety of roles: as a body
that dispensed millions of pounds in grant aid; that monitored the work
of the GLC as an employer and a political body; and, finally, that acted
as a source of policy itself. With respect to the last role, the Women's
Committee offered a fundamental rethink of urban policy from a

---

[87] GLC, Women's Committee, Report by the Director-General, 17 February 1982, LMA,
GLC/DG/PRE/223/01.
[88] GLC, Women's Committee, Report by Head of Women's Committee Support Unit,
'Promoting Equal Opportunities for Women – Procedures for Committees', 12 July 1984, LMA,
GLC/DG/PRE/223/14.
[89] GLC, Women's Committee, 'A Summary of the Achievements of the Women's Committee
to May 1984', 18 May 1984, LMA, GLC/DG/PRE/223/20.

feminist perspective, both in a general way and in particular areas such as housing, transport, and employment.

This was reflected in *A Programme for Women in London* (1983). The programme was a collection of statements from the consultative working groups established during the open meeting of July 1982, including those on housing, Black and ethnic minority women, transport, lesbians, women's centres, and pregnancy and motherhood.[90] The aim of all the working groups was to 'change the way London is run so that the interests and welfare of women are equally important'.[91] The task was an urgent one. To do nothing was to 'perpetuate existing male privilege'.[92] A city that oppressed women had to be made into a city for women.

Each of the reports in the programme reflected upon what the GLC could do as an employer and as the strategic authority for London to realize this aim. Reflecting upon 'Pregnancy and Motherhood', for example, the programme argued that the GLC should improve preconception care and working conditions for pregnant mothers, provide paternity leave for fathers and childcare for families, and, within London's schools, promote sex education. The 'Media and Arts' working group wanted to see a focus upon the representation of women in culture, including such topics as sexist advertising and pornography. This included important interventions by the English Collective of Prostitutes which sparked considerable debate within the Women's Committee. Women's safety in the city was also a concern. The Working Group on Violence against Women by Men highlighted the threat to women in the public sphere: 'Women make a vital contribution to the life of our city. They live, work and travel, shop and seek entertainment. Yet they are vulnerable, often fearful and ill-protected.'[93] This could also be seen in specific proposals on transport, which sought to mitigate the restrictions on 'women's mobility' by 'the threat of male violence'.[94]

---

[90] GLC, Women's Committee, 'Programme of Action for Women of London: Additional Sections', 19 January 1984, LMA, GLC/DG/PRE/223/14.

[91] GLC, Women's Committee, 'A Programme for Women in London', February 1983, LMA, GLC/DG/PRE/223/3.

[92] GLC, 'A Programme for Women in London', February 1983.

[93] GLC, 'A Programme for Women in London', February 1983.

[94] GLC, 'A Programme for Women in London', February 1983.

More generally, the programme wanted the GLC's policy and actions to be informed by an understanding of the problems of sexism. Pursuing positive discrimination in favour of women within the GLC was one aspect of this. Another was transforming the centre of gravity of all policy. The programme argued that planning policy should, for example, include thinking about women, particularly in their role as carers. Similarly, on the economy, the programme wanted policy shifted from concentrating only on manufacturing to concentrating on the service and retail sectors and towards 'the needs of women as workers and parents'.[95]

These efforts could be seen as an attempt to claim a place within the governing ideology of the GLC. But the programme also sought to claim physical space within the city for women's needs through the establishment of centres dedicated to women's issues. The Lesbian Working Party stressed the need for '[a] lesbian space... a place where they can go to be in the company of like women, whether it be for relaxing socializing, campaigning or just being there'.[96] The Women and Planning Group offered a vision of '[l]ocally managed centres [to] provide meeting spaces; communal restaurants, laundry services; childcare and any other activities and services required by the local community'.[97]

The most wide-ranging statement of this came, unsurprisingly, from the Working Group on 'Women's Centres'. It perceived that a women's centre could be 'a channel through which [a programme for women] can wage its attack on women's disadvantage in all areas':

Women are poor. Women need somewhere in their own neighbourhood from which to run campaigns for more nursery places, better housing etc. Where women can drop in for support, courage, advice, contacts before they apply for the first job in ten years or that slightly better job, or tackle the social security office. Access to paid work and to better paid work needs training schemes and advice. Women need childcare and work.... Women are abused. They need somewhere

---

[95] GLC, 'A Programme for Women in London', February 1983.
[96] GLC, 'A Programme for Women in London', February 1983.
[97] GLC, 'A Programme for Women in London', February 1983.

sympathetic and close at hand to get help, advice, collective strength, self-defence classes; referral to counselling, legal, medical, housing and other services; information on how and where to protest on advertising, street planning, transport provision etc... Women are isolated. Women's centres can help draw women into the community, into campaigns, recreational activities, adult education, and all sorts of women's groups.... Women are under-represented... Women's centres can form local links, controlled by women, between policy making bodies and local women and their organizations. All policies need to be backed (or restrained) by popular pressure, and pressure needs somewhere to organize, collect support, propagandize and so on.[98]

The programme hoped to see 'a network of women's centres, perhaps one in each borough'.[99]

Seeing the city through the lens of sexism involved reimagining particular issues and spaces. The problem of housing and the space of the housing estate provides one example. The GLC was, of course, a major provider of housing in London. To some, this made it culpable in the perpetuation of practices that discriminated against women. The housing estate was a particular focus of concern. A long report from 1986, based upon input from organizations such as the Child Poverty Action Group, Age Concern, and Gingerbread (an organization for lone mothers), as well as a variety of boroughs, outlined the problems faced by women on estates. These included 'security, design; lighting; maintenance... violence... homelessness; allocations policy, particularly in regard to relationship breakdown; access to rehousing'.[100] The very space of the housing estate deepened women's oppression. Another report, from Camden, emphasized the sense of threat to women on housing estates, sometimes written into the material environment: 'lifts, graffiti, noise disturbance (youth, parties), illegal parking, dog nuisance, et [cetera]'. This violated what Camden Council considered a basic aspiration for security: '[t]he assurance of personal safety... and the "quiet enjoyment"

[98] GLC, 'A Programme for Women in London', February 1983.
[99] GLC, 'A Programme for Women in London', February 1983.
[100] GLC, Women's Committee, Report by the Heads of the Women's Committee Support Unit, 'Women and Housing Report', 4 March 1986, LMA, GLC/DG/PRE/223/61.

of accommodation and the surrounding neighbourhood of the estate'. The evidence from almost all of the boroughs submitting evidence suggested that most women felt unsafe on estates. In Southwark, for example, 'over half the women said that they stayed at home at some point during the day or night because they were worried about their safety'. The solution to this included providing more refuges against sexual and domestic violence, as well as taking women's concerns into consideration when designing buildings and estates, from the provision of entryphones to what Lambeth noted as 'landscaping, lighting, footpaths and boundary definition'. In Southwark, for example, it was noted: 'women's security needed to be considered at every stage of design, development and the implementation of the Housing Investment Programme'. It was also believed that the allocations process had to give priority to women who needed accommodation as refuge from domestic violence, and specific groups, such as lesbians, older women, Black and ethnic minorities, and disabled women should also be given special attention.[101]

This also dovetailed with concerns about women and transport in the city. Just as women felt insecure in terms of their dwelling, moving about the city was also accompanied by a sense of threat. The 'Programme of Action for Women' stated, for instance, that '[w]omen's mobility is constantly restricted by the threat of male violence'.[102] Transport policy had to reflect the character and needs of women's lives, as workers, mothers, consumers, and carers. Towards this end, the Women's Committee funded a pilot project for Safe Women's Transport Ltd, which provided a minibus service. It was hoped that this would 'reverse the cultural, educational and social isolation of women who are afraid to go out alone in the evenings especially in those areas of inner London where statistics indicate that they are particularly vulnerable to attack'.[103] Other proposals included more flexible routes, attuned less to commuting to work than to the demands on women's life such as shopping and childcare. Thinking about transport and women also involved thinking about sexual

[101] GLC, 'Women and Housing Report', 4 March 1986.

[102] GLC, 'Programme of Action for Women in London', February 1983.

[103] GLC, Women's Committee, 'Safe Women's Transport Ltd', Funding Application, 13 April 1984, LMA, GLC/DG/PRE/223/19.

harassment, in a variety of ways. One proposal (which rebounded in the 2015 Labour leadership race) was to have women-only carriages on the Underground to provide a safe space against harassment; altering the physical experience of transport included confronting sexist advertising on London Transport.[104]

A distinctive element of the work of the Women's Committee was support for the establishment of women's centres throughout London. Of course, women's centres had existed before 1981 and were a critical aspect of the women's movement in London in the 1970s. This included Haringey Women's Centre, Cromer Street Women's Centre, Kentish Town Women's Workshop, Brent Women's Centre, North Paddington Women's Centre, and St Raphael's Women's Workshop in Harlesden. Many of these had received state funding through the Urban Aid programme. The needs that women's centres addressed were various, as advice centres, education (on health questions, for example, but also in things such as photography and carpentry), resources for teenage girls, childcare, and foundations for campaigning. But one need, as articulated as well in *Making Space,* arose from the spatial and emotional place of women in the city, specifically the way that women were often placed in isolation:

> Many women in London are lonely, especially when, as is often the case for women, their home is their workplace where they are engaged in repetitive work for long hours on their own. Particularly isolated are mothers looking after children below school age, women caring for dependents, elderly women and women with disabilities.... Loneliness is painful and a factor in mental breakdown. A higher proportion of women than men suffer ill health of this kind. There are not many places where women can meet one another and form friendships.... They may also be afraid of travelling by public transport late at night.

'By setting up a local women's centre,' the Women's Committee Support Unit argued, 'women provide for themselves a daily drop-in facility.'

[104] GLC, 'Programme of Action for Women in London', February 1983.

A women's centre could be 'a place of their own' in the city; this also meant having a space not 'controlled by men' but, rather, a 'women controlled space where they can be together to define themselves free from psychological or physical harassment'.[105]

An example was the Haringey Women's Centre, which applied to the Women's Committee for funding in 1982. The Haringey Women's Centre described itself as providing a 'meeting place exclusively for women', concentrating on health, housing, education, childcare provision and transport, workshops on welfare rights, language classes, self-help therapy, a library group, and a young women's project. About three hundred women a week used the centre, as did other groups, such as the Archway Women's Health Group, which provided reproductive information, as well as women's campaigning groups. Not least, the Centre was the 'only place available for women's meetings in the area where there is no possibility of male interference, and as such it is a unique and much needed venue'.[106]

Centres as a refuge from male interference or violence was a consistent theme of applications to the Women's Committee from women's centres. This speaks to the idea that these centres were radical interventions by women to claim a space in a man-dominated urban space. There were moments when this faced violent reaction. In 1982, for example, the Cromer Street Women's Centre in Camden was attacked by arsonists—an attack which women's activists struggled to get the police to take seriously.[107] The Women's Committee committed to establish, by various means, the 'development of a comprehensive network of essential resources for women in London'.[108] This would allow women a physical foothold in the city:

Women need somewhere in their own neighbourhood from which to run campaigns for more nursery places, better housing...Where

---

[105] GLC, Women's Committee, Report by the Head of the Women's Committee Support Unit, 'Women's Centres', 11 July 1983, LMA, GLC/DG/PRE/223/14.

[106] GLC, Women's Committee, 'Haringey Women's Centre', Funding Application, 22 September 1982, LMA, GLC/DG/PRE/223/1.

[107] See GLC Women's Centre, 'Women's Centre Attacked', September 1982, LMA, GLC/DG/223/2.

[108] GLC, Women's Committee, Report by the Chair, 'Funding of Women's Organisations in London – An Overall View', 16 September 1982, LMA, GLC/DG/PRE/223/1.

women can drop in for support, courage, advice, contacts... Women need childcare and work... they need somewhere sympathetic and close at hand to get help, advice, collective strength... Women are isolated... women's centres can help draw women into the community.[109]

By 1986, the publication of *The London Women's Handbook*, put together by the Women's Committee, listed a thirty-page directory of various women's centres. The resources that many women's centres needed were in terms not only of salaries and wages but also of property. Many of the centres had a precarious existence in terms of leases, and some sought a more permanent foothold in the city through the purchase or long-term rent of property. Perhaps the most ambitious aim of the Women's Committee, achieved in 1986, was the establishment of a metropolitan women's centre—the London Women's Centre—fully funded by the GLC, in Wesley House near Holborn Tube station. The centre offered a home to a variety of organizations, including the National Abortion Campaign, the English Collective of Prostitutes, and Women's Information and Resource Exchange.

The abolition of the GLC did not immediately end this project. The London Women's Centre existed until 2000. But once metropolitan funding for women's centres and organizations had been cut off, the remaining borough councils and the new Greater London Authority were either less able or less sympathetic as sources of funding for feminism.

As for Matrix, it continued until 1990. However, its ability to carry through its aims was more limited with the end of the GLC. Other factors also complicated its work. Housing association work became more commercial in the late 1980s. There was a sense that, with the abolition of the GLC, a moment had passed. There may also have been a sense of exhaustion within groups such as Matrix, as one former member suggested: 'I think that incredible kind of enthusiasm, you know thinking, "oh we can change the world" took a real beating and it became really quite survival towards the end, the end of the 80s.'[110] But this did not, of

---

[109] GLC, 'Programme of Action for Women in London', February 1983.
[110] Interview, Fran Bradshaw, 21 November 2017.

course, mean that the work done by Matrix did not continue in a different context. Its members moved in different directions in the 1990s, but there was a common thread of pursuing work with communities, with a sensitivity to the methods used in Matrix: true consultation with clients and to the needs of local communities, including environmental needs. Anne Thorne, for example, went on to have her own firm, which specializes in sustainable buildings designed in collaboration with clients. Many of the firm's projects parallel what Matrix did in the 1980s: 'community buildings, housing, education and children's buildings, urban studies and masterplans'.[111] The London that Matrix wanted to help construct in the 1980s is thus still being built.

With *Making Space* and with the work it had done on buildings across London, Matrix had mapped out many of the challenges of women in the late twentieth-century city: negotiating an environment not designed with them in mind, which not only caused women inconvenience but also threatened their safety. Perhaps most of all, Matrix had articulated that the problem of the urban environment was a problem of unequal power of men over women. The solution to that problem was, of course, to give women more power and more autonomy. The Women's Committee also pursued that aim. Making a city for women in the 1980s was, as both Matrix and the Women's Committee understood, about challenging the gender ideology and power relations that shaped that city.

London, 1984: Conflict and Change in the Radical City. Stephen Brooke, Oxford University Press.
© Stephen Brooke 2024. DOI: 10.1093/9780191895395.003.0005

[111] Anne Thorne Architects, https://www.annethornearchitects.com/about.

5

Gay's the Word

Cutting south through Bloomsbury, Marchmont Street has long been a centre of retail, its early nineteenth-century shops supplemented in the late twentieth century by the modernist ziggurat of the Brunswick Centre. In January 1979, at no. 66, a pioneering commercial venture appeared: Gay's the Word, Britain's first gay and lesbian bookshop, taking the name of a 1951 Ivor Novello musical. Gay's the Word became 'nothing less than a community centre' for gay people in London, an identity it has retained over five decades.[1]

But early in its life, in 1984, the existence of Gay's the Word was in jeopardy. On 10 April, Customs and Excise officers raided the shop and the homes of several of its directors. In the operation, code-named 'Tiger' (after the pet cat of Colin Woodgate, one of the officers), customs officers spent five hours seizing books, videos, and personal possessions under the 1876 Customs Consolidation Act, which prohibited the importation of 'obscene' or 'indecent' material.[2] In the case of Gay's the Word, the source of much of the seized material was the Philadelphia bookstore Giovanni's Room.

A precision operation, this was not. The bookshop's manager, Amanda Russell, suggested that 'the officers "didn't seem to know what they were looking for"... [t]he customs team repeatedly phoned their own office... to find out what they were supposed to take.'[3] Confusion apparently whetted appetites: a photograph from the raid shows a startled and heavily moustachioed customs officer bringing an armful of pork pies and sandwiches into the shop.[4] In went the food and out went about

---

[1] Letter to *Gay News* (London), 14–27 May 1981.
[2] Defend Gay's the Word Campaign, Witness Statement, Colin Woodgate, Regina v. Noncyp and others, Bishopsgate Institute Archives, DGWC, 1/1/8, 1985.
[3] 'Customs Raid Gay's the Word', *The Body Politic* (Toronto) (June 1984): 21.
[4] See photograph in *The Body Politic*, 'Customs Raid Gay's the Word'.

500 books, including Armistead Maupin's *Tales of the City* (1978),
Harvey Fierstein's *Torch Song Trilogy* (1978), novels by Janet Rule and
Rita Mae Brown, older work by Edward Carpenter and Oscar Wilde,
and even the fifteenth-century *Book of the City of Ladies* by Christine de
Pisan, until that point a work not known for its explicit erotic qualities.
Another raid on Gay's the Word in June 1984 saw the seizure of a further 200 titles.[5] The bookshop's directors subsequently faced 100 charges
of importing indecent material—charges which threatened heavy fines
and jail terms. Because £9000 of its stock had been seized, Gay's the
Word also faced potential financial ruin. In 1985, the case spilled across
the Atlantic when Giovanni's Room was named as a co-conspirator. One
commentator called it 'the most important literary case in several decades', but it never made it to court.[6] Before the case went to full trial in
1986, Customs and Excise withdrew all charges.[7]

The raid on Gay's the Word is a fascinating, if underexplored, episode
in the history of sexuality in late twentieth-century Britain. It was, in the
first place, a literal example of how sex was policed in London in the
1980s. The raid underlined the way the state (in the form of Customs
and Excise) continued to discipline same-sex sexuality—in this case,
identifying homosexuality with obscenity. More broadly, the raid illuminated the ambiguous position of gay and lesbian rights in the late
twentieth century. In the wake of the 1967 decriminalization of homosexuality and the emergence in the 1970s of gay liberation, gay people in
London experienced greater visibility and presence. But that visibility
and presence remained contested. The 1980s saw a counter-reaction to
the progress of gay rights, seen in policing, the media, and the policies of
the Conservative government. The last culminated in Section 28 of the
1988 Local Government Act, which forbade the 'promotion' of homosexuality through local government. The raid on Gay's the Word was
viewed through the prism of what was perceived to be increasing police
harassment of gay people and media vilification of the gay community.
The decade witnessed rising levels of homophobic violence and public

[5] 'Gay Raids', *Policing London*, 14 (September–October 1984).
[6] Nicholas de Jongh, 'Blue Pencil Blues', *Guardian,* 6 December 1984.
[7] See *The Body Politic*, August 1986, 17.

disapproval of gay relationships.[8] The events of 1984 also happened against the background of the unfolding AIDS crisis which devastated the gay community. Alan Hollinghurst's pioneering 1988 novel of same-sex desire, *The Swimming Pool Library*, was set in 1983, a year infused with a sense of ominous portent, 'a faint flicker of calamity', like flames around a photograph, something seen out of the corner of the eye.'[9]

The reaction to the raid on Gay's the Word nonetheless demonstrated the growing confidence and determination of the same-sex community in London. This can be seen in the success of the public campaign to defend the bookshop. Not only was this a definitive victory over Customs and Excise; it also demonstrated, in the period before the campaigning around Section 28, the determination of gay and lesbian activist groups in claiming rights and visibility in the city. Indeed, the campaign against the raid was a critical stepping stone on the road between gay liberation in the 1970s and the acquisition of civil rights in the 1990s and 2000s. This campaign also occurred at a moment when, for the first time in British history, a political body, the GLC, espoused gay rights as a policy. In 1984, the GLC committed itself to the promotion of gay rights and to fighting discrimination against gay men and lesbians. The following year, its Gay Working Party published a charter of gay rights, *Changing the World*, while the GLC opened the first centre for gay and lesbian people in Cowcross Street, Farringdon. This was not without controversy, but it did parallel a wider engagement between the Labour Party and gay and lesbian rights as part of a social democratic ideology in the late twentieth century.[10] The raid on Gay's the Word thus illuminated both the continuing restrictions on gay and lesbian life in the capital and the increasingly confident assertion of those rights. Gay and lesbian people were among the 'new social actors and new political actors' Kobena Mercer spoke of emerging with greater force in the 1980s; the raid on Gay's the Word underlined the importance of and counter-reaction to this development.[11]

---

[8] See Matt Cook, 'From Gay Reform to Gaydar, 1967–2006', in Matt Cook (ed.), *A Gay History of Britain* (Oxford: Greenwood, 2007), 192–3, 205.

[9] Alan Hollinghurst, *The Swimming Pool Library* (New York: Vintage, 1989), 5–6.

[10] See Brooke, *Sexual Politics*, ch. 8.   [11] Mercer, 'Welcome to the Jungle', 44.

5.1

In the 1970s, gay and lesbian life was more visible and less deferential than it had been before the decriminalization of homosexuality in 1967. The seventies have been described as a 'narrow window of particular freedom and possibility: after partial legalization...yet before AIDS'.[12] The short life of the Gay Liberation Front left an important legacy in an insistence upon the bold, undeferential, and unapologetic visibility of gay people. In 1972, the first pride parade occurred, as did a demonstration against police harassment on Highbury Fields. The Campaign for Homosexual Equality, while less radical than the Gay Liberation Front, nonetheless worked within the corridors of power on issues such as the equalization of the age of consent and the standardization of the 1967 Sexual Offences Act across the United Kingdom. On the left, the Gay Marxist Group tried to develop new ideologies of sexuality. The Gay Labour Group operated within constituency Labour parties from 1975 on to get the party to adopt a gay rights agenda.

The decade also witnessed the development of specifically gay media, such as the newspaper *Gay News,* and services, notably the London Lesbian and Gay Switchboard, which began in 1974. Gay nightclubs opened, such as Bang! in 1976 and Heaven in 1979. By the 1980s, the GLC's Gay Working Party could claim that London had become an accepted centre for gay life: 'young lesbians and gay men come to the metropolis in search of work and a large and diverse gay community which offers support and widespread social and sexual opportunities'.[13]

But if the post-1967 picture of gay and lesbian life was one of progress and greater visibility, constraints remained. The law remained fixed in the terms of the 1967 Act which sanctioned homosexuality in the private sphere. The formal and informal policing of homosexuality remained. Public expressions of homosexual affection could still violate the law on the grounds of public decency and order. Lesbians faced the

[12] Matt Cook, 'Capital Stories: Local Lives in Queer London', in Matt Cook and Jennifer V. Evans (eds.), *Queer Cities, Queer Cultures* (London: Bloomsbury, 2014), 50.
[13] GLC, GWG Employment Sub-Committee, 'The Employment of Lesbians and Gay Men: A Strategy for London', 11 November 1983, London School of Economics, Hall-Carpenter Archive, Gay Rights Working Party Papers [hereafter LSE, HCA/GWPP], 1/1.

possibility of legal sanctions, particularly in terms of child custody. The political world may also have been more, rather than less, hostile to the issue of gay rights after 1967. In the 1970s and 1980s, the Conservatives emphasized the family and rolling back what were seen as the excesses of the permissive era. This meant that homosexuality had a higher position in the Tories' demonology in the post-1967 period than before the decriminalization of homosexuality. Indeed, Anna Marie Smith argues that the 'promotion of homosexuality' was critical to the New Right in the seventies and eighties as a discursive foil to the idealization of the family.[14] The left was more conflicted. The far left, such as Militant Tendency, remained at best dismissive and at worst aggressive towards gay and lesbian issues.[15] The Labour Party began a cautious movement towards dealing more sympathetically with discrimination against gay and lesbian people in the mid-1970s, but progress was slow. Episodes such as the deselection of Maureen Colquhoun in 1977 because of her open lesbianism showed Labour could not be counted upon as a sympathetic political environment.[16]

A particular problem was the relationship between the gay and lesbian community and the police. In 1980, the Campaign for Homosexual Equality (CHE), a moderate gay rights organization, told a review of the Police Complaints Board that '[i]n the view of many gay people living in the United Kingdom the police cannot be trusted to do their job properly and fairly where a suspect or victim of a crime is a gay person'.[17] The CHE complained to Willie Whitelaw, Thatcher's Home Secretary, of 'police repression' against the gay and lesbian community, with relations 'never...worse'.[18] The complaints centred upon what the gay community saw as the over-policing of public behaviour and spaces, with raids on known gay pubs, crackdowns on public sex, 'sus', and importuning charges laid against gay men, and charges of public decency violations against things such as same-sex kissing or holding hands. The Gay

[14] Smith, *New Right Discourse*, 185.   [15] See Robinson, *Gay Men and the Left*.
[16] See Sarah Crook, 'The Labour Party, Feminism, and Maureen Colquhoun's Scandals in 1970s Britain', *Contemporary British History* 34/1 (2019): 71–94, doi: 10.1080.13619462.2019.1624166.
[17] Campaign for Homosexual Equality, Comments on the Triennial Review Report of the Police Complaints Board, 1980, London School of Economics, Hall-Carpenter Archives, Campaign for Homosexual Equality Archives, LSE, HCA/CHE2/9/23.
[18] CHE to William Whitelaw, 29 November 1980, LSE, HCA/CHE2/9/32.

London Police Monitoring Group (GALOP) was founded in 1982 by a group of lawyers. For GALOP, 1984 was a particularly important year in what was seen as the intensification of policing against gay and lesbian people:

> 1984 saw the curve for such offences begin to rise, and reports began to surface of increased attention to pornography by police and by Customs and Excise. Police were also harassing men on the streets... Not merely guilty of criminal sexual activity, we became illicit by our very presence on the civic landscape, and targets for surveillance and exclusion.[19]

GALOP saw the struggle of the gay and lesbian community against the police as an intrinsic element of a period of 'open warfare between the police and subaltern communities'.[20] GALOP and its lesbian counterpart, the Lesbians and Policing Project (LESPOP), dedicated much work to this problem, highlighting, for example, the issues involved in the Police and Criminal Evidence Bill (discussed further in Chapter 9) for gay and lesbian people.[21] In such ways, the concerns of the gay and lesbian movement in London in the late twentieth century were very material—the protection of physical space in the city and the protection of bodies against policing.

The year 1981 was an important turning point in the politics of gay and lesbian rights. In this respect, Ken Livingstone and the GLC played an undeniable role. The 1981 Labour manifesto had mentioned a commitment to gay rights almost in passing. But, by 1985, Livingstone could claim that opinion polls showed that 'the GLC's support for the lesbian and gay community is our best known policy'.[22] This change began in August 1981, when, in response to reports of police harassment of gay and lesbian people, Livingstone announced the Council's support for gay rights and equality. In a speech also suggesting that most people had a

---

[19] 'GALOP: Past and Future', unpublished paper, 1992, LSE, HCA/CHE2/12/14.

[20] 'GALOP: Past and Future', unpublished paper, 1992, LSE, HCA/CHE2/12/14.

[21] On LESPOP, see Glasgow Women's Library Archives, GL1534LP, The Lesbians and Policing Project, https://archive.womenslibrary.org.uk/the-lesbians-and-policing-project-lespop.

[22] GLC/Gay Working Group, *Changing the World* (London: GLC, 1985), 4.

fluid sexuality, Livingstone pledged that 'gay rights groups would be invited to County Hall to put their case and, where possible, the GLC would implement their proposals'.[23] A Gay Working Party was formed in 1982 (followed by a Lesbian Working Party), which, like the Women's Committee and the Ethnic Minorities Committee, was tasked with both formulating policy on sexual equality and dispensing grant funds to gay and lesbian community organizations. By 1984, nearly £1 million had been distributed to such organizations, a massive change from the pre-1981 period when no money had been given to gay and lesbian groups.[24] In 1984, the GLC committed to a wide-ranging policy of gay rights and equality. As mentioned, two material results of that commitment were the expansive policy statement *Changing the World* (1985) and the opening of a London centre for lesbian and gay men. In other spheres in London, one could also see greater visibility of gay men and lesbian women. Bob Crossman was the openly gay deputy mayor of Islington. In 1984, the Labour MP for Islington South and Finsbury, Chris Smith, announced he was gay—the first sitting MP to come out publicly.

But the GLC commitments and the greater openness of the gay rights movement in the context of London politics also saw a backlash against gay and lesbian rights and, indeed, against the GLC. Livingstone might have been right that the support for gay rights was the GLC's 'best-known' policy, but this might also be read as 'most notorious' policy. In August 1981, the political and media reaction was immediate and negative. It was dismissed as a 'charade', the 'political evangelization' of sexuality, and Livingstone himself was criticized for this being the latest in a series of outrageous comments about the police and Irish republicanism.[25] The London press identified the GLC with sexual extremism, with 'cash doled out to homosexual groups'.[26] The Tory Deputy Leader of the GLC decried the 'absolute nonsense of supporting groups like this with ratepayers' money'.[27] Homosexuality became another stick with

---

[23] *Guardian,* 19 August 1981.   [24] See comment in *The Times,* 19 August 1981.
[25] *The Evening Standard* (London), 19 August 1981; *Daily Telegraph* (London), 20 August 1981; *The Times,* 19 August 1981.
[26] *Daily Express,* 30 March 1984.   [27] *The Times,* 19 August 1981.

which the media beat the GLC. The growing AIDS crisis also encouraged intolerance and homophobia.[28] The Chief Constable of Manchester blamed the health crisis on the '"degenerate" behaviour of people swilling around in a cesspit of their own making'.[29] The GLC's espousal of gay rights did not gain support across the Labour movement. This is perhaps best seen in the divisive 1983 Bermondsey by-election, in which Peter Tatchell, the gay Labour candidate, was subjected to relentless homophobic abuse, not only from his Liberal opponent but also from Labour supporters; even the parliamentary leadership failed to support Tatchell. Four years later, Labour lost Greenwich in a by-election with the airing of similarly divisive sentiments. By the late 1980s, London had become identified with gay issues within the Labour Party, an association which some within the leadership, particularly under Neil Kinnock, resisted.

5.2

In 1977, Ernest Hole, a gay activist with the group Ice Breakers, floated the idea of a non-profit bookshop for gay and lesbian people. Charles Brown, a fellow activist in Ice Breakers, recalled that the idea for the bookshop was that it should nurture 'a positive image of homosexuals and women'.[30] A company was formed—Noncyo—and the premises on Marchmont Street acquired. Brown emphasized that the title of the bookshop was to underline that it would be an explicitly gay and lesbian space:

> It was the only space in London with a sign above the door saying it was gay... We knew that we were running the risk of harassment... an openness to the street [was] an important part of our approach.[31]

[28] See Matt Cook, 'Archives of Feeling: The AIDS Crisis in Britain 1987', *History Workshop Journal* 83/1 (2017): 51–78, doi: 10.1093/hwj/dbx001.
[29] Quoted in Martin Durham, *Sex and Politics* (Basingstoke: Macmillan, 1991), 123.
[30] Charles Brown, 'Statement', n.d. [1985], Bishopsgate Institute Archives, DGTW/2.
[31] Charles Brown, 'Statement', n.d. [1985], Bishopsgate Institute Archives, DGTW/2.

Early in its life, Gay's the Word acted as both a shop and a social centre for the gay and lesbian community, as an advertisement for it in 1980 suggested, providing 'a pleasant, comfortable and friendly central space for gay women and men to meet, relax, chat'.[32] A diverse group of organizations used the bookshop for meetings, such as Pride London and the Labour Campaign for Gay and Lesbian Rights. Most famously, it was the springboard for gay and lesbian support for the miners' strike.[33] The opening of Gay's the Word coincided with the growing importance of commercial culture for gay and lesbian people. It was claimed that it was the 'commercial wing...that has brought homosexuality so far out of the closet'.[34]

But a critical part of that commercial culture—stocking the shop with books—proved a challenge. Given that gay and lesbian publishing was still in its infancy in Britain—Millivres and Gay Men's Press were both founded in the mid- to late 1970s—most of the stock had to be imported from the United States. The US was perceived as a 'pace-setter' in gay publishing.[35] Not only did it boast several independent publishers and bookshops, such as Giovanni's Room, the Oscar Wilde Memorial Bookstore in New York, and A Different Light in San Francisco, the US also had mainstream publishers, like Random House and St. Martin's Press, which had developed gay and lesbian book lists. Philadelphia's Giovanni's Room was particularly important for the development of Gay's the Word. The management staff at Gay's the Word went for informal training there, and Giovanni's Room provided much of the stock for Gay's the Word when it opened.[36]

One thing that Gay's the Word did not want to be was a sex shop, rather than a bookshop. In October 1983, it successfully resisted being

[32] Handbill, 'Gay's the Word Open Seven Days a Week', n.d. [1980], Gay's the Word Campaign Archives.
[33] See Diarmaid Kelliher, 'Solidarity and Sexuality: Lesbians and Gays Support the Miners 1984–5', *History Workshop Journal* 77/1 (2014): 240–62, doi: 10.1093/hwj/dbt012.
[34] Peter Burton, quoted in Cook, 'From Gay Reform to Gaydar', 189.
[35] Defend Gay's the Word Campaign Information Pack, Bishopsgate Institute Archives, DGTW/3.
[36] See Ed Hermance, 'Giovanni's Room in the LGBT* Movement', *QED: A Journal in GLBTQ Worldmaking* 1/2 (Summer 2014): 100, doi: 10.14321/qed.1.2.0091; see also Marc Stein, *City of Sisterly and Brotherly Loves: Lesbian and Gay Philadelphia, 1945–72* (Chicago: University of Chicago Press, 2000).

forced to be licensed as such by Camden Council.[37] Nor did it wish to sell explicit pornography, as was available in some Soho sex shops, though there was some division among board members on this, particularly around what constituted pornography and what constituted erotica. There was a conscious policy in the stocking of printed works to avoid 'material which, in the opinion of the bookshop, is racist, sexist, pornographic or work which presents negative perspectives on gay or women's liberation.'[38] There was also a concern not to have material in the shop that would offend women. The issue was succinctly expressed by Glen McKee and Charles Brown at a Board meeting: 'the key question of whether we stock material "that you can wank off to". We did not stock such titles.'[39] The question of obscenity or indecency was, of course, not a certain one; or it was one in which such qualities were in the eyes of the beholder, as the raid of April 1984 later showed.

Importing stock from the United States presented difficulties. Almost from the beginning of the shop's opening, Customs and Excise seized books 'simply because they were gay', a problem *Gay News* had also faced in its own mail order service.[40] One of the directors, Jonathan Cutbill, had faced no problem, by contrast, in privately shipping material from America. The issue was having anything to do with 'gay' in the address. John Duncan, writing to Ed Hermance at Giovanni's Room, asked, '[u]nder no circumstance, please, mark Gay's the Word on the parcel'; otherwise, 'they will get seized by Customs.'[41] This was confirmed by testimony after the 1984 raid by Derek Riley, a customs official, who recalled that in February 1981 he was examining parcels and one caught his eye:

I selected it because of the address on the parcel being 'Gay's the Word'. This suggested a homosexual content so I decided to look into it. I had

[37] Gay's the Word, Board Meeting Minutes, 13 October 1983, Bishopsgate Institute Archives, DGTW/1/5.
[38] June Thomas, 'Gagging Gay's the Word', *Off Our Backs* 15/4 (April 1985): 3.
[39] Charles Brown, 'Comments on Exhibits', n.d. [1985?], Bishopsgate Institute Archives, DGTW/2.
[40] Charles Brown, 'Statement', n.d. [1985], Bishopsgate Institute Archives, DGTW/2.
[41] John Duncan to Ed Hermance, 24 January 1981, Bishopsgate Institute Archives, DGWC/1/4.

not heard of that title before. I associated 'Gay' with homosexuality, and I associate certain homosexual practices as within obscenity, so I decided to check…it was my opinion that certain homosexual acts could be indecent to a normal person: by that a [*sic*] mean a heterosexual person…As a heterosexual I considered homosexual activity to be abnormal.[42]

Derek had, of course, nailed the point. Customs and Excise defined homosexuality as obscene because it was not heterosexuality or perceived as 'normal'.

To avoid this problem, Gay's the Word adopted an informal policy of having books shipped from the United States to the private addresses of some of its directors. In late December 1983, there was some discussion among Gay's the Word board members about challenging Customs and Excise. One spark was the seizure of John Rechy's 1983 novel *Bodies and Souls*. This affirmed to some at Gay's the Word the double standard of Customs policy: 'I am sure that if it had been imported by Foyles or Dillons they would not have seized it…it was such a gross example of customs harassment.'[43] But commercial considerations and a lack of resources for court costs prevented Gay's the Word from immediately taking legal action.[44]

Customs and Excise itself provoked a confrontation. Operation Tiger had, apparently, been planned for six months before April 1984, though not at a high level. Colin Woodgate was not a senior officer. As already suggested, the raid had been based upon the seizure of materials under the Customs Consolidation Act 1876, which prohibited the importation of '[i]ndecent or obscene prints, paintings, photographs, books, cards, lithographs or other engraving, or any other indecent or obscene articles'. The directors of Gay's the Word—Charles Brown, Jonathan Cutbill, Peter Dorey, John Duncan, Paud Hegarty, Lesley Jones, Glenn McKee, Amanda Russell, and Gerard Walsh—were charged with 'on diverse

[42] Witness Testimony of Derek John Riley, n.d. [1984]. Bishopsgate Institute Archive, DGWC/1/5.
[43] Gerard Walsh, 'Statement', n.d. [1985], Bishopsgate Institute Archive, DGWC/2.
[44] Gay's the Word Board Meeting, 8 December 1983, Bishopsgate Institute Archives, DGWC/1/4.

days between 1st day of January 1981 and 1st day of August 1984 conspir[ing] together and with Ed Hermance and other persons unknown fraudulently to evade the provision imposed by Section 42 of the Customs Consolidation Act 1876 upon the important of indecent or obscene books'. The books included fifteen copies of Phil Andros's *Below the Belt and Other Stories*, ninety-two copies of *Roman Conquest*, twenty-eight copies of *Tricks*, twenty-five copies of *Native Issue 82*, ten copies of *The Joy of Lesbian Sex*, seventy copies of *The Joy of Gay Sex*, thirty-five copies of *Meat*, and five copies of *Now the Volcano: An Anthology of Latin American Gay Literature*.[45] The directors posed with some of the seized books, as seen in Figure 5.1.

The aftermath of the raid and the court proceedings served to illustrate two things more clearly than before. In the first place, it revealed the confusions from the perspective of the state (in the form of Customs and Excise) about the legal position of homosexuality and cultural material dealing with homosexuality. This revolved around the definition of what was 'obscene', 'indecent', or 'pornographic'. From the perspective of Customs and Excise, anything dealing with homosexuality was likely to occupy those categories, because homosexuality was, by its definition, 'abnormal' and therefore indecent.

This can be seen clearly in the evidence given by customs officers. Customs and Excise seized books from Gay's the Word that were either already for sale in other non-gay bookshops in Britain or already published, without controversy, in Britain. In some cases, the obscenity or the indecency of the work was established not by its innate content but, rather, by the context in which it was sold. Verlaine sold in Dillons on Gower Street was not obscene in 1984, but a few hundred yards away in Marchmont Street, it was obscene. As was noted by the Haringey Police Research Unit's report on the matter, '20 of the seized titles have already been published in Britain and would have been free from prosecution but for the fact that GTW imported them'.[46] This ambiguity became the nub of Gay's the Word's defence.

---

[45] See Formal charges, Bishopsgate Institute, DGWC/1/8.
[46] Report of Police Research Unit, 'Gay's the Word', 14 December 1984, Bishopsgate Institute, Makanji Papers, MAKANJI 74/1.

Figure 5.1 Gay's the Word directors with seized books, 1984.
Photo by Robert Workman, Defend Gay's the Word Campaign Archive, Bishopsgate Institute.

It was also clear, despite the apparent long planning of Operation Tiger, that Customs and Excise officers had 'received no training' in what obscene or indecent materials meant in the context of a bookshop.[47] The bookshop's manager had, as noted above, stated that, on 10 April, 'the officers "didn't seem to know what they were looking for"... [t]he customs team repeatedly phoned their own office... to find out what they were supposed to take'.[48] One customs officer, David Odd, was questioned, for example, about why a book about AIDS had been seized:

> Mr Odd said that he was unaware that it was a serious book and could not recall examining the contents. His judgement on detaining books during the raid had been 'based on what I could eliminate, rather than what was obscene'. The magistrate, Mr CJ Bourke, asked him: 'Did you open this book at all?' Mr Odd replied that he might have failed to do so.[49]

Another officer suggested that it was simply the 'luck of the draw' in terms of what was seized and that there had been no guidance. He added that a book of poems by Verlaine had been taken because it had the word 'cock' in the title.[50] The customs officers may have had little or no training in discerning what was indecent or obscene, but they were not confused at all about what they perceived to be an equivalency between gay texts and obscene and indecent ones. Under questioning at pretrial hearings, another Customs and Excise officer, Martin Clancy, stated that he could not say why a particular book had been taken except that it 'had a homosexual author on the cover'.[51] The Gay's the Word campaign noted, in 1985, that 'Customs Officers testified that they do automatically seize all literature sent to gay organizations and that they do have unpublished "secret guidelines" which have never been subject to judicial or parliamentary review'.[52]

[47] Defend Gay's the Word, Update 4 (November 1985), LSE, HCA/CHE2/9/32.
[48] 'Customs Raid Gay's the Word', The Body Politic, June 1984, 21.
[49] Guardian, 28 July 1985.   [50] Guardian, 24 June 1985.
[51] Guardian, 28 July 1985.
[52] Defend Gay's the Word, Update 4 (November 1985), LSE, HCA/CHE2/9/32.

Homosexuality was, thus, equated with indecency and obscenity. Indeed, at the court proceedings in 1985, 'an officer placidly said that he'd presumed any gay book to be obscene, unless and until "headquarters" ruled otherwise'.[53] Another officer was reported as saying 'that he judged material as a "normal, that is heterosexual" man'.[54] Photocopied guidelines circulated to customs officers on what could be considered indecent included 'various sexual activities (e.g. "masturbation", "group sex") but also the simple words "homosexuality" and "lesbians"'.[55] 'Sexual activities including masturbation, lesbianism, homosexuality and group sex', it was argued by Colin Woodgate, 'were matters that breached the prohibition', but he could not explain why *The Joy of Sex*, which dealt with some of these topics, was on sale at W. H. Smith or why *The Joy of Lesbian Sex* had been 'deemed not to be obscene'.[56] Woodgate's own witness statement during the preparation for the trial was more a testament to not knowing than knowing about what constituted obscenity:

In mounting Operation Tiger, I did not have any discussions with the obscene publications squad or the DPP nor did I consult any literary experts: I have not heard of M. Gene [sic] before this. I had heard of Oscar Wilde, but not Catulus [sic] or Ginsberg in the literary sense. Nor of Ezra Powell [sic]...I did not take any steps to seek the views of the gay community. No gay Customs officers that are known to me took part in this operation....One should not expect Customs officers to be fully aware of the day to day decisions about obscene books.... I am not an expert in this field. I have more experience in picture pornography.[57]

The testimony of other officers underlined a lack of knowledge about what constituted obscenity, but what filled that vacuum was an equating

[53] *New Statesman*, 5 July 1985.

[54] Defend Gay's the Word Campaign, 1 August 1985, LSE, HCA/CHE2/9/32.

[55] *New Statesman*, 5 July 1985.

[56] Witness Statement, Colin Woodgate, n.d. [1985], Bishopsgate Institute Archives, DGWC/1/5.

[57] Witness Statement, Colin Woodgate, n.d. [1985], Bishopsgate Institute Archives, DGWC/1/5.

of homosexuality and obscenity. 'I would detain a book if I thought there was something wrong with it,' stated David Woods, who worked in Oldham VAT office; '[i]t was the fact of homosexuality that caused me to think there may be something wrong with it'.[58] Another officer, Malcolm Clancy, noted:

> I have no guidelines on obscenity that I had read nor any training that I had received, nor any instructions that I had been given…I can't tell what it was about the book that made me judge it obscene. It might have been because it had the name of an author that I knew to be homosexual on the cover.[59]

The Defend Gay's the Word campaign can perhaps be forgiven the snobbish remark that '[m]any of the officers who had issued Seizure notices turned out to be young men of twenty who had left school at sixteen. These…were the people who had decided that poems of Verlaine were "indecent".'[60] But there is a point here that, in the absence of detailed guidelines about what constituted obscenity or pornography, what Customs and Excise were motivated by was a deeply held belief that homosexuality itself was worthy of surveillance and proscription through seizures. The contrast was summed up in a short exchange during the interview between Woodgate and Glenn McKee about the nature of the materials seized:

W: Pornographic.
McK: In your definition.[61]

The raid coincided with a spate of other anti-gay actions by the police. A Policy Studies Institute publication from 1983 had noted the deep homophobia in the Met, which let to both systemic and random

---

[58] Witness Statement, David Woods, n.d. [1985], Bishopsgate Institute Archives, DGWC/1/5.
[59] Witness Statement, Malcolm Clancy, n.d. [1985], Bishopsgate Institute Archives, DGWC/1/5.
[60] Defend Gay's the Word, Campaign Memorandum, 1 August 1985, Bishopsgate Institute Archives, DGWC/3.
[61] Interview, Charles McKee, 10 April 1984, Bishopsgate Institute Archives, DGTW/2.

oppression of gay people. This included the practice of 'pretty policing', by which police acted as sexual provocateurs.[62] This practice was perceived as such a threat that a legal counsel advised gay men not to enter a West End public convenience 'except in the direst emergency'.[63] The perception was of a 'wide-ranging escalation of discriminatory actions against lesbians and gay men...a shift towards "policing people" rather than "policing crime"'.[64] The raid on Gay's the Word in the spring of 1984 was paralleled by raids on the Edinburgh bookshop Lavender Menace and on gay pubs in London. Just as obscenity could be defined as being about homosexuality in print, homosexuality in public could also be seen as an act of disorder. In June 1988, for example, *Gay Times* reported that two men had been arrested outside Heaven nightclub and charged with disorderly conduct for 'kissing and fondling' each other, the crown prosecutor telling the court that the men's actions 'were causing a certain amount of alarm to people passing by'.[65]

In 1984, the police were poised to gain even more power in this regard. That year, the Police and Criminal Evidence Act was introduced, which formalized police powers of arrest and detention in relation to the committing or suspicion of committing 'arrestable offences'; this power rested on what the police's judgement of 'reasonable grounds'.[66] Gay rights groups, such as GALOP, saw it as a 'massive extension of police powers' which would 'give the state the means to exercise greater social control'. The way that this might play out on the street against gay and lesbian people was a particular fear:

They will also have a brand new power of arrest – they will be able to arrest you for any offence if they think you might cause 'an affront to public decency'. The Bill does not definite an affront to public decency – it is up to the individual officer to decide. He may decide that people

[62] See David Smith, *Police and People in London* (London: Policy Studies Institute, 1983).
[63] Defend Gay's the Word Campaign Information Pack, n.d. [1984], Bishopsgate Institute Archives, DGWC/3.
[64] Defend Gay's the Word Campaign Information Pack, n.d. [1984], Bishopsgate Institute Archives, DGWC/3.
[65] *Gay Times*, June 1988.
[66] See *Police and Criminal Evidence Act 1984* (1984, c. 60), Part III.

behaving in an overtly gay manner – for example kissing or holding hands in the street – constitutes an affront.[67]

The raid against Gay's the Word was thus the most public example of a range of events in the early to mid-1980s that crystalized concerns and resentments about the (literal) policing of sexuality and the ambiguities of same sex sexuality.

The passing of Section 28 of the 1988 Local Government Act later served as a powerful factor in the political mobilization of the gay and lesbian community. The reaction to the Gay's the Word raid served a similar purpose four years earlier. The first example of this came from within the gay and lesbian community within London. A Gay's the Word Defence Campaign (GTWDC) was quickly organized, under the direction of Graham McKerron, from *Capital Gay*, and David Northmore, who had worked with the National Council for Civil Liberties (NCCL). Recognizing the potential legal costs of a trial, the GTWDC set a goal of fundraising £75,000. The campaign raised £23,000 in the year following the raid and £53,000 by November 1985.[68] The money came from a variety of sources. There were some individual donations (the American writer Gore Vidal gave £1,000, for example), but much of it came from fundraising within the city's gay and lesbian community. There was a particular connection with culture in this regard. The nightclub Heaven gave £2000 in 1986, while the staff and cast of *Kiss of the Spiderwoman* at the Bush Theatre, starring Mark Rylance and Simon Callow, donated their services for one performance, which raised £7,000.[69] One of the most high-profile cultural contributions came from the four benefit gigs that the Communards played for Gay's the Word at venues such as the Fridge and the Shaw Theatre. The Communards' singer, Jimmy Somerville, had been in Bronski Beat, one of the first openly gay pop groups, who had a huge hit in 1984 with the gay-themed single 'Smalltown Boy', from an album called *The Age of Consent*, which tackled issues of gay inequality. Somerville left Bronski

---

[67] Gay London Police Monitoring Group, Gays and the Police Bill, n.d. [1984?], Garland Archives of Sexuality and Gender, MS International Vertical Files, Canadian Lesbian and Gay Archives, ID 7282.

[68] *Gay Times*, November 1985.   [69] *Gay Times*, November 1985.

Beat and formed the Communards with Richard Coles. Their first gigs were benefits for Gay's the Word. Such fundraising efforts connected the campaign and the issues of gay persecution to wider currents of popular culture and media in London.

An older, more established, and straighter culture also moved to support Gay's the Word. This was notable in terms of London's literary society—Angus Wilson, the President of the Author's Society, expressed his support, for example—as well as most mainstream and large publishers and booksellers. Publishing houses such as Chatto & Windus, Jonathan Cape, Thames & Hudson, Faber & Faber, and Virago all expressed support, as did the bookseller Waterstones. In such circles the raid appeared as a violation of liberal, progressive mores and absurd in its uneven application; *The Bookseller* asked, for instance, how 'an item [can be] obscene in one law office and not in another; indecent or obscene under one law but not under another'.[70] Support for the campaign was not limited to London. In Edinburgh, the bookshop Lavender Menace, which itself had endured raids seizing material (such as the American lesbian magazines *Sinister Wisdom* and *Common Lives, Lesbian Lives*), organized an 'uncensored fun week' among gay businesses in the city (such as Men Only Hair and Fire Island Disco), which raised £425.[71] Just as the legal case crossed the Atlantic, so too did support. In North America, bookshops such as A Different Light in San Francisco, A Brother's Touch in Minneapolis, and Gay Day Books in Toronto also organized fundraisers.

The campaign to defend Gay's the Word did not ignore mainstream politics. The coordinators of the campaign met with the Labour MPs Chris Smith, Jo Richardson, and Frank Dobson (the local MP for the bookshop). Smith and Richardson then went to Peter Brooke, a Treasury minister in charge of Customs and Excise, to lodge a protest about the raid and the prosecution.[72] Some Labour constituency parties also picked up the issue. In November 1984, for example, the Edinburgh

---

[70] Quoted in *New Statesman*, 9 November 1984.
[71] Lavender Menace, news release, 12 December 1984, Garland Archives of Sexuality and Gender, Canadian Lesbian and Gay Archives, 8864.
[72] 'Defend Gay's the Word Bookshop', News release, 5 May 1986, Garland Archives of Sexuality and Gender, Canadian Lesbian and Gay Archives, 8864.

Central Constituency Labour Party passed a motion condemning the raid as a 'major attack on the freedom of the gay community' and criticized Customs and Excise's abuse of 'arbitrary and far-reaching powers which are a danger to the civil liberties of all citizens'.[73]

The campaign to defend Gay's the Word lasted two years, between 1984 and the final dropping of the charges by Customs and Excise on 27 June 1986. The charges that were laid against the directors focused on a conspiracy 'fraudulently to evade the publication and importation of indecent or obscene material', thus highlighting two questions: whether this was a 'conspiracy' to smuggle, and what indecency amounted to.[74] The NCCL and the Law Society provided legal support. Committal proceedings made up of prosecution evidence were held in June 1985 and further evidentiary submissions in July 1985, which allowed much of the testimony by Customs and Excise and the directors to be heard.

Just as the raid foregrounded the state's approach to homosexuality—associating indecency with homosexuality—the aftermath of the raid and the campaign to defend Gay's the Word afforded an opportunity to articulate a claim for gay and lesbian rights in the city. This is particularly clear in campaign literature. The defenders of Gay's the Word evoked, in the first place, the peculiar place of homosexuality in British society in the 1980s:

> The legal attitude to homosexuality in the UK has always adopted the view that society must be protected from homosexuals; never has the principle been adopted legally that homosexuals are entitled to equal civil rights with other citizens, nor even that gay men and lesbians are entitled to protection from the excesses of the law and social attitudes in the same way as are non-gay people.[75]

The police and customs actions in 1984 were the predicable actions from such a stance. They were intended to discipline the gay and lesbian

[73] Lavender Menace, newsletter, 20 November 1984, Garland Archives of Sexuality and Gender, Canadian Lesbian and Gay Archives, 8864.
[74] Geoffrey Robertson, QC, Opinion, 10 December 1985. See Bishopsgate Institute Archives, DGTW/2.
[75] Defend Gay's the Word Campaign Information Pack, n.d. [1984], Bishopsgate Institute Archives, DGWC/3.

community, to draw the boundaries around the gay and lesbian claim to the city:

> All of these and similar incidents combine to create an atmosphere which circumscribes our community. It is an atmosphere which many would argue is used with conscious intent; that is, raids and arrests are used not only to proscribe those who are their immediate objects but also to deliver a message to the gay community, to make us aware that we cannot act with the same sense of freedom and security which other members of society expect as of right.[76]

If the campaign to defend Gay's the Word afforded an articulation of the place that gays and lesbians were positioned in by the law, it also allowed that community to offer what it felt its position should be. This began with the very material that had been seized. This comprised books and magazines that provided a basis for building gay and lesbian community, 'material which reflects our proud heritage, pleases us, entertains us, liberates us, affirms our gayness, and motivates us to be proud, and angry at our oppression'.[77] What was being defended, therefore, was a newly visible gay and lesbian culture: 'Gay's the Word's success since 1979 has been only one aspect of a widespread British and global phenomenon, the growth of an open lesbian and gay culture in place of the previous subterranean one'.[78] At stake in the case was the legitimacy of this culture in the city and the claim of gay and lesbian people to an open existence in the city. Defining gay and lesbian literature as obscene was only a way of undermining that claim. Police and customs, the campaign argued,

> do not recognise that we are capable of possessing a culture, a history of experience in common, which we have a right to share and enjoy... They characterise our literature and activities as being

---

[76] Defend Gay's the Word Campaign Information Pack, n.d. [1984], Bishopsgate Institute Archives, DGWC/3.

[77] Defend Gay's the Word Campaign Information Pack, n.d. [1984], Bishopsgate Institute Archives, DGWC/3.

[78] Defend Gay's the Word Campaign Information Pack, n.d. [1984], Bishopsgate Institute Archives, DGWC/3.

'indecent', 'obscene', or 'pornographic', as being about sex rather than a way of life.[79]

By 1986, it became clear that Customs and Excise would drop the case. They accepted that works that were already on sale in other bookshops in England could not be seized if also for sale in a gay bookshop. This admission did not stop the work of the Gay's the Word Defence Campaign from continuing to clarify the status of gay literature and information, attempting test cases.

While the events of the raid unfolded, there was greater political engagement with gay and lesbian rights in the capital. In 1984, the GLC formally committed itself to 'policies to eradicate discrimination against gay men and lesbians'.[80] In May, Livingstone had discussed the issue with the Council and had committees of the GLC discuss how this could be enacted. As already discussed, a turning point had come in 1981 with the election of the GLC and Livingstone's commitment in August of that year to doing something about gay and lesbian rights. The establishment of the Gay Working Party had followed in 1982, along with a notable increase in spending on gay and lesbian organizations across the capital, including groups such as Gay Switchboard. In 1984, in addition to the Gay Working Party, a number of GLC committees and units pursued work on gay and lesbian issues, including the Police Committee Support Unit and the Industry and Employment Committee. In 1985, the Gay Working Party published *Changing the World*. In it, Livingstone noted that the GLC was in a 'unique position to pursue policies that counteract discrimination and enable the gay community to develop its own range of services'.[81] The approach was similar to those adopted over race and gender, at once to set out a catalogue of specific policies as well as a vista of more wide-ranging proposals for sexual equality. The chair of the Gay Working Party, Jenni Fletcher, wrote, for example, of the need to 'to bring about a change in attitudes amongst the public to dispel ignorance and foster positive attitudes towards homosexuality'. 'Heterosexism',

---

[79] Defend Gay's the Word Campaign Information Pack, n.d. [1984], Bishopsgate Institute Archives, DGWC/3.
[80] GLC, *Changing the World*, 7.   [81] GLC, *Changing the World*, 7.

Fletcher remarked, 'should be condemned.'[82] The raid on Gay's the Word featured prominently in *Changing the World* as an example of 'organized police interference with the lives of lesbians and gay men'; the statement included a photograph of the bookshop staff. Following the publication of *Changing the World*, the GLC opened the London Lesbian and Gay Centre. The larger labour movement also reflected this move towards the political embrace of gay and lesbian rights. The Gay Labour Group had been founded in 1975, followed by the Labour Campaign for Lesbian and Gay Rights. Their efforts led to a commitment by the party's National Executive Committee (NEC) to the development of gay rights policies. In 1985, Labour's annual conference adopted a motion calling for the end of all discrimination and police harassment against gay and lesbian people, a motion supported by the National Union of Mineworkers. This was seen as the 'greatest single step for lesbian and gay liberation since the emergence of our movement fifteen years ago.'[83]

The developments with the GLC and the Labour Party certainly represented advancements in gay and lesbian rights. But such advances were nonetheless accompanied by a strong countervailing tide. In part, this was tied to the Conservatives and to the media (particularly the tabloid media). As has already been pointed out, Livingstone's commitment to gay and lesbian rights prompted an immediate backlash in 1981. The political excesses of the Labour GLC were identified with the perceived sexual excesses of the gay and lesbian community. In part, this was framed as an attack upon the family. Grass-roots conservative groups, such as the Conservative Family Campaign, the Haringey Parents' Rights Group, and Christian Action, Research and Education, organized in the 1980s to oppose what was perceived as the promotion of homosexuality in education by the GLC and the ILEA.[84] Metropolitan and local newspapers played up rumours that children were being educated in homosexuality.[85] In this, the Conservatives attempted to claim a middle ground by suggesting that gay rights were an assault upon the 'normal' or 'ordinary'. Just as works that touched upon gay life were seen

---

[82] GLC, *Changing the World*, 7.
[83] *Lesbian and Gay Socialist* (London), Summer 1985, 14.
[84] See Smith, *New Right Discourse on Race and Sexuality*, 187–8.
[85] See Susanne Bosche, 'Jenny, Eric, Martin...and me', *Guardian*, 31 January 2000.

as obscene by definition, gay life itself was divorced from the ordinary. That 'normal' or 'ordinary' continued to exclude same-sex sexuality. As Anna Marie Smith has claimed, homosexuality served a useful discursive purpose for the Conservatives. It allowed them to claim the middle ground of politics through a cultural conflict with perceived transgressors. This strategy gathered pace through the 1980s and gained a particular intensity between 1984 and the 1987 general election. Norman Tebbit railed against what he called 'sexual deviation' being 'treated as the norm'.[86] At the Conservatives' conference in 1987, Thatcher inveighed against children being taught that they had 'an inalienable right to be gay'.[87]

The resistance to gay rights was shared across the political spectrum. In 1983, for example, the Bermondsey by-election degenerated into toxic homophobia against Labour's candidate, Peter Tatchell; the attacks emanated from Labour as well as the party's rivals. The Labour leadership was itself notably hostile to Tatchell, though Michael Foot was more concerned about what he worried was Tatchell's penchant for extra-parliamentary politics than his sexuality. Neil Kinnock, who succeeded Foot, blatantly talked about 'fairies' when referring to the by-election.[88] Despite the movement towards the adoption of gay rights within the party in the 1980s, some within Labour saw this as alienating traditional working-class voters. After another by-election loss, in Greenwich in 1987, Frances Morrell, who led the ILEA, argued that the party needed to distance itself from the issue:

> ... [the] 'provocative presentation' of the gay and lesbian issue is alienating voters and damaging the interests of minority groups... [m]any electors, and in particular working-class electors, have formed a fixed impression of Labour's policy priorities. That fixed impression is incorrect, it makes Labour unpopular, and it causes us to lose elections... many voters... believe the campaign for gay rights has become the party's principal objective...[89]

---

[86] *Guardian*, 9 April 1986.   [87] *The Times*, 10 October 1987.
[88] Quoted in David Rayside, *On the Fringe: Gays and Lesbians in Politics* (Ithaca: Cornell University Press, 1998), 28.
[89] Quoted in *The Guardian*, 20 March 1987.

Surveys of public opinion did seem to show a rising level of public disapproval of gay relationships, from 62 per cent in 1983 to 74 per cent in 1987.[90]

The raid on Gay's the Word highlighted these ambiguities around same-sex sexuality in the city in the late twentieth century. It also demonstrated the continuing, and sometimes intensifying, policing of that sexuality. There was, of course, a central tension here. Gay and lesbian people and gay and lesbian culture were increasingly in the public sphere. Gay's the Word was a material example of that, a space in the city that demonstrated a new sexual culture and served a new community. But that visibility, as shown by the raid and the actions of the state in that raid, remained transgressive. Through Customs and Excise and the Met, same-sex sexuality continued to be literally policed. That policing gained greater force with Section 28. The raid on Gay's the Word illustrated the liminality of same-sex sexuality, poised between progress and visibility and counter-reaction and policing. The raid demonstrated both the challenges that still faced 'new social actors and new political subjects' emerging in the city in the 1980s and their determination to be seen and to claim a right to the city.[91]

London, 1984: Conflict and Change in the Radical City. Stephen Brooke, Oxford University Press.
© Stephen Brooke 2024. DOI: 10.1093/9780191895395.003.0006

[90] Cook, 'Capital Stories', 206.   [91] Mercer, 'Welcome to the Jungle', 44.

6

Dalston Children's Centre

Susan lived on Sandringham Road, Dalston, with her 19-month-old daughter, Lauren. She had noticed mothers and children 'coming in all the time' to a house at 80 Sandringham Road, which, she discovered, was a childcare centre. Susan decided to 'come and see what it was like', not least because she and Lauren were 'stuck at home, all the time'. Another neighbour on Sandringham Road, Karen, was an Irish mother of four, with her youngest, Kevin, not yet at school. Like Susan, Karen was grateful for the childcare on her street: 'It's just somewhere different for him to go, we get out of the kitchen for a while; you can have a cup of coffee and a natter. The workers are friendly and you come into a nice relaxed atmosphere.'[1]

The house to which Susan and Karen brought their children was the Dalston Children's Centre. As described in the Introduction to this book, the Dalston Children's Centre provided largely free childcare to local parents in Hackney 'in an anti-racist, anti-sexist, anti-heterosexist and anti-authoritarian way'.[2] In June 1984, it applied successfully to the Women's Committee of the GLC for a grant of £108,000 to renovate the Shacklewell Lane Baths as a 'permanent Children's Centre...to expand on their present activities and add other activities in response to the needs of local children and the adults who care for them'.[3]

The Dalston Children's Centre was an example of the alternative London of the 1980s, a small space carved out against both the discrimination faced by many in that city and the damage caused more

---

[1] Dalston Children's Centre, *Annual Report* (1982). Please note that efforts were made to obtain interviews with all of those involved with the Dalston Children's Centre between 1981 and 1985.

[2] Dalston Children's Centre, *Annual Report* (1983), Appendix A, Policy Statement.

[3] GLC, Women's Committee, 'Dalston Children's Centre', Funding Application, 22 June 1984, LMA, GLC/DG/PRE/223/22.

immediately by Thatcherism. It was an attempt to make something new. Childcare was its principal concern, but the Centre also explored women's issues, lesbianism, the problems of parenting, the challenges of working collectively, and, not least, the importance of creating an environment in which a diverse group of people, in terms of race, class, and sexual orientation, could feel comfortable. The Centre exemplified the 'new social actors and new political subjects' emerging in the 1970s and 1980s.[4] It also demonstrated that this new politics was rooted in both material needs—in this case, for childcare—and the desire to form new kinds of community, not least in terms of emotional sympathy and support, and to explore new ideas of living and working.[5]

What also emerged from the Dalston Children's Centre in 1984 was a collective of British Asian women's writing, *Breaking the Silence*, put together by one of the Centre's workers, Manju Mukherjee, with photographs by another worker, Anna Sherwin. The book was a pioneering collection, demonstrating how community organizations such as the Dalston Children's Centre were also centres for the articulation of new identities around gender, sexuality, and race in late twentieth-century Britain.

The Dalston Children's Centre emerged in part from second-wave feminism, in part from a belief in radical politics, and in part from a commitment to gay and lesbian rights. All helped build a strong sense of political, personal, and emotional bonds between the people working at the Centre. The Centre underwent a major upheaval in 1985, just as it was moving to the Shacklewell Lane Baths. This was rooted in a division over race, a tension that could be seen throughout the feminist movement in the 1970s and 1980s.[6] The Centre was thus an attempt to build a new kind of community in the city, but it also illustrated the tensions within that community-building.

---

[4] Mercer, 'Welcome to the Jungle', 44.

[5] On the latter, see Stephen Brooke, 'Space, Emotions and the Everyday: The Affective Ecology of 1980s London', *Twentieth-Century British History* 28/1 (2017): 110–42.

[6] See Natalie Thomlinson, *Race, Ethnicity and the Women's Movement in England, 1968–1993* (Houndmills: Palgrave Macmillan, 2016).

6.1

The Dalston Children's Centre began with discussions in the late seventies among a group of mothers in Hackney about the need for collective childcare. Up to the 1980s, childcare provision in Britain was minimal at best. Since the Second World War, a variety of pressure groups had argued for more comprehensive state childcare in Britain, and childcare was also central to the agenda of second-wave feminism.[7] Community childcare run by workers and parents became one favoured alternative within the feminist movement.

In Hackney, there were about 16,000 children under school age in 1974, 5,600 of which were from single-parent families or families with a working mother. But there were only 471 childcare places in the borough.[8] In 1978, a group of feminist photographers, Hackney Flashers, organized an exhibition, 'Who's Holding the Baby?', which highlighted this problem. Hackney Under Fives was founded in the same period, demanding 1,000 more childcare places in the borough.[9] Community nurseries such as the Market Nursery near Broadway Market and the Sandbrook Community Playgroup were established in the borough.[10] There was also a widespread squatting movement in Hackney, particularly near Broadway Market, which 'enabled radical experiments in collective living and shared childcare'.[11]

A key moment in the provision of community childcare in London came with the election of the Labour GLC. From its inception, the GLC Women's Committee made childcare a central part of its strategy for improving the lives of women in the city. Better childcare provision

---

[7] See Vicky Randall, *The Politics of Child Daycare in Britain* (New York: Oxford University Press, 2000).

[8] Statistics from 'Who's Holding the Baby?' exhibition (1978), https://hackneyflashers. co.uk/whos-holding-the-baby-1978/#:~:text=The%20resulting%20project%20 %27Who%27s%20Holding,this%20had%20on%20women%27s%20lives.

[9] On this, see http://www.hackneygazette.co.uk/news/heritage/parent-power-radical-stoke-newington-nursery-sandbrook-is-going-strong-40-years-on-1-4621746; https://www. ahackneyautobiography.org.uk/people/larraine-worpole; and http://radicalhistorynetwork. blogspot.ca/2016/01/activism-and-under-fives-meeting-report.html.

[10] https://www.ahackneyautobiography.org.uk/trails/community-action/10. Market Nursery, *Not So Much a Nursery* (London: n.d.; late 1970s?); thanks to Liz Khan for this pamphlet.

[11] Christine Wall, 'Sisterhood and Squatting in the 1970s: Feminism, Housing and Urban Change in Hackney', *History Workshop Journal* 83 (2017): 80, doi: 10.1093/hwj/dbx024.

would enable 'women with young children to...lead a full and active public and social life'.[12] The Women's Committee prioritized grant aid to community childcare and women's centres that provided childcare. By 1984, 60 per cent of the Women's Committee budget was being spent on funding childcare, and by the demise of the GLC two years later, it funded 12 per cent of all nursery places.[13]

In 1983, the journalist Paul Harrison wrote that Hackney was 'the most deprived inner-city area in London and one of the two or three most deprived in Britain'.[14] Hackney had the highest female unemployment rate in London, the highest proportion of single-parent families, the highest proportion of 'dwellings unfit for human habitation', and was second only to Tower Hamlets in other measures of deprivation.[15] Hackney had also been declared a Housing Aid Area, as a place of acute problems of housing.[16] The borough was also one of the most racially diverse areas in London. Forty per cent of its population were of Afro-Caribbean or South Asian origin. Ethnic minorities faced numerous challenges in the borough. These included organized political racism from the National Front, everyday racial harassment, poor relations between the police and ethnic minority people, and high levels of deprivation. There had been controversial deaths in police custody, such as those of Aseta Simms in 1972 and Colin Roach in 1983. In July 1981, following the Brixton disorders, there were disturbances between Black youth and the police on the Sandringham and Kingsland Roads.[17] Anne Thorne, one of the founders of the Dalston Children's Centre, remembered it as 'really quite a fearful time', when 'people feeling isolated in their own communities and wanted to find a different way forward'.[18]

The borough was home to a variety of radical grassroots initiatives. As already noted, there was a significant squatting movement in the borough. Unoccupied houses used by a variety of groups, including

[12] Women's Committee, Report from the Director General, 17 February 1982, LMA, GLC/DG/PRE/223/1.
[13] See Randall, *The Politics of Child Daycare in Britain*, 126; Mackintosh and Wainwright, *A Taste of Power*, ch. 5.
[14] Paul Harrison, *Inside the Inner City* (Harmondsworth: Penguin, 1983), 11.
[15] Harrison, *Inside the Inner City*, 31.
[16] See J. R. Short and Keith Bassett, 'Housing Action Areas', *Area* 10/2 (1978), 153–7.
[17] Harrison, *Inside the Inner City*, 33.   [18] Anne Thorne, interview, 20 February 2018.

all-female households. Later, some of these houses were allocated to squatters on a short-life basis.[19] Hackney was also a base for gay and lesbian liberation. Some of the squats, for example, were used by gay and lesbian households. The borough was also home to activism on sexual orientation, such as the Hackney Gay Liberation Front.[20]

New kinds of cultural work were being done in Hackney, based around collectives and the community arts movement.[21] One of the first was Centerprise, founded in 1971, which operated as a radical book-store and cultural centre aiming to break down barriers between classes and races. Hackney Flashers began in 1974 as a women's photography collective which included Liz Heron and Jo Spence; it mounted three exhibitions, 'Women and Work' (1975), 'Who's Holding the Baby?' (1978), and 'Domestic Labour and Virtual Representation' (1980). In 1976, the Lenthall Road Workshop was founded by a group of feminist photographers and screen printers.[22]

In 1979, a group of local mothers in Hackney began meeting to dis-cuss the need for collective childcare. Lesbian mothers played a critical part in these discussions.[23] As the previous chapter suggested, gay and lesbian rights were at risk in the 1980s, even before the chill cast by Section 28. Lesbians were particularly vulnerable. LESPOP, the policing project founded in 1985 and referred to in the previous chapter, empha-sized the range of harassment and discrimination faced by lesbians, from the police and other authorities.[24] An especially fraught issue was child custody. In 1983, a conference on Lesbian Mothers' Child Custody stated that 90 per cent of lesbian mothers lost custody of their children

[19] See Wall, 'Sisterhood and Squatting in the 1970s'.

[20] See Sarah Taylor, 'Queer Neighbourhoods: Lesbian Squats in London Fields', https://east-endwomensmuseum.org/blog/category/Protest.

[21] For a wider discussion of community arts, see Sam Wetherell, 'Painting the Crisis: Community Arts and the Search for the "Ordinary" in 1970s and '80s London', *History Workshop Journal* 76 (2013): 235–49, doi: 10.1093/hwj/dbt008.

[22] See https://hackneyhistory.wordpress.com/2011/05/19/lenthall-road-workshop-e8-1976/; on the work of Ingrid Pollard, see http://www.ingridpollard.com; see also Jo Spence, 'Women's Collective Work 1974 Onwards', in *Putting Myself in the Picture* (Seattle: Real Comet Press, 1988); see also BFI, *Somewhere in Hackney* (1980), https://player.bfi.org.uk/free/film/watch-somewhere-in-hackney-1980-online.

[23] Carol Ackroyd, written communication, 1 November 2017.

[24] Glasgow Women's Library Archives, GL1534LP, The Lesbians and Policing Project, https://archive.womenslibrary.org.uk/the-lesbians-and-policing-project-lespop.

because they were defined as 'unfit' in what was called an act of 'extreme oppression'.[25] A childcare centre free from threat and discrimination was an urgent political and material necessity. The Dalston Children's Centre was, in this respect, a refuge. The desire for collective childcare also grew out of a sense of isolation felt by mothers, as one remarked: 'the level of isolation in bringing up children, particularly in those days was actually far more than it is now in a way because I can remember going to cafés for example with my children in pushchairs and being turned away'.[26] This group put together the first meetings of the Dalston Children's Centre, using the hall at St Mark's Anglican Church.[27] Two people who became critical to the Centre's work joined soon after. Liz Khan lived in Stoke Newington and had worked as a nanny and child-minder. After the birth of her second child, she became involved with the nascent Dalston Children's Centre.[28] Manju Mukherjee had come to England from India in 1967. After working in the civil service, she had a child in 1979; a couple of years later, she began to work with the Dalston Children's Centre.[29]

A mosaic of funding from a variety of sources for community organ-izations in the 1980s was critical to the fledgling childcare centre. Initially, a grant of £9,720 was secured from an urban partnership scheme between local and central government. In 1982, the Centre received funding for six workers from the Manpower Services Community Enterprises Programme—designed for people who had been unemployed the previous year. Two years later, an Urban Aid grant of £65,650—again from central government—helped support running costs and the wages of six workers.[30] It is, of course, a lovely irony that a central Conservative government, in other respects ill-disposed to gay and lesbian rights, funded a centre founded on the principle of anti-heterosexism. In addition to these grants, between 1980 and 1985, the Dalston Children's Centre received support from a variety of

---

[25] Lynne Harne, 'Lesbian Mothers' Custody Conference', *Spare Rib* 129 (April 1983): 23.
[26] Anne Thorne, interview, 20 February 2018.   [27] Liz Khan, interview, 9 April 2018.
[28] Liz Khan, interview, 9 April 2018.
[29] Manju Mukherjee, interview, 21 November 2017.
[30] GLC, Women's Committee, 'Dalston Children's Centre', Funding Application, 28 June 1983, LMA, GLC/DG/PRE/223/7.

sources—local government and agencies such as Hackney Borough Council, the GLC Women's Committee, the Inner London Education Authority, and Hackney Adult Education, as well as private donors, including Marks & Spencer, NatWest Bank, and Sainsbury's. This support paid for wages, running costs, books, holiday playschemes, and equipment, including a darkroom set up by Anna Sherwin.[31]

The Centre was run as a collective made up of administrative and childcare workers, though there was sometimes a porous boundary between the two. There were about eight workers at the Centre, all of whom were on part-time contracts. Work at the Centre was supplemented by short-term contract workers. Though there were some men involved at the very beginning, the Dalston Children's Centre was predominantly run by women. Ethnically and in terms of sexual orientation, it was a diverse workforce and management team. People of Afro-Caribbean and South Asian descent were involved as workers and on the management committee. There were regular meetings to discuss both working practices and broader aims; one is pictured in Figure 6.1.

One of the workers, Nina Nissen, remarked that the Centre was 'more like a focus for a network or a variety of networks that drew on the children's centre, but also had its centres of gravity elsewhere.'[32] The Lenthall Road Workshop was an example of this, with people such as the photographer Ingrid Pollard moving between the two. In terms of political activism, Greenham Common and the women's peace movement attracted the participation of several workers.[33] Most of the mothers and children who used the Dalston Children's Centre came from the local Dalston area. The class composition of the Centre was mixed, with both middle-class and working-class parents and children.[34] Users of the Centre tended to be local. The mothers visiting the Centre were, according to Nina Nissen, 'literally women who lived down the road...who lived next door...who heard about the Centre through word of mouth.'[35] Dalston's substantial Afro-Caribbean and Asian population was reflected in the children and parents who used the Centre.[36] According to the

[31] Dalston Children's Centre, *Annual Report*, 1983.
[32] Nina Nissen, interview, 2 November 2017.   [33] Liz Khan, interview, 9 April 2018.
[34] Liz Khan, interview, 9 April 2018.   [35] Nina Nissen, interview, 2 November 2017.
[36] Helen Brown, interview, 22 November 2018.

Figure 6.1 Meeting at Dalston Children's Centre, *c.*1984.
Credit: Pam Isherwood.

GLC Women's Committee report on the Centre in 1984, there were 'equal proportions of black/ethnic minority and white children and parents'.[37] As Manju Mukherjee said, the Dalston Children's Centre brought 'together mothers and children, from different backgrounds, cultures, problems'.[38] Liz Khan called it a 'multicultural group of workers and parents'.[39]

After its beginnings in the hall of St Mark's Church, the Dalston Children's Centre worked out of four houses in the area between Dalston Lane and Kingsland Road. It began at 61a Greenwood Road, as short-life housing. The actress and singer Martine McCutcheon, the star of *Love Actually* (2003), remembered that, as a child coming home from school, she would 'hang around at the play centre' that was next door to her own flat on Greenwood Road.[40] The Children's Centre then moved

[37] GLC, Women's Committee, 'Dalston Children's Centre', Funding Application, 22 June 1984.
[38] Dalston Children's Centre, *Annual Report*, 1982.
[39] Liz Khan, interview, 9 April 2018.
[40] Martine McCutcheon, *Who Does She Think She Is? My Autobiography* (London: Arrow, 2000), 32–3.

to an end-of-terrace house at 80 Sandringham Road, licensed from the New Islington and Hackney Housing Association.[41] When the licence ran out in 1982, the Centre had nowhere to go. It threw itself into lobbying local government bodies. At the last minute, Hackney Borough Council provided another terraced house at 112 Greenwood Road, into which the Centre moved in October 1982. The Council also made a grant of £93,000 to buy another property at 68 Sandringham Road, but that sale fell through. At that point, the Dalston Children's Centre began exploring the possibility of a move to the Shacklewell Lane Baths, which the Council agreed to lease. The uncertainty about where the Centre would actually be situated remained its most 'demoralizing' problem and 'the main area of anguish'.[42]

The local circumstances of Dalston were crucial to the Centre's work. The Women's Committee report on a 1982 funding application from the Dalston Children's Centre relayed that it was a 'direct result of the desires and worries expressed by local parents'. Childcare was a 'local need'. Housing in the borough was in desperate straits. Hackney had a 'high proportion of single mothers', who needed support. The Centre thus provided a 'welcome release' to women who were 'under severe economic and environmental strain'.[43] In this context, the Centre's aim was to 'promote and advance the education of children and adults' in Hackney by improving the 'conditions of life for those children... who have need of such facilities by reason of their age or social and economic circumstances'.[44] Assessing an application by the Dalston Children's Centre to the Women's Committee of the GLC in 1983, the Committee noted that the Centre was an 'oasis of quiet from the severe overcrowding in the area'.[45]

Childcare was not the only activity at the Centre, but it did structure its daily life. There was a programme for under-fives between 10 a.m.

[41] Suzy Nelson, interview, 20 February 2018.

[42] Dalston Children's Centre, *Annual Report*, 1982.

[43] GLC, Women's Committee, 'Dalston Children's Centre', Funding Application, 14 December 1982, LMA, GLC/DG/PRE/223/3.

[44] GLC, Women's Committee, 'Dalston Children's Centre', Funding Application, 22 June 1984, LMA, GLC/DG/PRE/223/22.

[45] GLC, Women's Committee, 'Dalston Children's Centre', Funding Application, 28 June 1983, LMA, GLC/DG/PRE/223/7.

and 2 p.m.—up to seven children could attend unaccompanied.[46] Others could be accommodated if accompanied by a parent. Breakfast and lunch were provided. Liz Khan also noted that the Centre was 'one of the first places that recognized the importance of breakfast' for children.[47] At 3.30, older children were collected from four local schools (facilitated after 1983 by the purchase of a minibus funded by the GLC Women's Committee) and looked after at the Centre in an after-school programme until 6 p.m. A variety of activities were laid on for children during the day. This included craft and art, work, dance, and music, as well as outings to places both far afield, such as the seaside, and closer to home, such as the zoo and Dalston Library. The Centre also put on an under-fives theatre programme, first at a local church and later at a nursery, supported by the Greater London Arts Association (GLAA), which drew in children from other childcare centres in Stoke Newington and Hackney, as well as the Ickburgh Special School.[48] During school vacations, there were holiday playschemes run between 8 a.m. and 6 p.m., for which there was a small charge.

In its policy statement, the Centre stated that 'our society is profoundly authoritarian and children are oppressed by the authoritarianism of the adults with whom they have contact'.[49] The Centre wanted, as much as possible, to get children to make 'choices for themselves', in an environment that was free of 'competitiveness and bossiness' and 'physical violence'. The workers themselves did 'our best not to shout at them even we are hard pressed to think of other ways of dealing with them'.[50] Liz Khan remembered that she and Manju Mukherjee would 'set up activities' for the children, 'but there was no direction…we would follow children' rather than impose a rigid set of activities.[51] This anti-authoritarian commitment was partly rooted in influences from sixties French and German alternative politics.[52]

---

[46] The Centre had to limit its hours to four per day; more than that meant it would have had to be a regulated nursery.

[47] Liz Khan, interview, 9 April 2018.   [48] The GLAA existed between 1966 and 1996.

[49] Dalston Children's Centre, *Annual Report*, 1983, Appendix A, 'Policy Statement'.

[50] Dalston Children's Centre, *Annual Report*, 1983.

[51] Liz Khan, interview, 9 April 2018.

[52] Helen Brown, interview, 22 November 2017; the writer Christiane Rochefort and her 1961 novel *Les Petits Enfants du Siècle* were influential, as were alternative childcare approaches from Germany and France. See Marie-Luare Cadart, 'Des "crèches sauvages" à la structuration

Two evenings a week, a 'Girls' Night' was put on for girls between the ages of 6 and 18. Activities included ice-skating, disco dancing, self-defence, drama, and juggling. There was a regular attendance of up to twenty girls. The reaction of one of the girls, Jeanette, gives us some sense what 'Girls' Night' offered: 'the boys would think you were mad if you messed around like this at the club'.[53] Nina Nissen remembered these nights as 'completely wild... really, really lively', with lots of music and dancing.[54] Transport was provided for the girls, 'taking into account how unsafe the streets are for women and girls of all ages'.[55]

The Dalston Children's Centre worked hard to include children with disabilities in the childcare it offered.[56] Its policy statement noted that 'people who have disabilities' were among those who were most oppressed by society.[57] Anne Thorne felt that 'we really broke the boundaries' by 'looking at disabilities'.[58] Among the Centre's founders were mothers with children with disabilities. Early on in the Centre's existence, children with disabilities were integrated into the care of all children. This was part of the inclusive approach adopted by the Centre. A book made for the Centre was entitled 'Everybody's Different'. Liz Khan also noted this point as critical—that the children, parents and workers at the Centre saw children with disabilities as part of the community and for those children to know that they were 'part of something... for the other children, this was normal'.[59] To further develop a programme for children with disabilities, the Centre organized a disability awareness workshop and met with people involved with children with disabilities, including parents, teachers from special schools, workers with the Hackney Play Association, and activists with groups such as

au réseau associative (1968–1986)', in *Des Parents Dans Les Crèches, Utopie ou Réalité* (Toulouse: ERES, 2006), 11–24; Timothy Scott Brown, *West Germany and the Global Sixties: The Anti-Authoritarian Revolt 1962–78* (Cambridge: Cambridge University Press, 2013), 314; Sheila Rowbotham, *Promise of a Dream* (London: Penguin, 2000), 243.

[53] Dalston Children's Centre, *Annual Report*, 1983.
[54] Nina Nissen, interview, 4 November 2017.
[55] Dalston Children's Centre, *Annual Report*, 1983.
[56] I am grateful to Carol Ackroyd for her helpful comments on this section; written communication, 1 November 2017.
[57] Dalston Children's Centre, *Annual Report*, 1983, Appendix A, 'Policy Statement'.
[58] Anne Thorne, interview, 20 February 2018.
[59] Helen Brown, interview, 22 November 2017; Liz Khan, interview, 9 April 2018.

the Liberation Network of People with Disabilities.[60] A hearing-impaired woman came to advise on integrating children with disabilities at the Centre. Later, two workers, one visually impaired, did a job-share dedicated to the disability issue. There were, of course, problems. Accessibility to the buildings was one. Transporting children with disabilities from outside the immediate neighbourhood of the Centre was another. The limitations of space were another. It was hoped that moving to new premises at the Shacklewell Lane Baths would facilitate disabled access and a more expansive space.

Childcare was certainly at the heart of what the Dalston Children's Centre did. But those who had founded the Centre and those who worked there saw childcare in a larger context. '[Y]ou cannot consider the needs of children', the Centre stated in an application for funding to the GLC Women's Committee in 1982, 'without giving thought to the needs of those who are responsible for childcare – mostly women.'[61] As Anna Sherwin remarked, a pressing question was '[w]hat do women need, what do women want, what do they want to do?'[62] The Dalston Children's Centre served as a fulcrum for a number of disparate activities which addressed women's needs. Childcare was also provided, for example, on Saturdays between 10 a.m. and 1 p.m. to help women with shopping, not least to avoid adding the 'hustle and bustle' of the Ridley Road Market to the other stresses of parenting.[63] In one of its locations, the Centre provided not only a room for parents to rest but also use of the washer and dryer to do laundry.[64] One of the most successful courses put on at the Centre was a six-week sleep workshop for parents with a specialist from Great Ormond Street.[65]

The isolation of women was a particular concern for the Centre. Liz Khan noted that among workers at the Centre there was 'an

[60] On the last, see Allan Sutherland, 'The Other Tradition: From Personal Politics to Disability Arts' (2006), http://citeseerx.ist.psu.edu/viewdoc/download?doi=10.1.1.548.565&rep=rep1&type=pdf (accessed 20 October 2017).

[61] GLC, Women's Committee, 'Dalston Children's Centre', Funding Application, 14 December 1982, LMA, GLC/DG/PRE/223/3.

[62] Anna Sherwin, interview, 21 November 2017.

[63] Liz Khan, interview, 9 April 2018.

[64] Helen Brown, interview, 22 November 2017; GLC, Women's Committee, 'Dalston Children's Centre', Funding Application, 22 June 1984, LMA, GLC/DG/PRE/223/22.

[65] Liz Khan, interview, 9 April 2018.

understanding that when you had this new baby it was quite isolating'.[66] In the 1984 application to the GLC Women's Committee, the Centre wrote of the importance of ameliorating women's 'isolated lives'.[67] The Centre allowed such women a way out of 'their own environment, where they are surrounded by constant reminders of household chores'.[68] The Centre provided not only childcare but also community to help with this isolation: 'somewhere for mothers with children up to five years to go as often as they wish...a relaxed atmosphere for the children to play in and for the mothers to get to know one another'.[69] Requesting funds from the GLC Women's Committee to expand its premises in 1982, the Centre stated that a larger building would afford 'space where the women can meet, read, talk, share their experiences'.[70]

The desire to address maternal isolation and build community among women formed a pattern that was repeated across London in community childcares and women's centres in the 1980s, using such spaces to address women's material and emotional needs and to build community. The Kingston Women's Centre in south-west London argued that it sought to relieve the 'frequently expressed feelings of isolation' and 'loneliness' among women.[71] Such work was also perceived as building community for women. On the Pepys Estate in Deptford, for example, an outreach programme for women wanted to 'create a community spirit on the estate...to make the community more self-articulate and aware, to raise consciousness on the estate around issues like provision for under-fives, problems of unemployed women, lack of community resources'.[72] Anne Thorne remarked that the question of the emotional value of the Centre for parents was 'very explicit'. There was the hope, she said, that the Centre would provide a place that was 'warm and

[66] Liz Khan, interview, 9 April 2018.
[67] GLC, Women's Committee, 'Dalston Children's Centre', Funding Application, 22 June 1984, LMA, GLC/DG/PRE/223/22.
[68] Dalston Children's Centre, *Annual Report*, 1982.
[69] Dalston Children's Centre, *Annual Report*, 1982.
[70] GLC, Women's Committee, 'Dalston Children's Centre', Funding Application, 14 December 1982, LMA, GLC/DG/PRE/223/3.
[71] GLC, Women's Committee, 'Kingston Women's Centre', Funding Application, 31 January 1984, LMA, GLC/DG/PRE/223/22.
[72] GLC, Women's Committee, 'Combination Outreach Project [Pepys Estate, Deptford]', Funding Application, 14 December 1982, LMA, GLC/DG/PRE/223/3.

friendly' and a community: 'a place that was part of your community and part of your life and that was a warm and friendly place for your children to be brought up by the village not by yourself'.[73]

The Dalston Children's Centre also offered women a substantial slate of courses in a variety of subjects—women's health, Asian cooking, self-defence, and photography. Hackney Adult Education also worked through the Centre. There were workshops on questions such as feminism and heterosexism. In this way, as already noted, the Centre was as much a women's centre as a childcare centre, designed to address women's questions from a feminist perspective.

In the registration form for children attending the Dalston Children's Centre, it described itself as a 'radical alternative' to existing childcare provision for 'children of all ages and their adults'.[74] This radicalism was rooted in 'trying to develop' childcare for children and parents 'in an anti-racist, anti-sexist, anti-heterosexist and anti-authoritarian way'.[75] The aim was to 'provide an open, supportive environment in which women, young women and children are free to grow and develop in their own ways'.[76] A particular social analysis grounded this aim:

The Children's Centre exists within a society in which many people do not have this freedom. Our society is racist and people of colour and other ethnic groups are oppressed by that racism. Our society is sexist and women and girls are oppressed by the patriarchal attitudes that underlie sexism. Lesbians and gay men are oppressed for example, by the pervasive assumption that only heterosexual relationships are acceptable: that is what we call heterosexism, why we believe that society is heterosexist. Our society is profoundly authoritarian and children are oppressed by the authoritarianism of the adults with whom they are daily in contact. In our society people who have disabilities, people who are unemployed, people who do not conform to middle class values, are all considered to be less than fully human.[77]

[73] Anne Thorne, interview, 20 February 2018.
[74] Dalston Children's Centre, *Annual Report,* 1983, Appendix A, Policy Statement.
[75] Dalston Children's Centre, *Annual Report,* 1983, Appendix B, Registration Form.
[76] Dalston Children's Centre, *Annual Report,* 1983, Appendix A, Policy Statement.
[77] Dalston Children's Centre, *Annual Report,* 1983, Appendix A, Policy Statement.

The Centre was not only a means to provide help to children and parents but also a space to confront such social problems:

> At the Children's Centre, we want to provide positive alternatives to the prevailing attitudes around us. We want to fight oppression in all its forms, and to enable the women, young women and children who use the Centre and the women who work and the Centre to grow without fear.[78]

The focus on race, gender, and sexual orientation spoke to the most powerful currents running through radical politics in the 1970s and 1980s. It also had a particular local purchase, given factors such as the presence of a lesbian community within Hackney and the difficult conditions faced by ethnic minorities. In this light, the Dalston Children's Centre could be perceived as a space within which the everyday practice and meaning of anti-racism, anti-sexism, and anti-heterosexism could be worked out on the ground. The feminism that guided the Centre was a kind of canopy under which these issues were explored—what was later called intersectionality. This is not to suggest that feminism was able to contain such questions, but that within the feminist movement after 1970 they were critical reference points.[79]

One of the most important ways this manifested itself at the Centre was in relation to lesbianism. The Dalston Children's Centre strove to integrate lesbian issues into the running of the Centre. In May 1982, it held a special meeting for lesbian mothers. Carol Ackroyd wrote in that year's annual report of the special challenges facing lesbian mothers:

> Lesbians face the oppression of all women in very direct and brutal ways. To be a lesbian is to risk losing custody of children and to face contempt as well as physical attacks. While we may be out with our friends, many of us feel we have to hide our lesbianism at our children's school, from neighbours, with doctors and other professionals.[80]

---

[78] Dalston Children's Centre, *Annual Report*, 1982.
[79] See Thomlinson, *Race, Ethnicity and the Women's Movement in England, 1968–1993*.
[80] Dalston Children's Centre, *Annual Report*, 1982.

The meeting led to a commitment to other discussions for lesbian mothers, as well as the organization of summer holidays for lesbians and their children at a Welsh holiday home. A year later, the Centre's policy statement set out its commitment to providing 'a space where lesbians can meet and provide support for lesbian mothers. We encourage an open, sensitive sharing between lesbian and heterosexual women.' The Centre also helped organize heterosexism awareness workshops.[81]

The Dalston Children's Centre saw its work as an explicit reaction to Thatcherite politics. The Centre understood that it was operating 'at a time when savage cuts and inflation meant that bad housing, lack of childcare provision, a poor health service, unemployment…put intolerable strains on most people who live around here.'[82] Not least, it decried the Thatcher government's view of gender: '[t]he present government believes the best place for women and their children is in the home – the basis of the Children's Centre is an opposition to this ideology.'[83] The Dalston Children's Centre was aware that its provision was, in many ways, but a small bandage on a larger social wound caused by rising unemployment and swingeing cuts to government spending, particularly within Dalston:

> We know we'll never be able to do more than scratch at the surface of all the needs in the area…We strongly believe that people should have a say in what is provided for them and that they have a right to a decent life. We are a voluntary organization. We don't want to be providing, at low cost, a sop to what people really want and need.[84]

The Centre was, in practice and approach, a response to Thatcherite cuts to social services and to market-driven solutions to social need. It provided, after all, free childcare. It did not exist in the market. But it would be wrong to think of it in terms of older forms of social democracy. Like many other organizations funded by the GLC and other municipal bodies, the Centre was not a product of state centralism or corporatism.

---

[81] Dalston Children's Centre, *Annual Report*, 1983, Appendix A, Policy Statement.
[82] Dalston Children's Centre, *Annual Report*, 1983.
[83] Dalston Children's Centre, *Annual Report*, 1982.
[84] Dalston Children's Centre, *Annual Report*, 1982.

Rather, it was an alternative to that kind of statist approach. The Dalston Children's Centre was an example of this radical decentralization. It provided social services through the receipt of state (or, at least, local state) funding, but did so outside the ambit of the state and without reference to the free market.

What did the commitment to anti-racism, anti-sexism, anti-heterosexism, and anti-authoritarianism mean in practical terms, in everyday practices at the Centre? The first point of reference was the children themselves. It meant dealing with racist comments made by children in as gentle and effective a way as possible: 'if children make racist remarks, we will try to explain to them why such remarks are objectionable, in terms that the children will understand'.[85] The same was true of gendered stereotypes:

> We've tried to make sure that we work against sexism and racism during the scheme – for example, we don't want to encourage the girls to be 'nurses' and the boys 'warriors' when acting out plays…We employ women workers now, so that boys can see that women can arrange all sorts of activities, not just traditional ones.[86]

Resources and toys that reflected anti-racist and anti-sexist values were sought from organizations such as Lambeth Toys and Oxfam. The Centre organized an under-fives theatre series in 1982, which led to a determination to seek non-traditional fare in children's plays:

> We had a Judy and Punch show, which most women in the audience found very offensive. We now feel that even if the performer says there is no violence to women in the show, the whole story of Judy of Punch is so violence-orientated that it's best if we don't show it. We are trying to find shows which are consciously anti-racist, anti-sexist or dealing with other important issues.[87]

---

[85] Dalston Children's Centre, *Annual Report*, 1983, Appendix A, Policy Statement.
[86] Dalston Children's Centre, *Annual Report*, 1983.
[87] Dalston Children's Centre, *Annual Report*, 1982.

The commitment to anti-racism, anti-sexism, anti-heterosexism, and anti-authoritarianism was taken up not only with 'the children, with adult users' but also 'in its internal organization.'[88] The Centre's Annual Report of 1983 stated, for example, that it sought 'to challenge racism wherever it occurs: in ourselves, in the children, in young women and women who use the Centre and whenever and however we become aware of it in the larger society outside the Centre.'[89] The remark 'in ourselves' is particularly striking, coming to grips with racism as an internal, as well as external, problem. In this regard the Dalston Children's Centre saw itself as trying to provide a space 'in which white people can become aware of and challenge the historic roots of their racism.'[90] Natalie Thomlinson has written that in the 1970s and 1980s some white feminists may have perceived racism as an external phenomenon, 'rather than as a category that structure both society and their own subjectivity.'[91] This was not the case at the Dalston Children's Centre, where workers accepted that racism was something to be confronted within, as well as beyond the Centre. There were particular moments when white workers at the Centre were asked to reflect upon the Centre's views of race and identity; both were difficult but important experiences. The Centre was, in this way, an example of the self-critical or self-reflexive radicalism of the 1980s. Ultimately, however, this dynamic proved untenable.

The Centre made a conscious effort to hire more ethnic minority workers and get more ethnic minority people on the management committee. The 1982 annual report noted that 'our area has a high proportion of Afro-Caribbean, and Asian residents and we believe it's important that a high proportion of our workers are black so that we can be, as a whole, responsive to issues concerning our lives like racism, sexism etc.'[92] The year 1984 was a particular turning point in this regard. Advertising for administrative, fundraising, and welfare rights officers that year, for example, the Centre stipulated that '[a]ll workers need an

[88] GLC, Women's Committee, 'Dalston Children's Centre', Funding Application, 22 June 1984, LMA, GLC/DG/PRE/223/22.
[89] Dalston Children's Centre, *Annual Report*, 1983.
[90] Dalston Children's Centre, *Annual Report*, 1983.
[91] Thomlinson, *Race, Ethnicity and the Women's Movement in England, 1968–1993*, 17.
[92] Dalston Children's Centre, *Annual Report*, 1982.

understanding of the particular needs and experiences of Black women and Black children, of lesbians and the children of lesbians, and of people of all ages and disabilities'.[93] In another advertisement in June 1984, the Centre stated that 'Black/lesbian/working-class women [are] encouraged to apply'.[94] Such positive discrimination resonated with similar initiatives within local and metropolitan government. But it also courted controversy. Following the June advertisement, the *East London Advertiser* reported on what it called a 'rumpus' surrounding a "Black women and lesbians ad." According to the *Advertiser*, complaints were made by 'parents and councillors' to the Commission for Racial Equality. It responded by stating that '[i]t is allowable to advertise for black people, but many circumstances must be considered'. Hilda Kean, then Labour leader of the local council, also became involved, going to the Centre 'to discuss rewriting the advert'.[95] The metropolitan tabloid media also plunged into the controversy, doorstepping workers at the Centre.[96] Nonetheless, despite this opposition the initiative succeeded in making the Centre more diverse.

6.2

The Dalston Children's Centre had a profound effect on those who worked there. Some, like Liz Khan, felt that the Centre shaped their political outlook in a deep way. After the birth of her daughters, Khan became more feminist. Working at the Centre, she found herself able to grow further and explore new political directions and questions: '[w]hat was good about the Centre was that you could explore safely, you could discuss issues that you had never discussed or never thought through'. It was, she said, 'an amazing time for discovery as a person'.[97] Among the issues she remembered encountering were those of race and sexuality. She also became involved in the women's peace movement around the

---

[93] *Guardian*, 17 October 1984.   [94] *Spare Rib* 143 (June 1984).
[95] Ken Hayes, 'Black women and lesbians ad starts rumpus', *East London Advertiser*, 13 July 1984.
[96] Nina Nissen, correspondence, 1 August 2023.
[97] Liz Khan, interview, 9 April 2018.

time she worked at the Centre and was among those going to Greenham Common. Khan thought of the Centre as a place that facilitated personal growth and freedom through an empathetic and tolerant environment. This was echoed by other workers. Anne Thorne talked of the importance of 'learning [from] and respecting each other' on an 'equal basis regardless of sex, gender, race or whatever'.[98] Manju Mukherjee suggested that at the centre of this was a feeling of 'real sisterhood'.[99] That the Centre was, after its beginning, run entirely by women was felt to have contributed to this sense of respect. Nina Nissen suggested, for example: 'I think the issue around the relationships and the way we worked collectively in a really respectful way I think that also very much had to do with it being women only'.[100]

According to Nina Nissen, one of the most important aspects of the Centre was the way it wound together ideology, process, and everyday life. '[W]e were determined to be different,' she said, 'and the way to start that was by us doing it differently.' Nissen spoke of the variety of people involved in the Centre—'women with children, with disabilities, single mothers, single fathers'—brought together in a single space grounded in a feminist approach, a 'gathering of different political streams around feminism to create something that was different'. The politics of this moment was also rooted in the everyday life of its protagonists: 'these were politics that we were living...they had real...importance and meaning and significance for us, because they were reflecting also how we envisaged not only how to work, but how to live and how to be with children and how to be with each other'. This contained the aim of creating something larger: 'we had that great hope that bringing up children in different ways would also lead to a different kind of society and we as adults would be changed through engaging with children and with each other in different ways'.[101]

Emotion lay at the centre of the Dalston Children's Centre. It was concerned with the emotional welfare and development of children (seen in the commitment to anti-authoritarianism) and the emotional

---

[98] Anne Thorne, interview, 20 February 2018.
[99] Manju Mukherjee, interview, 21 November 2018.
[100] Nina Nissen, interview, 2 November 2017.
[101] Nina Nissen, interview, 2 November 2017.

welfare of parents, particularly women. The approach to the latter was inflected with empathy, a moment when the personal—the acknowledgement of the emotional cost of parenting, loneliness, and isolation—was political and could be ameliorated through a collective initiative, the provision of childcare and a sympathetic environment. To echo Karen, quoted at the beginning of this chapter, the Dalston Children's Centre was a place where 'you can have a cup of coffee and a natter'.

But that work also existed within a particular kind of community, one in which emotion was an important part.[102] This was not only about the emotional labour of childcare and working for women but also about the relationships between workers. Anne Thorne remarked, for example, that emotion was an 'explicit' aspect of the Centre's work and that a central aim was to create a 'place that was warm and friendly…a place that was part of your community and part of your life and that was a warm and friendly place for your children to be brought up by the village, not by yourself'.[103] Even when the discussions became intense, there was a sense that this also existed within a particular emotionally supportive framework. Helen Brown said, for example, '[t]here were lots of discussions, very intense discussion at times, but basically the idea was that…you could be free and open and accepted for who you were in that place'.[104] Nina Nissen expressed a similar view:

> We had long discussions and heated discussions…they were very engaged but never nasty…that makes a huge difference in terms of the learning process, the engagement…nobody really had it in for anybody, and I think that is something that is really very special.[105]

6.3

Hackney was home to a number of community arts organizations and collectives, such as Hackney Flashers, Centerprise, the Lenthall Road

---

[102] See Barbara Rosenwein, *Emotional Communities in the Early Middle Ages* (Ithaca: Cornell University Press, 2006).
[103] Anne Thorne, interview, 20 February 2018.
[104] Helen Brown, interview, 22 November 2017.
[105] Nina Nissen, interview, 2 November 2017.

Workshop, and Freeform.[106] This work was committed to facilitating the production of culture by local communities.[107] The Dalston Children's Centre was not formally a community arts organization, but its work paralleled some of that movement's ideals. Most notably, the Centre made an important cultural contribution through an initiative pursued by Manju Mukherjee and Anna Sherwin.

In 1984, the Dalston Children's Centre and the community cultural organization Centerprise published *Breaking the Silence*, a pioneering collection of Asian women's writing. There were accounts of the lives of young South Asian women and a photo-essay on a particular day, taken by Anna Sherwin of Manju Mukherjee and her daughter. Mukherjee was the force behind *Breaking the Silence*. It was, in her words, 'a great adventure'.[108] The original idea was to have Asian women in the area come into the Centre to write their stories, through 'a workshop to get them to write their own thoughts', and to learn how to make photographs of their lives, using resources such as the darkroom. Mukherjee put up about two hundred leaflets in Hackney. But the initial response was negligible. This left Mukherjee 'very frustrated'.[109] The problem was that many Asian women in the area were apprehensive about participating in such a project, afraid of 'offending their families'.[110] To get around this, Mukherjee went to women, approaching them at bus stops, at the nearby Dalston Market, wherever she could find them, and wrote down their stories, using pseudonyms.[111] Mukherjee remarked that 'most of the young women were really frightened to express their true feelings living in between two cultures'.[112] The resulting book was a challenging portrait of that in-between position. This was particularly important in terms of younger women: 'most of them didn't want to reject their traditional culture – just want some understanding and support from their

---

[106] For a visual record of this activity, see BFI, *Somewhere in Hackney* (1980) https://player. bfi.org.uk/free/film/watch-somewhere-in-hackney-1980-online; see also *The Rio Tape/Slide Archive: Radical Community Photography in Hackney in the 80s* (London: Isola, 2020).

[107] On the community arts movement, see Wetherell, 'Painting the Crisis'; Philip Wolmuth, 'Radical Losses', *British Journal of Photography* (June 2010), 87–8.

[108] *Breaking the Silence: Writing by Asian Women* (London: Centerprise, 1984), 1.

[109] *Breaking the Silence*, 1.   [110] *Breaking the Silence*, 1.

[111] https://www.ahackneyautobiography.org.uk/people/manjula-mukherjee (accessed 2 October 2017).

[112] Dalston Children's Centre, *Annual Report*, 1983.

parents'.[113] The book was also a portrait of the racism facing Asian women in British society. Mukherjee reflected upon this position herself:

> One thing I noticed, we are taken for granted: nice, soft, and sari clad, timid little things, by white society. It is not going to be the same with the next generation. They will question this expectation of them and want a clear answer.[114]

Breaking the Silence reflected many of the themes apparent in writing by British South Asian women in the 1970s and 1980s: the difficulties faced, particularly by second-generation South Asian women, in reconciling Asian and British identity around questions of marriage, social life, and gender roles and expectations. Life in Britain was both an opportunity, in terms of personal freedom for women and education, and a challenge, most clearly from the different forms of racism encountered on a daily basis.[115] One writer in *Breaking the Silence* summed up this position: 'I am an Indian girl in England'.[116] *Breaking the Silence* remains a compelling account of the challenges facing South Asian women in 1980s Britain, between two worlds.

6.4

A photograph from 1984, published in a later pamphlet by Matrix, shows a group of women from the Centre clustered around a model of the Shacklewell Baths renovation.[117] But that same year, tensions began to appear within the Centre. Discussions at the regular Wednesday morning meetings became increasingly intense in 1984 and 1985, specifically around questions of class and race within the Centre and its

---

[113] *Breaking the Silence*, 2.   [114] *Breaking the Silence*, 3.
[115] See Chris Weedon, 'Migration, Identity, and Belonging in British Black and South Asian Women's Writing', *Contemporary Women's Writing* 2/1 (2008): 17–35, doi: 10.1093/cww/vpn003.
[116] Rita, in *Breaking the Silence*, 30.
[117] See Matrix, *Building for Childcare* (London: Matrix/GLC, 1986).

priorities with respect to the local Black community in Hackney.[118] The Centre's approach, which might now be termed intersectional—comprising a focus on sexuality, disability, gender, and race—became more focused on the question of race.

This development was not surprising given the character of political radicalism in the 1980s. The desire to build new communities was simultaneously marked by the appearance of divisions along lines of gender, sexuality, class, and race. The last was a particularly important tension running through the feminist movement in the 1970s and 1980s.[119] In 1982, Hazel Carby published 'White Women Listen! Black Feminism and the Boundaries of Sisterhood', a sharp critique of white feminism and the possibilities of unity between Black and white feminists. Two years later, *Feminist Review* ran a series of similar critiques.[120] Gail Lewis was involved with the Brixton Black Women's Group and the Organization for Women of African and Asian Descent in the 1970s and 1980s. She recalled how 'incredibly fraught' the racial divide was within the feminist movement by the 1980s. What was 'configured as racism' in this context, Lewis suggested, was the failure of white feminists to challenge their own privilege and assumptions: '[white feminism] signals itself both as the universal topic – so there is no other kind of womanhood, but it's also that the moral project is to bring all those other women – black women...into, up to, develop them up, a form of tutelage'.[121] Few areas of feminist work were left untouched by this criticism. In 1984, for example, the GLC Women's Committee Support Unit itself faced accusations of racial bias, a charge it accepted.[122]

In the eyes of Black feminists, the division with white feminists was revealed through particular issues. One was the family. Amrit Wilson,

---

[118] Private information.
[119] See Thomlinson, *Race, Ethnicity and the Women's Movement in England*, ch. 5.
[120] Hazel L. Carby, 'White Women Listen! Black Feminism and the Boundaries of Sisterhood', in Centre for Contemporary Cultural Studies, *The Empire Strikes Back* (London: Hutchinson, 1982), 110–28; Valerie Amos, Gail Lewis, Amina Mama, and Pratibha Parmar, 'Many Voices, One Chant: Black Feminist Perspectives', *Feminist Review* 17 (Autumn 1984): 1–2.
[121] Gail Lewis, interviewed by Rachel Cohen, British Library, *Sisterhood and After*, Interview 4.
[122] GLC, Report by the Director-General, 'Women's Committee Support Unit – Management Structure', 18 May 1984, LMA, GLC/DG/PRE/223/20.

who was also involved with the Organization of Women of Asian and African Descent, remarked, for example, that white feminists were often in 'denial' about racial violence.[123] A particular problem for the Black community in London was the racist policing of young men. Gail Lewis argued that an understandable priority for Black feminists was to 'protect the younger generation, predominantly sons.'[124] Rather than exploring alternatives to traditional or heteronormative family structures (as the Dalston Children's Centre did), the protection of Black families was perceived as urgent. In Lambeth, for example, the West Indian Parents Action Group shared many of the same aims as the Dalston Children's Centre but focused more upon the traditional family as the unit that needed help with 'often depressive and discriminative issues faced from day-to-day.'[125]

Wider tensions within feminism and radicalism over race must also be linked to the urgency of the local circumstances facing Black people in Hackney in the 1980s. Those circumstances were shaped by deprivation and racism. Policing was an issue. Sandringham Road itself was the site of tense encounters between Black people and the police. It was an area targeted by Kenneth Newman, the head of the Met, a place he considered where 'the racial ingredient is at its most potent.'[126] The death of Colin Roach inside Stoke Newington police station in 1983 and the subsequent movement to determine the cause of his death were indictments of the police's relationship with the Black community in the area. The police were not the only source of racism. The Commission for Racial Equality also documented a shocking degree of discrimination against Black families in housing allocation in Hackney in 1984.[127]

Given these broader and local contexts in 1984, some within the Dalston Children's Centre wanted to make it more attuned to questions

---

[123] Amrit Wilson, interviewed by Margaretta Jolly, British Library, *Sisterhood and After*.

[124] Gail Lewis, interviewed by Rachel Cohen, British Library, *Sisterhood and After*, Interview 4.

[125] GLC, Ethnic Minorities Committee, 'West Indian Parents Action Group (Lambeth)', Funding Application, 22 April 1985, LMA, GLC/DG/PRE/49/50.

[126] Quoted in Michael Keith, '"Policing a Perplexed Society?" No-go areas and the mystification of police-black conflict', in Ellis Cashmore and Eugene McLaughlin (eds.), *Out of Order: Policing Black People* (London: Routledge, 1991), 204.

[127] See Commission for Racial Equality, *Race and Council Housing in Hackney* (London: CRE, 1984); Ken Hayes, 'New Deal for Black Families', *East London Advertiser*, 20 January 1984.

of race and, specifically, more focused upon the specific needs of Black people in Hackney.[128] Other aims within the Centre, such as concerns about fighting discrimination on the basis of sexuality (and in particular protecting the rights of lesbian mothers) or addressing the needs of children with disabilities, may have been eclipsed by this desire. In 1985, discussions within the Centre became increasingly fractious. The issue finally came to a head when some workers, both white and Black, were sacked by management, citing racial bias. These charges were refuted after an intervention by the National Council for Civil Liberties and reinstatements followed, but the Centre was never the same, and many of the original workers and management had left before the Centre moved to the Shacklewell Lane Baths in 1985.[129]

The former workers of the Dalston Children's Centre took various paths after 1985. Helen Brown, for example, was a Community Liaison Officer with Hackney Council, then worked with Matrix before moving on to the Citizens' Advice Bureau. Liz Khan went to university and became a social worker. Nina Nissen qualified as a medical herbalist, then, after working in the feminist health movement and adult and further education, became an academic with an interest in health care. What linked these different paths away from the Dalston Children's Centre was a common interest in social issues such as environmental sustainability, disability, refugee rights, the peace movement, and feminism. What also connected the former workers was a strong bond of friendship over the decades that followed. This even touched the children of workers, some of whom kept up with those with whom they had been together as children at the Centre.

The Centre's importance and legacy lay in what Nina Nissen called 'an absolute commitment to have [a] different kind of childcare and to bring together, or use childcare in a way as a political way to live our lives.'[130] The Centre brought together a number of different commitments— meeting the everyday demands of childcare while believing that a different kind of world for children and adults could be built from doing childcare in a new way. Its effect was not only external but internal as well,

[128] Private information.   [129] Private information.
[130] Nina Nissen, interview, 2 November 2017.

shaping the lives of its children, parents, and workers.[131] Of course, this did not come without tension, as, ultimately, the demise of the original iteration of the Centre in 1985 demonstrated.

In its short life, the Dalston Children's Centre achieved something distinctly new. In the 1970s, Sheila Rowbotham had reflected that childcare lay at the intersection between the demands of everyday life and the promises of a different political world. It was a 'practical need', particularly for women, but also offered the 'possibility of developing new relationships and consciousness', of 'how we want to work, care for children and play and indeed to love'.[132] The Centre saw such 'new relationships and consciousness' worked out through the material issue of childcare. 'To me', Nina Nissen recalled, 'it never felt like an experiment, but a practical vision, an ongoing endeavour aimed at producing social and political change, both individual and structural, based on the notion of "the personal is political".'[133] 'We did think', Anna Sherwin remarked, 'that we were changing the world a bit.'[134]

London, 1984: Conflict and Change in the Radical City. Stephen Brooke, Oxford University Press.
© Stephen Brooke 2024. DOI: 10.1093/9780191895395.003.0007

---

[131] Dalston Children's Centre, *Annual Report*, 1983.
[132] Sheila Rowbotham, 'Storefront Day Care Centres: The Radical Berlin Experiment' (1974) and 'Who's Holding the Baby?' (1979), in *Dreams and Dilemmas*, 94, 128.
[133] Nina Nissen, personal correspondence, 1 August 2023.
[134] Anna Sherwin, interview, 20 November 2017.

7

The Anti-Apartheid March

June 1984: a sea of banners and marchers flows into Trafalgar Square.[1] The focus of the crowd is an imposing interwar building, South Africa House. Scuffles break out between marchers and the police around a float, sponsored by the *Caribbean Times,* carrying the Mangrove Community Steelband.[2] The Steelband hails from the All Saints Road in Notting Hill and is named after the struggle of the Mangrove Restaurant and the so-called Mangrove Nine against police racism and harassment in Notting Hill. Beer cans are thrown at the police. People in the crowd accuse them of snatching and arresting protestors.[3] And indeed three policemen do bundle a young Black man away from the Square, his hands held tightly behind his back, his head pushed down. In another part of the Square, five white policemen, one with his helmet comically askew as if in some grotesque Punch and Judy show, another smiling wryly, carry a struggling Black man away. The protest had begun in Hyde Park, with appeals to free the imprisoned Nelson Mandela and to condemn the South African Prime Minister, 'Botha the Butcher' (as is shown in Figure 7.1). The crowd eventually moves out of Trafalgar Square, through Whitehall, crossing the Thames at Westminster Bridge, and ends up at Jubilee Gardens on the South Bank, near County Hall, where the demonstrators are entertained with music and speeches.

Wembley Stadium, April 1990: a 72-year-old man, dressed in a double-breasted jacket, with a pullover underneath to protect against the cold on a wet Easter Monday, takes the stage to an eight-minute standing

---

[1] This account is reconstructed from photographs of the march from the Getty Agency and the AAM archives and newspaper reports, https://www.aamarchives.org.

[2] *Guardian,* 4 June 1984.

[3] *Observer,* 3 June 1984; see also https://mangrovesteelband.wordpress.com/history/ (accessed 21 May 2021).

Figure 7.1 Anti-apartheid rally, 2 June 1984.
Credit: Cameron Brisbane/Anti-Apartheid Archives.

ovation and the strains of 'You'll Never Walk Alone'.[4] He begins his
speech to those he calls 'dear friends here' on a note of gratitude: '[w]e
are here because you took the humane decision that you could not
ignore the inhumanity represented by the apartheid system'.[5] The
speaker was, of course, Nelson Mandela. The occasion was a tribute concert, marking the first international appearance of the African National
Congress leader since being released from prison two months earlier.
Mandela's presence at the concert had not been certain. He had hesi-
tated about visiting 'Thatcher's country' because of that prime minister's
long-standing opposition to sanctions against South African's racist

[4] See http://tonyhollingsworth.com/?q=content/nelson-mandela-international-tribute-free-south-africa; Robin Denselow, 'Mandela Magic', *Guardian*, 17 April 1990.
[5] Transcript found at https://www.mylondon.news/news/local-news/read-full-text-nelson-mandelas-6379415.

government.[6] But, despite this, Mandela wanted to acknowledge the role that the anti-apartheid movement in Britain and, especially, London had played in opposing the South African government.

There is a clear trajectory between the two moments—between the protest at the anti-apartheid regime and the celebration of the release of Mandela. In the 1980s, the efforts of British anti-apartheid groups and activists made London a centre of global opposition to apartheid South Africa.[7] Between 1986 and 1990, there was a non-stop picket of the South African embassy in Trafalgar Square mounted by the City Anti-Apartheid Group. In June 1986, a massive anti-apartheid concert was held on Clapham Common, featuring some of the biggest British pop and rock stars of the day. A quarter of a million people attended that concert. Two years later there was another huge concert, this time broadcast worldwide, during which stars such as Whitney Houston, Stevie Wonder, Sting, Simple Minds, and the Special AKA celebrated Mandela's birthday and called for his release.

Nineteen eighty-four was a turning point in the anti-apartheid campaign in Britain. The Anti-Apartheid Movement (AAM), Britain's most important anti-apartheid campaigning organization, noted, for example, that '1984 has seen some of the most effective campaigning activities by the AAM, emphasizing as never before the extent of public support for the Movement and its policies'.[8] This public support and activity could also be seen beyond the political sphere. In March, 'Free Nelson Mandela', a single by the Special AKA, reached no. 9 in the charts, and the song was featured on Top of the Pops, the BBC's flagship popular music programme. The following month, the apartheid issue was also highlighted by the campaign, undertaken by both the anti-apartheid movement and local authorities such as the GLC, to prevent the white South African-turned-British 1500-metre runner Zola Budd from participating in athletics meets. But perhaps the most important event

---

[6] Information from http://tonyhollingsworth.com/?q=content/nelson-mandela-international-tribute-free-south-africa.

[7] See Susan Dabney Pennybacker, 'A Cold War Geography: South African Anti-Apartheid Refuge and Exile in London, 1945–94', in Nathan Riley Carpenter and Benjamin N. Lawrence (eds.), Africans in Exile: Mobility, Law and Identity (Bloomington: Indiana University Press, 2018), 185–99.

[8] AAM, Annual Report 1983–4, AAM Archives.

happened on 2 June 1984. Over 25,000 people marched through the streets of central London to protest against the official state visit of the South African Prime Minister, P. W. Botha. This was the biggest demonstration in the history of the anti-apartheid movement in Britain and one of the largest public demonstrations in the history of twentieth-century London. It was officially supported by the GLC and was part of its 1984 Anti-Racist Year programme.

The anti-apartheid march in 1984 underlined a convergence between local and global anti-racist struggles in London. In this way, there was a trajectory in the event between London and South Africa. The incident in Trafalgar Square during the march is telling in this respect. The struggles between police and protestors, which led to the arrest of Black demonstrators, were centred around a float sponsored by a leading Black British newspaper which featured a steel band linked explicitly to a famous local anti-racist struggle. Local and global anti-racism thus orbited one another in 1984: the struggle against racism in Britain overlapped with the struggle against apartheid in South Africa. As Elizabeth Williams has pointed out, the anti-apartheid movement of the 1980s witnessed, more than ever before, the involvement of local Black British groups and campaigns.[9]

In 1984, London lay at the centre of a constellation of different developments in local and global anti-racism, gathered around the anti-apartheid campaign and symbolized by the 2 June march. Recent work has stressed London's place not only as an imperial centre but also as a 'locus of resistance to empire', particularly through the communities of colonial reformers from the African diaspora and beyond who lived there, even before Windrush.[10] In the 1980s, the work of the

    [9] Elizabeth M. Williams, *The Politics of Race in Britain and South Africa: Black British Solidarity and the Anti-Apartheid Struggle* (London: I. B. Tauris, 2015).

    [10] Marc Matera, *Black London* (Berkeley: University of California Press, 2015), 2: see also Philip Zachernuk, *Colonial Subjects* (Charlottesville: University Press of Virginia, 2000); Ann Spry Rush, 'Imperial Identity and Colonial Minds: Harold Moody and the League of Coloured Peoples, 1931–50', *Twentieth-Century British History* 13/4 (2002): 356–83, doi: 10.1093/tcbh/13.4.356; Susan D. Pennybacker, *From Scottsboro to Munich: Race and Political Culture in 1930s Britain* (Princeton: Princeton University Press, 2009); Daniel Whittall, 'Creating Black Places in Imperial London: The League of Colonial Peoples and Aggrey House, 1931–43', *London Journal* 36/3 (2011): 225–46, doi: 10.1179/174963211X13127325480316; Hammond Perry, *London is the Place for Me*.

anti-apartheid movement in Britain showed once again the centrality of London as a space that linked local, national, and global political movements. In this case, the anti-apartheid movement brought together local anti-racist and Black rights campaigns with the global campaign against apartheid.

The GLC made a crucial contribution to this, not only providing material support for the anti-apartheid movement in Britain but also symbolically linking its own anti-racist campaign with the global anti-apartheid movement. Nineteen eighty-four was not only Anti-Racist Year; it was also a year in which London was declared a 'zone' against apartheid. Anti-Racist Year itself foregrounded the anti-apartheid struggle. The GLC supported the new emphasis upon consumer, cultural, and sporting boycotts, notably lending its support to barring the use of its facilities to cultural figures or athletes who either were associated with the apartheid regime or had violated the boycott against South Africa. With some borough authorities, the GLC brought the anti-apartheid struggle to London's cartography, renaming streets after anti-apartheid figures such as Mandela.

7.1

Since the establishment of a formal apartheid policy by the National Party in South Africa in 1948, London had served as a centre for international campaigns against the apartheid regime.[11] Through the 1960s, the anti-apartheid cause was a powerful example of a number of social movements that challenged the boundaries of traditional British politics, while, at the same time, it helped construct a new kind of transnational politics and a sense of global citizenship in the postcolonial period.[12] In Britain, until the 1970s, the AAM was largely a white movement, drawing upon progressives and sympathizers in the Labour

[11] See Rob Skinner, *The Foundations of Anti-Apartheid* (Basingstoke: Palgrave Macmillan, 2007); Roger Fieldhouse, *Anti-Apartheid* (London: Merlin Press, 2005).
[12] See Lent, *British Social Movements Since 1945*; Håkan Thörn, *Anti-Apartheid and the Emergence of a Global Civil Society* (Houndmills: Palgrave Macmillan, 2006); Jodi Burkett, *Constructing Post-Imperial Britain* (Houndmills: Palgrave Macmillan, 2013).

and Liberal parties; ethnic minority groups in London began associating themselves with anti-apartheid work in the 1970s.[13] As Williams has demonstrated, though there was some coolness towards the AAM from Black organizations such as the West Indian Standing Committee, there were particular moments, such as the 1970 'Stop the Seventies' attempt to boycott South African sports teams and the reaction to the 1976 Soweto massacre of schoolchildren, when Black organizations in Britain began to firmly identify with the anti-apartheid struggle. A clear connection was made between racism in South Africa and racism in Britain. In particular, the experience of policing in Britain was a touchstone, as the publication *West Indian World* stated in 1973: '[o]ur feeling of security has been shattered...It never occurred to any of us that we will be stopped by an official policeman...like the blacks of South African [and] have to produce the British version of the pass – the passport.'[14] Williams quotes Lee Jasper on the connection made on the ground between Black British people and the struggle in South Africa: 'it resonated with our own experience of policing in largely poor black working class areas of Liverpool, Manchester, Handsworth, Brixton', becoming '[a] universal metaphor for black experience'.[15] In 1976, as a mark of this increasing sense of connection between Black Britain and South Africa, the West Indian Standing Committee organized a march from Notting Hill to the South African Embassy to protest against the killings in Soweto.

London was an important site for the international apartheid movement, and not only because it was the founding home of the AAM; it was also the centre of British government and the symbolic home of the Commonwealth, in which the wider politics around South Africa played out. As already noted, London's role as a locus of global finance lent a particular sharpness to the question of economic sanctions against South Africa. Britain was also the largest supplier of arms to apartheid South Africa. And finally, and not least important, London was home to

---

[13] See Williams, *The Politics of Race in Britain and South Africa.*
[14] Quoted in Elizabeth Williams, 'Anti-Apartheid: The Black British Response', *South African Historical Journal* 64/3 (2012): 696, doi: 10.1080/02582473.2012.675809.
[15] Quoted in Williams, 'Anti-Apartheid: The Black British Responses', 695.

anti-apartheid South African exiles, working through the African National Congress (ANC) and the Pan-Africanist Congress (PAC).[16]

The anti-apartheid movement gathered greater strength in the 1980s. Much of this was due to the intensification of the struggle in South Africa, the growing isolation of its government, and, in South Africa itself, the unceasing efforts of the ANC, the PAC, and, after 1983, the United Democratic Front (UDF). The years 1984 and 1985 were particularly violent in the townships.

In Britain, an important factor in the heightened visibility of the anti-apartheid movement in the 1980s was Margaret Thatcher herself. The Thatcher government was more clearly identified with support for and tolerance of the apartheid regime in South Africa. Thatcher was steadfastly opposed to abandoning trade with South Africa, pursuing, instead, 'constructive engagement' with the regime. As late as 1987, she referred to the ANC as a terrorist organization, though she was sympathetic to the plight of its imprisoned leaders, especially Nelson Mandela. Ironically, the Thatcher government did the anti-apartheid movement an enormous, if unintended, service by initiating talks on Zimbabwe which led to majority rule there; this freed up the energies of the anti-apartheid movement to focus on South Africa.

Another political factor in the strengthening of the anti-apartheid movement in 1980s Britain was local government. To the new urban left of the 1970s populating municipal government in places like London and Sheffield in the 1980s, apartheid was a critical issue. When the Labour Party came to power in London in 1981, it was not surprising that a commitment to the anti-apartheid movement was carried into government.

With its stance on apartheid, the GLC wound together local, national, and global politics. It was not the only local authority to do this, nor the only Labour body to do so. Sheffield had been the first local authority to commit to the anti-apartheid cause.[17] In February 1982, the

---

[16] See Saul Dubow, *Apartheid 1948–1994* (Oxford: Oxford University Press, 2014), 134 ff.; Pennybacker, 'A Cold War Geography'.

[17] See Daisy Payling, ' "Socialist Republic of South Yorkshire": Grassroots Activism and Left-Wing Solidarity in 1980s Sheffield', *Twentieth Century British History* 25/4 (2014): 602–27, doi: 10.1093/tcbh/hwu001.

Labour National Executive Committee sanctioned Labour local authorities to pursue concrete action, such as disinvestment and boycotts. Local Authorities Action Against Apartheid was formed in March 1983.[18] Throughout the 1980s, the trade union movement also dedicated itself more strongly to the anti-apartheid cause.[19] The GLC was committed, as we have seen, to anti-racism in its policy and governance. This was a policy adopted in London but also seen as a critique of Britain's racial situation, one that had been exacerbated by the Thatcher government. A commitment to the anti-apartheid cause was a natural parallel to this. Indeed, anti-racism in London and anti-racism on the world stage were inextricable from one another.

On 20 December 1983, the Council adopted a declaration on apartheid. This set out the GLC's 'abhorrence of the racist regime of South Africa and its illegal occupation of Namibia'. It was also an expression of a commitment 'to the cause of freedom in South Africa, to pay tribute to Nelson Mandela and all other prisoners of apartheid, and in recognition of the struggles and sacrifices of the African National Congress of South Africa and South West People's Organization of Namibia and others to liberate their peoples'. In specific terms, the declaration committed the GLC to the boycott of South African and Namibian goods, the withdrawal of Council investment in South Africa and Namibia, the refusal to have GLC representatives at any event that included representatives of either the South African government or the Bantustans, and the support of the cultural boycott of South Africa, in particular refusing to allow any GLC facilities to host events that included South African sports or cultural figures.[20] The commitment to the anti-apartheid cause included literally remaking the map of London:

> [the Council will] encourage the naming of streets and buildings after prominent opponents of apartheid, and the commemoration of historical connections between the Southern African liberation struggle

---

[18]   See Fieldhouse, *Anti-Apartheid*, 364 ff.   [19]   Fieldhouse, *Anti-Apartheid*, 391.
[20]   On cultural boycotts, see GLC, Report by Controller of Operational Services, Director of Recreation and the Arts, PRRA, 'London Against Racism in the Arts: Use of Council Facilities and Premises', 18 June 1984, LMA, GLC/DG/PRE/49/28.

and London, including the unveiling of blue plaques in honour of such connections.[21]

The GLC's support for the anti-apartheid cause was meant to have both local and global effects. On the one hand, it would 'lend strength to the international struggle for eradicating racial discrimination from our society'. On the other, it would help 'Londoners to understand the financial, political and cultural links between London and apartheid South Africa and how racism underpins the two countries' existence'.[22] Towards that end, a pamphlet was proposed that would detail London's double identity as a place that was home to 'many financial and industrial concerns based in the City [that] have considerable investments in South Africa and Namibia' as well as 'members of liberation movements involved in the struggle against apartheid'.[23] This had international resonance. The Secretary-General of the UN, Javier Pérez de Cuéllar, told the GLC that its action on apartheid lent 'strength to the international struggle for eradicating racial discrimination from human society throughout the globe'. Similarly, Oliver Tambo, a leader of the ANC, stated that, with this commitment in 1984, 'all Londoners, men and women alike, drawing inspiration from the indelible contribution to the salvation of humanity, will once more transform into right redoubts for the victory of the cause of equality, friendship and peace'.[24]

In other ways in the 1980s, London was marked by the anti-apartheid struggle, from the quotidian to the dramatic. As noted above, the GLC announced its intention to make the connection between London and the South African struggle explicit. One example was in the renaming of streets. In 1981, Brent Council named a street in a new development 'Mandela Close' to honour the imprisoned ANC leader. Over the next decade or so, a number of similarly named streets appeared in Britain.

[21] GLC, Ethnic Minorities Committee, GLC Council meeting, 20 December 1983, LMA, GLC/DG/PRE/49/41.
[22] GLC, PRRA, 'Anti-Apartheid Policy for the GLC: Progress Report', 14 June 1984, LMA, GLC/DG/PRE/49/28.
[23] GLC, Ethnic Minorities Committee, PRRA, 'Anti-Apartheid Declaration: Proposal for Ceremonial Booklet', 14 June 1984, LMA, GLC/DG/PRE/49/28.
[24] GLC, Ethnic Minorities Committee, PRRA, 'Anti-Apartheid Declaration: Proposal for Ceremonial Booklet', 14 June 1984, LMA, GLC/DG/PRE/49/28.

In London, there was also a Mandela Way (Bermondsey), Mandela Road (Lewisham), Mandela House (Woolwich), Nelson Mandela House (Stoke Newington), Steve Biko Way (Hounslow), Steve Biko Road (Islington), and a Desmond Tutu Drive (Lewisham). These initiatives were embedded in popular culture, beginning in 1981 with the popular television comedy *Only Fools and Horses*, whose main characters, Del Boy and Rodney, resided in a fictional Peckham tower block, Nelson Mandela House. Owen Hatherley has argued that few of the Mandela streets offered much in the way of architectural or aesthetic distinction to honour Mandela, but they did nonetheless literally situate the ANC leader's name in the map of London.[25]

The most high-profile example of this occurred in 1983.[26] That year, to mark Mandela's sixty-fifth birthday, Camden Council and the GLC proposed to rename Selous Street in Camden Town, to which the AAM had recently relocated its offices from Charlotte Street in Fitzrovia, as Mandela Street. This change was not without controversy. Selous Street was largely commercial, and the Post Office and businesses on the street objected to the name change, arguing that it would confuse customers and pose extra administrative costs. The South African Embassy also protested to Camden Council, saying that Mandela was a criminal. Despite such opposition, the renaming went ahead in July 1983.

Apartheid also affected London through state-sanctioned violence. On a Sunday morning in March 1982, the explosion from a 10-pound bomb ripped through the headquarters of the ANC, destroying part of the building and injuring a research officer. The bombing coincided with a planned rally in Trafalgar Square. It was erroneously believed that the President of the ANC, Oliver Tambo, would be at that rally, and there was speculation that the bomb might have been a failed assassination attempt, particularly given the targeted killings of anti-apartheid activists such as Ruth First. Later evidence showed that the bomb materials had been brought into Britain through the diplomatic pouch of the

---

[25] See Owen Hatherley, *A Guide to the New Ruins of Great Britain* (London: Verso, 2011).

[26] For accounts of the renaming of Selous Street, see https://theconversation.com/how-resistance-led-to-londons-selous-street-becoming-mandela-street-100770; https://www.bbc.com/news/magazine-20663509; https://www.hamhigh.co.uk/news/camden-so-proud-to-have-one-of-two-street-named-3460072.

South African Embassy and that those who planted the bomb were directly associated with the South African security services.[27] The bombing was followed in 1983 by burglaries at the offices of the ANC, PAC, and South West Africa People's Organization, and on May Bank Holiday weekend at the AAM offices. In 1985, there was a serious arson attack on the AAM headquarters in Mandela Street which caused tens of thousands of pounds of damage.

The renaming of streets and the attacks made on anti-apartheid organizations by the South African government were examples of how the apartheid issue permeated the space of London in the 1980s. There are, as already discussed, cultural examples of this influence, particularly if we look at popular music and sport. Nineteen eighty-four was an especially significant year in this regard.

On 5 March 1984, the Special AKA released the single 'Free Nelson Mandela'. Jerry Dammers was one of the founders of the Specials, a biracial ska band from Coventry on the 2-Tone label, which had enjoyed considerable success as chroniclers of the racial tension and economic blight of the early Thatcher years. Dammers had long been politically engaged—the Specials themselves had been partly inspired by Rock Against Racism—and in 1983, after going to a concert promoting the anti-apartheid movement, he decided to write a song about Nelson Mandela.[28]

'Free Nelson Mandela' was, of course, about the plight of an individual political prisoner, 'twenty-one years in captivity...his body abused but his mind is still free', but, without naming apartheid South Africa, the song did not shy away from associating that individual with a specific collective cause, the ANC, with Mandela as 'one in a large army'. There were other anti-apartheid songs, such as Little Steven's 'Sun City', released in 1985, but 'Free Nelson Mandela' succeeded at being both

---

[27] See Memorandum from the Anti-Apartheid Movement for Meeting with the Home Secretary, 13 October 1982, AAM Archives, MSS AAM 818; Submission to the Truth and Reconciliation Commission on South Africa's Illegal and Covert Activities in the United Kingdom, TRC Seminar, Cape Town, South Africa, 10 November 1997, AAM Archives Committee.

[28] https://www.bbcamerica.com/anglophenia/2013/06/nelson-mandela-and-the-most-potent-protest-song-ever-recorded; https://www.theguardian.com/music/2013/dec/09/jerry-dammers-free-nelson-mandela.

explicitly political and eminently danceable and did not separate the two. Music video was still in its first blush in 1984, and the video for 'Free Nelson Mandela', shot in a church basement with dancers, offered an assertion of both the politics of the song and its dynamism. The song was a commercial success, reaching the top ten in the charts in the UK. This meant an appearance on *Top of the Pops*, Britain's marquee pop music show, broadcast on Thursday evenings. On 19 April 1984, the Special AKA performed 'Nelson Mandela' on the show. It was a remarkable moment, perhaps in the incongruity between an overtly political song, about the politics of another country with an implicit anti-racist message, and mainstream British popular culture, with young people dancing and some of the young women with hairstyles inspired by Princess Diana. But perhaps this is not an incongruity at all but, rather, a moment that the anti-apartheid message permeated mainstream British culture, even while the British government were insisting that the ANC was a terrorist organization and that it would refuse sanctions against South Africa.

'Free Nelson Mandela' represented the breakthrough of the apartheid issue into mainstream popular culture. But there had been important preludes to this change. The most important was the way Black music in Britain had for some years before that song foregrounded the problem of apartheid. Indeed, music had provided a link between Black organizations at home and the global struggle represented by the anti-apartheid movement.[29] The Birmingham reggae band Steel Pulse had, for example, made an explicit connection between the anti-apartheid struggle—the 'brothers in South of Africa'—and the anti-racist struggle in Britain in their 1978 album and title track *Handsworth Revolution*. Other reggae bands such as Ladbroke Grove's Aswad also emphasized the African connections of British Black communities in songs such as 'Back to Africa' (1976) and 'African Children' (1981). The embrace of a kind of global African identity in Black British music was an important way in which the anti-apartheid struggle could be articulated outside of formal politics.

In another direct way, popular music could be one focal point of anti-apartheid or radical politics in the 1980s. A particularly important

[29] See Williams, 'Anti-Apartheid: The Black British Response', 685–706.

development was Dammers's involvement in establishing Artists Against Apartheid, which helped put together a series of concerts after 1984, including a massive concert on Clapham Common in 1986. Of course, this was not the first time popular music had been linked directly to popular music. Rock Against Racism (RAR) had effectively pioneered the use of pop music in radical political campaigns, responding to the rise of the National Front and racism in the music industry, the latter represented by Eric Clapton's anti-immigrant comments in 1976 and David Bowie's apparent flirtation with fascism the same year.[30] RAR had been a multiracial effort, bringing together both Black and white acts. However, RAR was somewhat more limited in that its acts tended to come from two genres of pop music—reggae and punk.[31] Artists Against Apartheid included artists who were more mainstream and well known than those associated with RAR, such as Sade, Simple Minds, Peter Gabriel, and Sting. Mainstream music was therefore pulled in a new way into politics.

Sport also highlighted the apartheid issue in the spring of 1984. The sporting links between Britain and South Africa had been a focus of the AAM since the early 1960s. The AAM focused on encouraging disengagement between British sports events and South African teams and athletes and boycotting South African teams coming to Britain, particularly in cricket and rugby.[32] In 1984, around the time of the release of 'Free Nelson Mandela', it was a young, female, white South African runner, Zola Budd, who became the focus of attention.[33] She was known as a talented 1500-metre runner who competed barefoot but whose chances of capturing international attention at the 1984 Los Angeles Olympics in a match-up with the American Mary Decker were

[30] On Bowie, see https://au.rollingstone.com/music/music-lists/the-50-worst-decisions-in-music-history-44119/david-bowie-sort-of-suggests-hes-cool-with-nazis-44152/ and https://www.politico.com/magazine/story/2016/01/david-bowie-death-politics-213529/.

[31] On RAR, see David Renton, *Never Again: Rock Against Racism and the Anti-Nazi League 1976–1982* (London: Routledge, 2019); Ian Goodyer, 'Rock Against Racism: Multiculturalism and Political Mobilization, 1976–81', *Immigrants and Minorities* 22/1 (2010): 44–62, doi: 10.1080/02619288.2003.9975053.

[32] See Geoff Brown, 'Not Just Peterloo: The Anti-Apartheid March to the Springbok Match, Manchester, 26 November 1969', *Socialist History* 56 (2019): 19–42.

[33] On Zola Budd, see Matthew P. Llewelyn and Toby C. Rider, 'Sport, Thatcher and Apartheid Politics: the Zola Budd Affair', *Journal of Southern Africa Studies* 44 (2018): 575–92, doi: 10.1080/03057070.2018.1464297.

threatened by South Africa's ban from Olympic competition. At this point, a right-wing British tabloid intervened. The *Daily Mail* began a campaign to get Budd British citizenship so that she could compete under the Union Jack at the 1984 Olympics. The argument used was both opportunistic—a way of bringing potential sporting glory to Britain—and rooted in a white 'kith and kin' perspective—that as a white South African, albeit as an Afrikaner South African—she had a deep connection with her 'homeland'. Despite some reservations within the government, the Home Secretary deployed his discretionary powers under the 1981 Nationality Act to grant citizenship quickly. This was controversial for a number of reasons, not least because the 1981 Act was otherwise restrictive. As Matthew P. Llewellyn and Toby C. Rider have argued, Budd, unlike Black migrants, 'fit seamlessly within the constructed boundaries of an "imagined community" of Britishness' in Thatcher's Britain because of the young athlete's whiteness.[34] Budd received British citizenship in April 1984 and began appearing at meets in Britain. This set off a series of confrontations between the British athletics authorities, anti-apartheid activists, and local authorities. The first two fought over the link between sport and politics, the first arguing there was no link, and the second that there had to be a link. The GLC tried to use its authority of ownership of facilities to prevent Budd appearing. She was, for example, supposed to appear at the Crystal Palace National Sports Centre, to which the GLC contributed significant running costs and on which it held the freehold. The GLC tried unsuccessfully to execute its ban on appearances at its facilities by people with a known link to South Africa. This failed. But the Budd controversy in the spring and summer of 1984 nonetheless highlighted the centrality of a global issue such as apartheid to local and national politics in different spaces, such as sports stadia.

In 1984, one could see increased pressure on the British government from anti-apartheid groups and community activism. This was provoked by events in southern African, including a constitutional reform in 1983 which still left Black South Africans unrepresented and the incursion of South African forces into Angola. In March 1984, for

[34] Llewelyn and Rider, 'Sport, Thatcher and Apartheid Politics', 586.

example, a parliamentary lobby was organized by a coalition of groups including the British Black Standing Conference, War on Want, and the National Union of Students.

7.2

On 4 May 1984, it was announced that Margaret Thatcher would host P. W. Botha on the latter's tour of Western Europe—a tour that was intended, according to Botha, to 'find a place for South Africa in the international community of nations'.[35] It would be the first time since South Africa had been expelled from the Commonwealth in 1961 that a South African prime minister had paid an official visit to Britain. The AAM saw the visit as 'one of its most important challenges'.[36] Its executive launched a campaign entitled 'No to Botha! No to Apartheid!' and, with the support of a large mobilizing committee, decided to hold a march in central London on 2 June, the day that Botha was scheduled to meet with Thatcher, though that meeting eventually took place at the country retreat of Chequers rather than Downing Street because of security concerns. The preparations and energy devoted to the march were considerable. Eight hundred and fifty thousand leaflets, as well as thousands more badges and stickers, were distributed promoting the campaign and march, and more than 15,000 posters were put up. The march received sponsorship from the Labour and Liberal parties and the trade union movement, and political support from across the political spectrum, even including a lone Conservative body, the Conservative Council in Brent. Television coverage of Botha's visit and the preparations for the march were also considerable. The week before, organizers of the march had told television reporters that 'people will want to be together to express their anger', nonetheless maintaining that there would be no violence.[37]

---

[35] Memorandum to the Prime Minister, 30 May 1984, AAM Archives, MSS AAM 818.
[36] *Annual Report of Activities and Developments October 1983–September 1984* (London: AAM, 1984), 3, AAM Archives.
[37] ITN News, 30 May 1984.

In 1984, there was clear evidence of the growing connection between anti-racist politics in London and among Black organizations and the anti-apartheid movement. As Elizabeth Williams has shown, Black organizations reacted strongly to the invitation to Botha. She quotes one Black activist as saying: '[b]y 1984 people felt strong and they had enough young black kids born in this country who knew no other country who felt "this is my home, and I'm going to fight for it!" They could go on the streets which we could not have done in the 1960s, plus the [1980s] urban disturbances had emboldened people.'[38] In a press release, the West Indian Standing Committee emphasized the connections between the treatment of Black people in Britain and that meted out to Blacks in South Africa:

> Black people fought in the last war, under the British flag, when Great Britain fought to destroy racism in the form of Nazism which was based upon the concept of the so-called superior race. Apartheid South Africa is similar in its practical intention of degradation of man. It delimits black fellow human beings who are capable of unlimited achievement, to the role of sub-animal status without rights in their inherent country. Therefore, Great Britain *must destroy* it and not accommodate it. Britain must practise what it preaches or it shall lose its customary position of credibility.[39]

The Thatcher government's invitation was seen as 'an illustration of their contempt for black people.'[40] In this way the anti-apartheid struggle became a means not only of expressing 'solidarity with the struggle of our brothers and sisters' but also of articulating the position of Black people in Britain.[41]

In the weeks leading up to the march, a variety of groups made public protests and demonstrations across London. They included demonstrations outside the embassies of Switzerland, Portugal, and West Germany

---

[38] Dame Jocelyn Barrow, quoted in Williams, 'Anti-Apartheid: The Black British Response', 699.
[39] Quoted in Williams, 'Anti-Apartheid: The Black British Response', 700.
[40] Quoted in Williams, 'Anti-Apartheid: The Black British Response', 700.
[41] Quoted in Williams, 'Anti-Apartheid: The Black British Response', 700.

and vigils outside Downing Street. A day before the march, for example, women wearing the black sash, a symbol of resistance to apartheid, marched outside the Prime Minister's residence. These preludes to the march demonstrated the breadth of the support for the anti-apartheid cause. South Africa House in Trafalgar Square was one focus of these efforts, with the City Anti-Apartheid Group mounting a 'non-stop picket' of the building, Kent miners dumping a sack of South African coal there, and Christians Against Racism holding a vigil at nearby St Martin-in-the-Fields. The GLC pledged material support to the march. It planned to sponsor a festival on the South Bank following the march, it put up a huge anti-apartheid banner at County Hall, and as the time of the march approached held a press conference featuring Livingstone, Boateng, and Trevor Huddleston.

But the campaign was not only on the streets: this moment connected different spaces of power. On 30 May 1984, for the first time, a British Prime Minister received a delegation from the AAM. Trevor Huddleston and Abdul Minty made clear the importance of the moment and the danger that the visit might represented to the 'future of British policy towards Southern Africa', with respect to the end of apartheid, attacks upon 'front-line' states such as Angola and Mozambique, and the arms embargo, warning that 'the present tour of P. W. Botha is intended to rehabilitate the apartheid system rather than destroy it'.[42]

On Saturday, 2 June, the march began at Hyde Park, moving down Piccadilly under the black, yellow, and green banner of the African National Congress and thousands of placards reading 'No to Botha', 'Mandela', and 'South Africa—Time to Act'. As already described, the march stopped in Trafalgar Square, where there were a few confrontations with the police. It ended up in Jubilee Gardens, where, into the early summer evening, music and speeches entertained a large crowd.

London's involvement with the anti-apartheid cause in 1984, as symbolized by the anti-apartheid march on 2 June, illustrated several important issues. In the first place, it underlined the importance of the city as a space of political spectacle, particularly for progressive or radical causes. In 1984, the streets of central London were a space for the

---

[42] Memorandum to the Prime Minister, 30 May 1984, AAM Archives, MSS AAM 818.

articulation of protest, as those streets had been for centuries, whether in the 1880s over unemployment or in 1968 over the Vietnam War—or would be later in 1990 over the poll tax. The June 1984 march also saw a different kind of progressive protest, linked with cultural politics as well. It is significant that, like the protests on the Thames and the unemployed campaign, the anti-apartheid march ended with music. With 'Free Nelson Mandela', it also had an anthem. Six years later, the birthday concert for Nelson Mandela was an expanded version of this, a hybrid moment of political spectacle and modern pop culture and celebrity.

What the anti-apartheid march also demonstrated was the winding together of the local and the global in 1980s London. The anti-apartheid march was, of course, concerned with a global issue. But it was, in the first place, also grounded in a framework of political campaigning within London. Of course, this included the AAM. But it also increasingly drew upon local Black organizations, which integrated the anti-apartheid cause with their own efforts to fight racism and to nurture Black culture in 1980s London. And, as suggested throughout, the anti-apartheid issue was one that found a place within local government politics, whether this was the GLC or local boroughs. In this way, local community organization and activism and local government were not only local; they had a global component.

London, 1984: Conflict and Change in the Radical City. Stephen Brooke, Oxford University Press.
© Stephen Brooke 2024. DOI: 10.1093/9780191895395.003.0008

8

Lincoln Estate

On 18 September 1984, members of the GLC Women's Committee, its Housing Committee, and the head of its Race and Housing Action Team met with a group of Bangladeshi tenants of the Lincoln Estate, Tower Hamlets. There had been alarming reports the previous July of the daily harassment suffered by ethnic minority tenants on the estate. These included attacks

> on children...spitting; jostling; name-calling...lighted fireworks [and] lighted matches...being put through the letter box....Two tenants have been fired at by air guns....The Bangladeshis...claimed that racial harassment had become an integral part of their everyday life on Lincoln [estate]. Women live like prisoners. They do not dare to go out....Children are often not allowed to play outdoors unless in very large groups outside the flats because of the risk of abuse and attacks. Bangladeshi men often do their shopping in groups and come back in a taxi.[1]

The point of the harassment, perpetrated by youths, men, and women, was to 'drive the Bangladeshis off the estate'.[2] The meeting in September had to be held in the home of one of the ethnic minority families because 'the women were afraid to go to any public building'. The tenants complained of isolation because of the racial harassment and the 'agony of seeing their children attacked and abused and being unable to protect them'. But the September 1984 meeting itself became a horrific demonstration of the intensity of racial enmity on the estate:

[1] GLC, Ethnic Minorities Committee and Head of Housing Services, 'Racial Harassment on Lincoln Estate', 18 July 1984, LMA, GLC/DG/PRE/49/31.
[2] GLC, Ethnic Minorities Committee and Head of Housing Services, 'Racial Harassment on Lincoln Estate', 18 July 1984, LMA, GLC/DG/PRE/49/31.

> White women tenants abused Bangladeshis and officers in the landing…
> As the head of the Race and Housing Team, who was wearing a sari,
> was standing at street level, a van swerved towards her forcing her to
> leap to safety and the driver yelled abuse at the group.[3]

What happened on the Lincoln Estate in September 1984 was not exceptional in 1980s London. In the previous year, there had been 245
reported cases of racial harassment of tenants over 42 GLC estates, most
of which were in Tower Hamlets. Ninety-seven per cent of the victims
were Bangladeshi. A report by the GLC's Housing Committee, again in
September 1984, reviewing the estates in Tower Hamlets under GLC
control, set out what was termed '[a]n appalling chronicle of racist
intimidation'. The racial divide was stark. Among ethnic minority tenants, most of whom were of Bangladeshi origin, there was 'real fear',
while '[m]any white men and women tenants of the GLC were overtly
hostile' to Bangladeshi tenants.[4] A report from the previous year characterized the situation on East London estates as one of 'unalloyed race
hatred'.[5]

Unsurprisingly, the GLC was deeply concerned about such racial harassment. The GLC was not only committed to anti-racism but was also a
major provider of housing in the capital, with 30,000 council properties,
many of them on estates in Tower Hamlets and Thamesmead. In this
role, the GLC was implicated in the problem of racial harassment as a
landlord. The problem of racial harassment sparked concern at other
levels of government in the 1980s.[6] In 1986, the parliamentary Home
Affairs Committee's report on 'Racial Attacks and Harassment' called
the problem the 'most shameful and dispiriting aspect of race relations
in Britain'.[7] The Home Office and the Metropolitan Police also published

---

[3] GLC, Ethnic Minorities Committee and Housing Committee, 'Racial Harassment on GLC
Estates in Tower Hamlets – Emerging Patterns (Nov. 1983–Aug. 1984)', 20 September 1984,
LMA/GLC/DG/PRE/49/34.
[4] GLC, Ethnic Minorities Committee and Housing Committee, 'Racial Harassment on GLC
Estates in Tower Hamlets – Emerging Patterns (Nov. 1983–Aug. 1984)', 20 September 1984,
LMA/GLC/DG/PRE/49/34.
[5] GLC, Police Committee, Report by the Panel of Inquiry into Racial Harassment,
29 September 1983, LMA, GLC/DG/PRE/49/17.
[6] See Benjamin Bowling, *Violent Racism* (Oxford: Oxford University Press, 1998).
[7] Home Affairs Committee, *Racial Attacks and Harassment* (London: HMSO, 1986), iv.

reports. The Met told the Home Affairs Committee in 1985 that there had been 1,877 racial 'incidents', with particular problems in Tower Hamlets and Newham—495 incidents in Tower Hamlets alone.[8] Racial 'incidents' described a variety of encounters motivated by racial difference, including verbal abuse, property damage, theft, and physical violence. At this point, the concept of a 'hate crime' did not have legal meaning, only acquiring it in 1998 with the Crime and Disorder Act, which introduced 'racial and religious aggravation' into crimes against the person and property.

Reflecting on the 1993 Stephen Lawrence murder, Stuart Hall wrote of the 'repetitive persistence' of racist violence in late twentieth-century Britain paralleling the growth of a multiracial and multicultural society.[9] Racial violence was a dark current running through 1980s London, flowing from a broader history of such violence in post-war Britain. This tenebrous landscape included everyday harassment and abuse, riots such as in Notting Hill in 1958 and Brixton in 1981, and racially motivated murders, from Kelso Cochrane in 1959 to Stephen Lawrence in 1993. The 1980s were a particularly grim period. Everyday violence and harassment also 'intensified' in the 1980s according to official statistics.[10] It was a particularly bad period for Asian people. At the end of the decade, the Home Affairs Committee remarked that 'the vulnerability of the Asian community had worsened between 1981 and 1987'.[11] The reflexive, spontaneous violence appalled the writer of one Home Office report on attacks on Asians and West Indians: '[i]n such incidents strangers may simply approach others and hit them, kick them, throw stones at them or even use knives and bottles to assault them'.[12] Perhaps most disturbing was the horrific spike in racially motivated killings in the early 1980s. In 1976, there were five reported such murders. In 1981,

[8] Home Affairs Committee, *Racial Attacks and Harassment* (London: HMSO, 1986), iv.

[9] Stuart Hall, 'From Scarman to Stephen Lawrence', *History Workshop Journal* 48 (1999): 188, doi: 10.1093/hwj/1999.48.187.

[10] See *Annual Report of the Commission for Racial Equality 1980* (London: HMSO, 1981); *Annual Report of the Commission for Racial Equality 1981* (London: HMSO, 1982).

[11] Home Affairs Committee, *Racial Attacks and Harassment* (London: HMSO, 1989), vi.

[12] Roy Walmsley, *Personal Violence: Home Office Research Study 89* (London: HMSO, 1986), 26.

twenty-six were reported, during what the anti-fascist journal *Searchlight* called 'the year of racist terror on Britain's streets'.[13]

Famously, Joseph Conrad's *Heart of Darkness,* written at the end of the nineteenth century, begins its tale of colonial madness and brutality on the Thames. London, as the narrator, Marlowe, says, was one of the 'dark places of the earth', a place bound in violence with the far-flung empire.[14] As London neared another fin de siècle, what happened on the Lincoln Estate in 1984 is another story of darkness, but one that illuminates the working out of the end of empire, where racial difference and animosity were experienced not at the periphery, but in the heart of the metropole. This existed within a culture of fear and hatred, which shaped lives, spaces, and politics in London at the end of the twentieth century.

The Lincoln Estate was built over two decades, beginning in the 1960s. It lay north of the Docklands, between Tower Hamlets Cemetery Park, Limehouse Cut, and the River Lea. The estate was a mixture of low-rise and tower blocks, with about 1,200 dwellings rehousing East End families. In 1984, the GLC Housing Management committee noted that this included 'a number of "notorious East London criminal families"'.[15] The estate was largely white, though there were a few families of Afro-Caribbean, Turkish, Maltese, Chinese, and Vietnamese origin. In the late 1970s, Bangladeshi families began to move into the estate, thanks to a Homeless Families programme.

By the mid-1980s, there were over 17,000 Bangladeshis in inner London, 12,600 of whom were in Tower Hamlets.[16] This represented, in areas such as Spitalfields, a dominant part of the local population. In 1981, for example, of the population of Spitalfields, 44 per cent were Bengali in origin. A significant fall in population since the end of the

[13] 'Racial Attacks Not Policing Problem: Review of Home Office Report', *Searchlight,* January 1982.

[14] Joseph Conrad, *Heart of Darkness and Other Tales* (Oxford: Oxford University Press, 1899, 1990), 138.

[15] GLC, Ethnic Minorities Committee Report by the Head of Housing Services, Housing Management, Tower Hamlets Sub-Committee, 'Racial Harassment on Lincoln Estate', 8 July 1984, LMA, GLC/DG/PRE/49/51.

[16] S. E. Curtis and P. E. Ogden, 'Bangladeshis in London: A challenge to welfare', *Revue Européenne des Migrations Internationales* 2 (1986): 138; see also Anne Kershen, *Strangers, Aliens and Asians* (London: Routledge, 2005).

Second World War underscored the change in ethnic composition. Most of the Bangladeshis in Tower Hamlets originated from the rural Sylhet region of east Bengal and most came in the 1960s and 1970s.[17] Once in London, they joined the pool of semi-skilled or unskilled labour in the textile industry. They were among the most disadvantaged sections of the population. A 1986 parliamentary report remarked that the migrants 'tend to occupy the worst and most overcrowded housing, their recorded unemployment rate is exceptionally high...the language barrier and cultural factors restrict their access to health and social services, and they appear to be disproportionately affected by racial violence.'[18]

Housing was a particular problem. In the 1970s, Bangladeshi migrants were dependent upon often poor private housing (which one study called 'housing of the lowest standard') or became involved in the squatting movement in Spitalfields.[19] In 1985, 90 per cent of those classified as homeless were Bangladeshi.[20] The Bengali Housing Action Group was formed as a response to this problem. In 1977, the Housing (Homeless Persons) Act prioritized the needs of homeless people for council housing, and this meant, particularly in Tower Hamlets, that Bangladeshi people began to get such housing. This was against the background of already high existing demand for council housing; in 1985, the waiting list for such housing in Tower Hamlets stood at 9,000.[21]

Bangladeshi people experienced the sharp edge of racism in Tower Hamlets. The racially motivated murders of Altab Ali and Ishaq Ali in 1978 focused attention on the community as victims of racial violence. Both the Commission for Racial Equality and the Bethnal Green and Stepney Trades Council issued major reports on racial violence and harassment in the late seventies.[22] This coincided with mobilization against racism within the Bangladeshi community, particularly among a

[17] See Glynn, *Class, Ethnicity and Religion in the Bengali East End*, ch. 1.
[18] Home Affairs Committee, *The Bangladeshis in Britain: Volume I* (London: HMSO, 1986), iv.
[19] Curtis and Ogden, 'Bangladeshis in London', 145; on squatting, see Glynn, *Class, Ethnicity and Religion in the Bengali East End*, 121.
[20] Home Affairs Committee, *The Bangladeshis in Britain*, ix.
[21] Home Affairs Committee, *The Bangladeshis in Britain*, viii.
[22] CRE, *Brick Lane and Beyond* (London: CRE, 1979); Bethnal Green and Stepney Trades Council, *Blood on the Streets* (London: Bethnal Green and Stepney Trades Council, 1978).

younger generation, in groups such as the Bangladesh Youth Movement (BYM).[23] The Bengali Housing Action Group sought to protect Bangladeshi families from racial harassment by arguing (against the opposition of groups like the BYM) that Bangladeshi estate tenants be allocated to 'safe areas', meaning estates with established Bangladeshi communities.[24]

The Lincoln Estate was not such an estate. By 1984, there were only about twenty-five Bangladeshi families on the Lincoln Estate, mostly clustered in one area around the Knapp Road in the north-east part of the estate, with a few more 'isolated' in the Belton Way area to the south.[25] The GLC viewed the estate, even before the Bangladeshi families moved in, as 'rough', with a 'reputation for violence':

> The crimes committed by tenants on the estate include murder, violent physical assault, arson attack, armed robbery involving some tenants and local youths, tenants threatening other tenants with an axe, attacks with shotguns, baseball bats, and an electric carving knife...[26]

The north-eastern part of the estate was particularly 'notorious for criminal activities'.[27] The GLC referred to the 'Hobbesian state of nature prevailing on the Estate', where 'aggression', the GLC Estate Officer noted, was 'a way of life'.[28]

All of this made it surprising to some GLC officers that 'vulnerable people like Asian homeless people were introduced' to the estate. The Bangladeshis became the object of abuse by tenants on the estate. Youths

---

[23] See Ali Riaz, *Islam and Identity Politics Among British Bangladeshis* (Manchester: Manchester University Press, 2013), 92–5.

[24] Glynn, *Class, Ethnicity and Religion in the Bengali East End*, 123.

[25] GLC, Ethnic Minorities Committee, Report by the Head of Housing Services, Housing Management (Tower Hamlets), Sub-Committee, 'Racial Harassment on Lincoln Estate', 8 July 1984, LMA, GLC/DG/PRE/49/51.

[26] GLC, Ethnic Minorities Committee, Report by the Head of Housing Services, Housing Management (Tower Hamlets) Sub-Committee, 'Racial Harassment on Lincoln Estate', 8 July 1984, LMA, GLC/DG/PRE/49/51.

[27] GLC, Ethnic Minorities Committee, Report by the Head of Housing Services, Housing Management (Tower Hamlets) Sub-Committee, 'Racial Harassment on Lincoln Estate', 8 July 1984, LMA, GLC/DG/PRE/49/51.

[28] Quoted in GLC, Ethnic Minorities Committee Report by Peter Dawe, Chair, Race and Housing Advisory Group, 'Lincoln Estate Racial Attacks', 9 July 1984, LMA, GLC/DG/PRE/108/02.

from outside the estate were also involved. The isolation of the
Bangladeshi families compounded the problem. There was no halal
butcher on the estate, and the nearest mosque was a fifteen-minute walk
and bus ride away, a journey that was 'risky and dangerous'. They were
similarly cut off from a larger Bangladeshi community by a 'dangerous'
walk through the Devons Road.[29]

By 1984, the GLC acknowledged that 'racial harassment has become
an everyday affair' on the Lincoln Estate.[30] That year, a group of
Bangladeshi tenants petitioned the GLC's Race and Housing Advisory
Group concerning the 'level of racial attacks they were facing'. They said
their families were 'subjected to a barrage of racial attacks' on a daily
basis and were 'living in a state of siege'.[31] The nature of the attacks
visited upon the Bangladeshi families has already been noted at the
beginning of this chapter, but it is worth detailing other examples of the
pervasive violence:

The Bangladeshis…claimed that racial harassment had become an
integral part of their everyday life on Lincoln…white women also
harass Bangladeshi men and women by verbally abusing them, by trying
to spit on them or at them and on one occasion a white woman, having
failed to spit at a Bengali man, allegedly openly encouraged her son to
attack his two and a half-year-old daughter. One of the Bangladeshi
tenants was allegedly threatened by a white youth with a knife. In
addition, some white people in cars and on motorcycles have been
reported as driving forward at tremendous speed to run over black
people when they are in public areas in front of their blocks of flats.[32]

<hr/>

[29] GLC, Ethnic Minorities Committee, Report by the Head of Housing Services, Housing
Management (Tower Hamlets) Sub-Committee, 'Racial Harassment on Lincoln Estate', 8 July
1984, LMA, GLC/DG/PRE/108/02.
[30] GLC, Ethnic Minorities Committee, Report by the Head of Housing Services, Housing
Management (Tower Hamlets) Sub-Committee, 'Racial Harassment on Lincoln Estate', 8 July
1984, LMA, GLC/DG/PRE/108/02.
[31] GLC, Ethnic Minorities Committee Report by Peter Dawe, Chair, Race and Housing
Advisory Group, 'Lincoln Estate Racial Attacks', 9 July 1984, LMA, GLC/DG/PRE/108/02.
[32] GLC, Ethnic Minorities Committee, Report by the Head of Housing Services, Housing
Management (Tower Hamlets) Sub-Committee, 'Racial Harassment on Lincoln Estate', 8 July
1984, LMA, GLC/DG/PRE/108/02.

In the light of such incidents, a Race and Housing Action Team (RHAT) met with the Lincoln Estate Tenants Association in March 1984 to discuss racial harassment on the estate. The result was mixed. Though the majority of the tenants' association members were 'aware and sympathetic' and 'offered their support', 'some members voiced strong opposition to the Asian families being there in the first place and stated that if they saw incidents of harassment, they certainly would do nothing to stop it'.[33] Two months later, a group of members from RHAT, the District Office, the police, the tenants' association, and other community groups met again with Bangladeshi people from the estate.

The police completely failed to deal with incidents of racial harassment on the estate. During the May 1984 meeting, the police assured the Bangladeshi people that they would take forward their complaints, but that they could not prosecute those committing racial harassment without evidence or identification. But the police did not seem committed to pursuing such prosecutions, nor did they seem to take the situation seriously. It was suggested, for example, that the police took twenty to thirty minutes to respond to emergency calls, that they tended to believe 'the alleged white perpetrators', and that they were not willing to even give a 'stern warning' to alleged perpetrators.[34] In July 1984, for example, there was a disturbing incident at the meeting:

A white woman tenant who was present at the meeting declared that if the Bangladeshis could be collected together, she would put a petrol bomb on the Bangladeshis. None of the police reacted to this statement. When asked after the meeting what action the police would take against such people, the Senior police officer laughed the matter off and said the woman had not dropped the bomb after all. Action would be taken after she had done so.[35]

[33] GLC, Ethnic Minorities Committee, Report by the Head of Housing Services, Housing Management (Tower Hamlets) Sub-Committee, 'Racial Harassment on Lincoln Estate', 8 July 1984, LMA, GLC/DG/PRE/108/02.
[34] GLC, Ethnic Minorities Committee, Report by the Head of Housing Services, Housing Management (Tower Hamlets) Sub-Committee, 'Racial Harassment on Lincoln Estate', 8 July 1984, LMA, GLC/DG/PRE/108/02.
[35] GLC, Ethnic Minorities Committee, Report by the Head of Housing Services, Housing Management (Tower Hamlets) Sub-Committee, 'Racial Harassment on Lincoln Estate', 8 July 1984, LMA, GLC/DG/PRE/108/02.

Convincing the police that racial harassment was a crime that had to be taken seriously was the most urgent task in solving the problem of racial harassment. But there were also questions about what to do for both the victims and perpetrators, as tenants, of the GLC. The victims of racial violence wanted to be moved out to estates 'where the Bengali community is already established'.[36] This was a solution, but some worried that if this was the first resort, there would be little chance of 'building a multiracial community on the estate'.[37] For tenants who were found to be perpetrators of racial harassment, the GLC felt that threatening eviction would be appropriate and, in the future, that tenancy agreements had to include a clause that made racial harassment a cause for eviction. The GLC also sought to make life on the estate more hospitable for Bangladeshi people by funding the opening of halal butchers and a mosque, as well as establishing mother tongue and English classes.

Across London, there were stories of racial violence like those on the Lincoln Estate. On another Tower Hamlets estate, for example, 'vicious looking dogs' were set on people; '[s]tones steeped in dogs' excreta are thrown at them; children are beaten up; at times, air guns are fired at the Bangladeshis; windows are broken[;] doors are kicked in at any hour of the day or night'.[38] It was often suggested that white youths were the main protagonists of this violence and abuse, but the hostility towards ethnic minority tenants moved across generational and gender divides. Parents were 'motivating their children to abuse and harass Bengalis' or getting 'dogs to attack young children playing outside'.[39] As the episodes already related suggest, older people and women were also involved. On the Mountmorres Estate in 1984, it was reported that 'the Estate Officer and prospective Bangladeshi tenants were met by what cannot be

[36] GLC, Ethnic Minorities Committee, Report by the Head of Housing Services, Housing Management (Tower Hamlets) Sub-Committee, 'Racial Harassment on Lincoln Estate', 8 July 1984, LMA, GLC/DG/PRE/108/02.

[37] GLC, Ethnic Minorities Committee, Report by the Head of Housing Services, Housing Management (Tower Hamlets) Sub-Committee, 'Racial Harassment on Lincoln Estate', 8 July 1984, LMA, GLC/DG/PRE/108/02.

[38] GLC, Ethnic Minorities Committee and Housing Committee, 'Racial Harassment on GLC Estates in Tower Hamlets – Emerging Patterns (Nov. 1983–Aug. 1984)', 20 September 1984, LMA/GLC/DG/PRE/49/34.

[39] GLC, Ethnic Minorities Committee and Housing Committee, 'Racial Harassment on GLC Estates in Tower Hamlets – Emerging Patterns (Nov. 1983–Aug. 1984)', 20 September 1984, LMA/GLC/DG/PRE/49/34.

termed as anything other than a "mob" of women shouting abuse. When the family were actually viewing the inside, these women chanted such things as "pigs"; "curry eaters"; and "black bastards".'[40]

Individual accounts evoked the exhaustion of living with racial harassment on a daily basis. A teenage girl from West Ham, Nasreem Saddique, wrote of her family huddled for safety in one room, night after night:

> There was a violent knock at the front door and an enormous crash against the boarded-up window. Voices echoed through the letterbox: 'Fucking Pakis'. I was upstairs peering through the bedroom curtain, lights out, hoping it wouldn't be like the previous night, hoping they would disappear into the darkness and leave me and my parents alone. Experience told me that it was unlikely. This had been happening every night for weeks. There seemed to be no end to it all.[41]

Saddique's journal had the unrelenting quality of a wartime diary: '26 January, "Trouble. Got no sleep"; 27 January, "Trouble. Got no sleep".'[42] Chronic, everyday harassment could explode into moments of appalling violence, as a report from Southwark in 1983 suggested: 'People on the estate attacked the family over a long period until it culminated in a serious incident when a young Asian baby was attacked by having hot water poured over its body.'[43] Homes were also continually vandalized, as shown in Figure 8.1.

Another individual story set out the horrific physical and emotional toll of harassment and violence. It was told by a father who was out shopping with his two daughters, aged 4 and 2:

> Three men came up behind me and threw tins of either Pepsi or beer, which hit me on my back...They came towards me and started

---

[40] GLC, Ethnic Minorities Committee, Report by the Head of Housing Services, 'Unlawful Intimidation of Ethnic Minority Families', 20 October 1984, LMA, GLC/DG/PRE/49/37.

[41] Quoted in Keith Tompson, *Under Siege: Racial Violence in Britain Today* (Harmondsworth: Penguin, 1988), 2.

[42] Quoted in Tompson, *Under Siege*, 4.

[43] GLC, Police Committee, Southwark Black Workers Group: Southwark Monitoring Project Annual Report 1982/3, LMA, GLC/DG/ISG/PC/2/2/22.

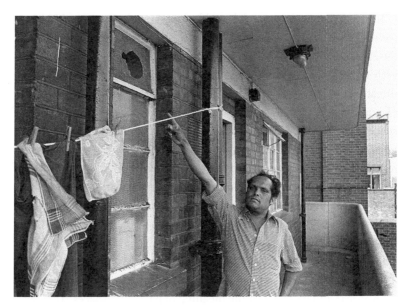

Figure 8.1 Racist vandalism on an East End estate.
Credit: Andrew Scott.

threatening me...I became frightened...They each picked up large pieces of wood and started hitting me with them. They hit me so violently that I fell to the ground and became unconscious. Many people witnessed the attack, but no one came forward to help. My two small daughters watched helplessly and cried with shock.

The victim later received death threats from the fathers of his attackers and became 'too afraid to go outside at all'.[44] For that man, racial harassment was written on the body through injury and upon the psyche through fear. A similar fear shaped the everyday life of most ethnic minority people. In 1986, a spokesperson for the Bangladeshi community told a parliamentary committee: '[m]uch has been made of "Terrorism" but Bangladeshis daily suffer from acts of terrorism'.[45]

---

[44] GLC, Police Committee, Report by the Panel of Enquiry into Racial Harassment, 29 September 1983, LMA, GLC/DG/ISG/PC/2/2/22.
[45] Home Affairs Committee, *The Bangladeshis in Britain: Volume II* (London: HMSO, 1986), 32.

Reconstructing the material world of the Lincoln Estate in 1984 is to reconstruct a dark emotional world. Indeed, the social, the physical, and the emotional were wound together in the experience of racism. To live with the experience of racial harassment and violence or under their threat was to live with fear and the effects of hatred. Fear became a way of understanding the physical world, a way in which the meaning of space was changed. Ethnic minority people in London in the 1980s had to navigate a material environment that had been organized through fear. This could be compared to the effects on women in urban spaces of the Yorkshire Ripper murders, on gay people by incidents of gay-bashing or hate crime in the city, or on communities on both sides of the sectarian divide in Northern Ireland.[46] One witness to the 1985 Home Affairs Committee relayed the toll of such spatialized fear succinctly: 'the daily walk to and from work and school becomes a never-ending nightmare.'[47] The material environment and emotion were thus intertwined. Emotions such as fear and hatred shift the meaning of particular spaces. The meeting in September 1984 was, for example, about specific private and public spaces—the home, the shared space of an estate, the landing, and the street—and intense encounters within those spaces—the verbal abuse shouted at both tenants and GLC representative, the physical intimidation of the van driver, the intensity of the fear that prevented the ethnic minority tenants from wishing to leave their homes. In 1984, the street, the stairwell, and the home were where racial politics were made and lived on a daily basis. A point of racial violence was to imbue those spaces with fear, through potential harm and humiliation. The compressed nature of some of these spaces intensified such fear. Little room was left, literally, to avoid racism. At the same time, ethnic minority communities were made in these spaces, not just by ethnicity, but by the shared experience of fear and harassment, by being objects of hatred.

[46] See Judith Walkowitz, *City of Dreadful Delight* (Chicago: University of Chicago Press, 1992); Leslie Moran and Beverley Skeggs, with Paul Tyrer and Karen Corteen, *Sexuality and the Politics of Violence and Safety* (London: Routledge, 2004); Karen Lysaght and Anne Basten, 'Violence, Fear and "the Everyday": Negotiating Spatial Practice in the City of Belfast', in Elizabeth A. Stanko (ed.), *The Meanings of Violence* (London: Routledge, 2003).

[47] Quoted in Home Affairs Committee, *Racial Attacks and Harassment* (1986), vi.

And if fear was one dominant aspect of the emotional ecology shaping places like the Lincoln Estate in 1984, hatred was the other. Looking into racial intimidation in 1984, the GLC's Housing Services committee spoke of 'unalloyed racial hatred' as driving racial harassment.[48] Understanding racial animosity on the Lincoln Estate in 1984 involves making some sense of both fear and hatred. This means understanding the views of white, working-class tenants that lay behind racial harassment and violence. Not all white working-class people on estates engaged in racial harassment, of course. Nor were they all racist. There were many white tenants who were appalled by the violence or were seen as potential allies in the construction of better relations between the races. Within the East End, for example, an organization such as the Tower Hamlets Federation of Tenants Associations—a group dominated by white tenants—sought to find ways to combat racism.[49]

But even with those qualifications, violence was disproportionately suffered by non-white people and was disproportionately perpetrated by white people. Racial animosity—hatred—moved white tenants to action, including violence. Such animosity seems to have been a unifying factor within the working class, bridging generational and gendered divides. David Ost has written of the 'exclusive solidarities' produced by anger in Polish politics in the 1980s; we can see the same solidarity built out of racial enmity in 1980s London.[50] In this racial ecosystem, hatred arose from white fear: of demographic and social change; of the shrinking boundaries of state provision; and of difference itself.

Racial animosity in the East End of London was not, of course, a new thing.[51] Anti-alien feeling had been strong in Edwardian London, and, between the wars, anti-Semitism fuelled British fascism. But there were particular social and economic contexts to the racial hatred of the 1980s. The decline of manufacturing jobs in London and the closure of the docks had a dramatic effect upon one kind of working-class labour

[48] GLC, Ethnic Minorities Committee, Report by the Head of Housing Services, 'Unlawful Intimidation of Ethnic Minority Families', 20 October 1984, LMA, GLC/DG/PRE/108/02.
[49] See Tower Hamlets Federation of Tenants Associations,… *Get Together and Get Things Done* (London: Tower Hamlets Federation of Tenants Associations, 1984).
[50] David Ost, *The Defeat of Solidarity* (Ithaca: Cornell University Press, 2005).
[51] See C. T. Husbands, 'East End Racism 1900–1980', *London Journal* 8/1 (1982): 3–26, doi: 10.1179/ldn.1982.8.1.3.

market, foreclosing opportunities and security, particularly for young working-class men. An air of social decline hung over working-class London in the eighties, underlined by factors such as global economic restructuring and government cuts to social services since the 1970s. Such social decline was sometimes interpreted in racial terms.[52] This produced anger: at ethnic minorities; at a political class that seemed to favour ethnic minorities over the white working class; and at the local authority that allocated housing. All could be blamed for the perceived 'death of the community'.[53]

Another factor contributing to the confusions of the late twentieth-century London might be termed 'post-imperial Britain and its discontents'. Camilla Schofield has noted the sense of anger, anxiety, loss, and nostalgia that suffused letters of support to Enoch Powell after his 'Rivers of Blood' speech in 1968, an 'expression of postwar shame and indignation' that was related through racist hatred.[54] In the 1980s, racial difference became a means of interpreting these various economic, social, and cultural changes. As Paul Gilroy has written, 'many people in Britain have actually come to need "race" and perhaps to welcome its certainties as one sure way to keep their bearings in a world they experience as increasingly confusing'.[55]

The violent manifestations of such white fear and hatred were obvious on the Lincoln Estate in 1984, on the bodies of ethnic minority people,

---

[52] Geoff Dench, Kate Gavron, and Michael Young, *The New East End: Kinship, Race and Conflict* (London: Profile Books, 2006), 4–5; see also Harold Carter, 'Building the Divided City: Race, Class and Social Housing in Southwark, 1945–95', *London Journal* 33 (2008): 155–85, doi: 10.1179/174963208X307343; Jon May, 'Globalization and the Politics of Place: Place and Identity in an Inner London Neighbourhood', *Transactions of the Institute of British Geographers* 21 (1996): 194–215, doi: 10.2307/622933; Paul Watt, 'Respectability, Roughness and "Race"', *International Journal of Urban and Regional Research* 30/4 (2006): 776–97, doi: 10.1111/j.1468-2427.2006.00688.x.

[53] Les Back, *New Ethnicities and Urban Culture* (New York: St. Martin's Press, 1996), 45, 42; see also Annie Phizacklea and Robert Miles, 'Working Class Racist Beliefs in the Inner City', in Robert Miles and Annie Phizacklea (eds.), *Racism and Political Action in Britain* (London: Routledge & Kegan Paul, 1979), 118.

[54] Camilla Schofield, *Enoch Powell and the Making of Postcolonial Britain* (Cambridge: Cambridge University Press, 2013), 8; see also Bill Schwarz, '"The only white man in there": the re-racialisation of England, 1956–68', *Race & Class* 38 (1996): 73, doi: 10.117 7/030639689603800105; see also Camilla Schofield, 'In Defence of White Freedom: Working Men's Clubs and the Politics of Sociability in Late Industrial England', *Twentieth Century British History* 38/1 (2023): 1–37, doi: 10.1093/tcbh/hwad038.

[55] Paul Gilroy, *Postcolonial Melancholia* (New York: Columbia University Press, 2005), 106.

and on the walls and doors of the estate itself. Their verbal expression came in brief, intense bursts. One occurred after the July 1984 meeting on the estate:

> … when the officers and Bangladeshis came out on to the balcony of a block of flats on Fairfoot Road, a white woman living next door came out and accused the GLC of giving unfair priority to the Bangladeshis. She also said that there was no racial harassment on Lincoln. These Bengalis, she said, wanted to go to the Spitalfields area where they had a mosque; why did the GLC put them in this estate and not in Spitalfields?[56]

After the September meeting, in addition to the 'abuse' aimed at GLC officers and Bangladeshis and the near attack on one officer, there was a similar encounter during which one white tenant told GLC officers, 'if they [the Bangladeshi tenants] are asking for harassment, they will get harassment'.[57]

From other estates in the same period there were similar examples, both verbal and physical, of white hostility to ethnic minority estate tenants. The hand of right-wing political organizations could be seen behind some of this. Tenants' associations were dominated by white residents, and there was, for example, a belief that some associations were 'a centre for National Front influence'.[58] The National Front and the Conservative Monday Club were also involved in a group called Fairplay, which demanded 'fair play for whites' in the East End.[59] 'Reception committees' made up of white tenants and white outsiders, sometimes organized by the National Front, showed up to intimidate prospective ethnic minority tenants on estates. In 1983, for example, an older Somali

<hr/>

[56] GLC, Ethnic Minorities Committee, Report by the Head of Housing Services, Housing Management (Tower Hamlets), Sub-Committee, 'Racial Harassment on Lincoln Estate', 8 July 1984, LMA, GLC/DG/PRE/108/02.

[57] GLC, Women's Committee, Housing Management Committee, Concurrent report by Director General, 18 September 1984, LMA, GLC/DG/PRE/49/36.

[58] GLC, Police Committee, Report by the Panel of Inquiry into Racial Harassment, 29 September 1983, LMA, GLC/DG/PRE/49/17.

[59] *Tenants Tackle Racism: An Account of a Series of Workshops Held in Stepney* (London: no publisher, 1985), 5.

couple being shown a flat in Solander Gardens, Wapping, were 'abused' by elderly white residents who 'lined the stairs and balcony shouting threatening and racist remarks'.[60] On another East End estate, prospective tenants were greeted with a 'well organized reception committee com- posed of women' who 'prevented the tenant from entering'. Prospective properties were vandalized and pigs' trotters—explicitly designed to offend Bangladeshi people—nailed to doors, racist graffiti daubed on the outside of flats, and potential tenants threatened with violence.[61] It was suspected that someone within the GLC housing department was tipping off white tenants when a viewing appointment was made.

White tenants expressed their opposition to ethnic minorities in other ways. They wrote to the GLC requesting that Bangladeshi people not be given housing on 'their estates'.[62] Petitions were also presented to the GLC opposing the housing of Asian families on estates; one such petition was found to be in contravention of the Race Relations Act.[63] Another from the Exmouth Estate demanded that no Asian families should be moved into the estate for fear that 'the violence would intensify'.[64]

Another fear was that the admission of any ethnic minority families to an estate would lead to an influx and 'eventually the place would be "flooded with them"'. This would make a 'slum' of any estate. And there was a sense of repulsion at the 'lifestyle' of Asians. This focused on a variety of things: the size of Asian families; the sound of the Bengali lan- guage; and Asian cooking. The last was a consistent reference point: '[t]he most common complaint was that of the smell of the cooking. Effects of such smells varied from feeling nauseous to having to take Valium to calm the nerves.'[65]

---

[60] GLC, Police Committee, Report by the Panel of Inquiry into Racial Harassment, 29 September 1983, LMA, GLC/DG/PRE/49/17.

[61] GLC, Ethnic Minorities Committee, Report by the Head of Housing Services, 'Unlawful Intimidation of Ethnic Minority Families', 20 October 1984, LMA, GLC/DG/PRE/108/02.

[62] GLC, Ethnic Minorities Committee, Housing Committee, 'Racial Harassment on GLC Estates in Tower Hamlets—Emerging Patterns (Nov. 1983–Aug. 1984)', 20 September 1984, LMA, GLC/DG/PRE/49/34.

[63] Tenants Tackle Racism, 4.

[64] GLC, Ethnic Minorities Committee, Report by the Head of Housing Services, 'Unlawful Intimidation of Ethnic Minority Families', 20 October 1984, LMA, GLC/DG/PRE/108/02.

[65] GLC, Ethnic Minorities Committee, Report by the Head of Housing Services, 'Unlawful Intimidation of Ethnic Minority Families', 20 October 1984, LMA, GLC/DG/PRE/108/02.

Similar sentiments were found in the letters pages of local newspapers. Some letters highlighted a sense of white injustice and grievance felt by what was called the 'indigenous population' of the East End, focusing, in particular, upon housing policies:

> What about the needs of people who have lived here all their lives?... I can show you hundreds of people who have been in the borough all their lives and haven't had a chance of getting accommodation suited to their needs....Local people do not get a chance when it comes to housing....If something is not done soon to give local people their rights I predict a riot.[66]

Other complaints centred on what was perceived as the degradation of estates by the presence of ethnic minority people, 'a growing army of degenerate families moving into council flats'.[67]

There was a remarkable series of workshops organized in 1984 by the Limehouse and Tower Hamlets tenants' associations. The hopeful title for published transcripts of these workshops was *Tenants Tackle Racism*, but, unfortunately, a more accurate name would have been 'Tenants Express Racism'. The workshops were dominated by white voices—at most meetings, white tenants outnumbered Asians or Afro-Caribbeans. The tenor of discussion was dominated by white fear, anger, disgust, and animosity, directed against ethnic minority people, particularly Bangladeshis. At the first meeting in June 1984, '[m]any white people [gave] vent to "anti-Bengali feelings" in a "noisy meeting".'[68] An underlying sense of white grievance and powerlessness ran through these discussions. 'We are being swamped, and losing our cultural heritage,' one tenant told a meeting, '[w]e now feel under threat as a minority group.'[69] Many denied that South Asians were the victims of racism. Rather, they argued, it was the white population of the East End that was being

---

[66] Letters from Charles F. Davidson, *East London Advertiser*, 13 July 1984; Mr Douman, Stepney, 13 July 1984; John Bradshaw, Stepney, 27 July 1984.
[67] Letters from D. M., Isle of Dogs, *East London Advertiser*, 13 July 1984; E. A. McCann, Mile End, *East London Advertiser*, 13 July 1984.
[68] *Tenants Tackle Racism*, 9.   [69] *Tenants Tackle Racism*, 15.

victimized: '[i]t's our people that are being trodden on – it's us'.[70]
Grievance focused on housing allocation, the allocation of GLC funds,
and education; of the last, for instance, someone remarked, 'in our
schools our kids are getting pushed out'.[71] And there was a sense that the
GLC and other institutions had abandoned them: '[w]e've got nobody
on our side'.[72] Resentment and fear were coloured by particular perceptions of the South Asian population. South Asians were negatively
compared to previous waves of immigrants, such as Jews and Afro-
Caribbeans, who had integrated.[73] They were also accused of being
'dirty' and unable to keep their flats in order.[74] Once again, the smell of
Asian food was complained about. Family size also attracted criticism:
'[w]e don't breed like that'.[75] This was perceived to be a degradation of
housing estates and a 'burden on the state'.[76] Resentment and fear also
revolved around misconceptions about education. One speaker said, for
instance, '[i]n the schools you can't say you want white coffee or
black... You have to say with or without milk'.[77] There was a widely held,
utterly groundless belief that children were being forced to learn Bengali
in schools; that, for example, ' "Janet and John" books are being printed
in Bengali'.[78]

Housing was a recurring subject of white resentment. In 1986, the
Home Affairs Committee wrote: '[i]t is hard to imagine anything more
damaging to racial harmony in Tower Hamlets than competition
between different communities for increasingly scarce housing'.[79] White
tenants believed that, because of initiatives to house homeless people or
multiracial policies, ethnic minority people were being given flats ahead
of white tenants. On the Lincoln Estate, for example, a woman haranguing
GLC officers talked of 'unfair priority' being given to Bangladeshi

---

[70] *Tenants Tackle Racism*, 13.   [71] *Tenants Tackle Racism*, 13.
[72] *Tenants Tackle Racism*, 16.
[73] See, for example, letters from Marsha Gordon, *East London Advertiser*, 15 June 1984, and
from R. W. Mackman, *East London Advertiser*, 29 June 1984.
[74] *Tenants Tackle Racism*, 16.   [75] *Tenants Tackle Racism*, 15.
[76] *Tenants Tackle Racism*, 14.   [77] *Tenants Tackle Racism*, 43–4.
[78] *Tenants Tackle Racism*, 13.
[79] Home Affairs Committee, *The Bangladeshis in Britain*, I, xi; see also Carter, 'Building the
Divided City', 155–85.

tenants. From the nearby Ocean Estate, one member of the white Fairplay organization wrote:

> Why is it that all the Indians get all the good houses and flats like the new houses in Columbia Road? The whole row is Indians, and what do I get offered – rubbish…I waited years and that's what you give me I want a decent flat clean not high rise.[80]

In the spring of 1984, the GLC discontinued a long-standing 'sons and daughters' policy which favoured the children of existing tenants on estates. This contributed to a sense of grievance against a shift towards prioritizing homeless families.[81] There was a belief that ethnic minority people were jumping the housing queue, as one local complained to the *East London Advertiser* in 1985: '[o]ur children are being forced to find homes outside the borough and families are splitting up as they watch a steady stream of coloured people moving into flats and houses'.[82]

Housing allocation was certainly racially biased in the 1980s, but, contrary to the perceptions of white people, it was biased towards white tenants. A survey done in 1985 by the GLC found that racial bias against ethnic minority tenants ran through the entire allocation process.[83] In the 1980s, several surveys found that white tenants were overwhelmingly favoured in the allocation of newly built flats.[84] Ethnic minority tenants were consistently given older, poorer flats. In Hackney, for example, a 1984 Commission for Racial Equality report suggested that, while 80 per cent of all new properties were given to white applicants, 75 per cent of all interwar properties were allocated to black applicants; the CRE concluded that this was 'the result of direct discrimination by

[80] Deborah Phillips, *What Price Equality? Report on the allocation of GLC housing in Tower Hamlets: Housing Research and Policy Report No. 9* (London: GLC, 1986), 44.

[81] See, for example, 'It's Till Bed Do Us Part', *East London Advertiser*, 3 August 1984.

[82] Ken Hayes, 'Housing Fury Erupts', *East London Advertiser*, 26 August 1985.

[83] D. A. Phillips, 'Race and Housing: GLC Policy and Practice in Tower Hamlets', 1985, in GLC, Ethnic Minorities Committee, Concurrent Report by Head of Housing Services, 'Race and Housing: Consultants Report on GLC Policy and Practice in Tower Hamlets', 18 March 1985, LMA, GLC/DG/PRE/49/50.

[84] See also Runnymede Trust and Radical Statistics Race Group, *Britain's Black Population* (London: Heinemann, 1980), ch. 4.

housing staff".[85] Similar patterns could be found in Tower Hamlets.[86] It was not that white tenants objected to a racial bias in housing allocation; it was that they wanted to protect the normative racial bias. This was alluded to in a 1983 Police Committee enquiry into racial harassment:

> It [housing allocation] encourages [white] tenants to feel that it is 'their right' to have exclusive access to the best housing.... It appears to them that the local authority itself is saying that race and not housing need is the criterion which gives you the key to rehousing.... The first Asian tenant on the estate then appears as an aberration of the system, and smashing their windows and firing pellets at them will be...a way of ensuring that the housing system returns to normal.[87]

The placement of ethnic minority people on housing estates was perceived as a violation of territoriality, community, and normality. Petitions, reception committees, abuse, and violence might have been seen simply as protecting normality—a normality that had been achieved through white privilege in the first place.

Sociologists of affect write of a 'passion in hate'.[88] The stories told by white Britons about Asian Britons in the 1980s East End show all the markers of such passion in hate: a deep desire for distance from a devalued and repugnant object—the Asian Briton—articulated through repulsion at the physical presence of Asian Britons, the sound of their language, and the smell of their food. That passionate hatred became a way of understanding the world of the East End in the 1980s. And such knowledge was then translated into violence, against persons and property, as the material manifestation of emotion, 'expressive' of fear, shame,

---

[85] GLC, Ethnic Minorities Committee, Report by Head of Housing Services, 'Commission for Racial Equality – Report on "Hackney Housing',' 23 January 1984; LMA, GLC/DG/PRE/108/02; see also CRE, Race and Council Housing in Hackney.

[86] GLC, Ethnic Minorities Committee, Report by Anti-Racist Year Housing Working Group, 'GLC Allocations in Tower Hamlets', 16 May 1984, LMA, GLC/DG/PRE/108/02.

[87] GLC, Police Committee, Report by the Panel of Inquiry into Racial Harassment, 29 September 1983, LMA, GLC/DG/PRE/49/17.

[88] Robert J. Sternberg and Karin Sternberg, The Nature of Hate (Cambridge: Cambridge University Press, 2008), 59–65.

disgust, and anger.[89] Richard Price has written of the 'pervasive violence that was part of the imperial encounter', a violence that was 'endemic to the quotidian life of empire'.[90] The racial harassment of the kind witnessed in the 1970s and 1980s might be seen as a post-imperial manifestation of this quotidian imperial violence. Paul Gilroy characterized the racist killing of Stephen Lawrence as a kind of 'pre-emptive strike' by white Britons against ethnic minorities.[91] The everyday racial harassment experienced in places like the Lincoln Estate in 1984 was an unceasing series of such 'pre-emptive strikes', always disciplining encounters between different kinds of Britons.

The far right in Tower Hamlets unsurprisingly fed on white hatred, fear, and resentment.[92] Perhaps more surprising is the way that such sentiments found a place within the mainstream right at the national level in the 1970s and 1980s. As already suggested, a sense of confusion and threat ran through white reaction to the growth of Black Britain in the post-war period.[93] Between the 1960s and the 1980s, there was also some validation of such feelings within mainstream British politics. Early in the 1980s. Martin Barker wrote of how the fear of migrant others became validated, often by politicians, as a 'genuine fear' worked into the idea of 'ordinary' views of the nation, or a kind of 'new common sense' about national and local community, a fear played upon by Powell's talk of 'the transformation of whole areas...into alien territory' (November 1968) and legitimated by Thatcher's later remarks in 1978 about the 'fear that [the British nation] might be swamped', which, according to Thatcher, make it understandable that 'people are going to react and be rather hostile to those coming in'.[94] 'Rather hostile' is a frighteningly accurate, if understated, description of the climate on the

---

[89] Larry Ray, David Smith, and Liz Wastell, 'Understanding Racist Violence' in Stanko (ed.), *The Meanings of Violence,* 125; see also Sara Ahmed, 'The Organization of Hate', *Law and Critique* 12/3 (2001): 345–65, doi: 10.1023/a:1013728103073.

[90] Richard Price, 'One Big Thing: Britain, Its Empire, and Their Imperial Culture', *Journal of British Studies* 45/3 (2006): 626, doi: 10.1086/503593.

[91] Paul Gilroy, *Post-Colonial Melancholia,* 101.

[92] See Christopher T. Husbands, *Racial Exclusionism and the City: The Urban Support of the National Front* (London: George Allen & Unwin, 1983), 146.

[93] See Chris Waters, '"Dark Strangers in Our Midst": Discourses of Race and Nation in Britain, 1947–63', *Journal of British Studies* 36 (1997): 216, 222, doi: 0.1086/386134.

[94] See Martin Barker, *The New Racism* (London: Junction Books, 1981), 16, 25, 39, 15.

ground in housing estates in the 1980s. This did not originate with Thatcher's governments. It was in place before 1979, but the hostile environment seems to have been intensified in the 1980s with Conservative government.

In his book *Distant Strangers* (2014), James Vernon has argued that an aspect of modernity was the emergence of a 'new society of strangers' which demanded '[i]ncreasingly abstract and bureaucratic forms' to 'address the challenges of living around, doing business with, and governing (often distant) strangers'.[95] At the local level, on 1980s housing estates, we might think that an aspect of late modern Britain was a society of proximate strangers, people alien to one another but living close together. What was missing were the social, economic, and political mechanisms to mediate that relationship. Indeed, though a parlous state of race relations in London existed before 1979, the legislation of the Conservative government, particularly seen in, for example, the 1981 Nationality Act, was perceived as restrictive by migrant communities.

Race relations in places such as the Lincoln Estate produced a particular kind of politics at the local level. The Bangladeshi community did not remain passive victims in response to the violence. As already noted, on the Lincoln Estate groups of Bangladeshi tenants went to the GLC to alert it of the situation. Some Bangladeshis also asked for transfer off the estate, something that the GLC viewed with considerable ambivalence—at once, it recognized the dire situation of ethnic minority tenants and, at the same time, worried that acceding to such transfers would mean acknowledging that there were 'no-go' estates for ethnic minority people, a point that was made specifically about the Lincoln Estate.[96]

As Sarah Glynn has pointed out, Bangladeshi people had mobilized in the 1970s in response to problems of housing and racial violence.[97] It was a younger generation that was particularly represented in

---

[95] James Vernon, *Distant Strangers* (Berkeley: University of California Press, 2014), 274.

[96] 'GLC Plans to Curb Racism', *East London Advertiser*, 10 August 1984; GLC, Ethnic Minorities Committee, Report by the Head of Housing Services, 'Unlawful Intimidation of Ethnic Minority Families', 20 October 1984, LMA, GLC/DG/PRE/108/02.

[97] See Glynn, *Class, Ethnicity and Religion in the Bengali East End*; Stephen Ashe, Satnam Virdee, and Laurence Brown, 'Striking back against racist violence in the East End of London, 1968–1970', *Race & Class* 58/1 (2016): 34–54, doi: 10.1177/0306396816642997.

organizations like the Bangladesh Youth Movement and the Bangladesh Youth League. The Institute of Race Relations' Race Today collective helped form the Bengali Housing Action Group and the Anti-Racist Committee of Asians in East London (ARC-AEL). The strategies taken up by such groups focused upon self-defence (in ARC-AEL's case, street patrols) and sometimes vigilante actions against white racists. The Pakistani Welfare Society also formed 'militant street patrols' to protect ethnic minority people in the East End.[98] In 1983, East London Workers Against Racism (ELWAR), created by the Revolutionary Communist Party, committed to patrols in Spitalfields to 'defend Asians against these attacks'.[99] But self-defence strategies could also fall foul of the police. In 1982, eight young Bangladeshi men—the 'Newham 8'—were arrested by plain-clothes police after attempting to protect Bangladeshi schoolchildren. A later campaign defended the right 'to take reasonable precautions to defend their group, particularly in situations where they would be unable to have immediate police protection'.[100] The BHAG, as we have already seen, focused on arguing for 'safe areas'; this was a controversial move, with groups like the Bangladesh Youth Movement concerned that it would create Bangladeshi ghettos.[101] Umbrella groups were also formed, such as the Tower Hamlets Association for Racial Equality (THARE), which worked with the Bangladesh Youth Movement and the Bangladeshi Welfare Association.[102]

In 1984, Nadira Hura and Kumar Nurshid wrote of the efforts of the Federation of Bangladeshi Youth Organizations and ordinary Bangladeshi people to fight back against racist attacks. In April 1984, there was an attack by twenty 'thugs' on an Asian home in Stepney Green; the police arrived late and left early, 'with the attackers...still hanging around the back of the house' and with 'white neighbours shout[ing]

[98] GLC, Police Committee, 'Racist Attacks: The Community Response', May 1985, LMA, GLC/DG/ISG/PG/2/5/48.
[99] East London Advertiser, 9 September 1983.
[100] See New Statesman, 24 September 1982; Amrit Wilson, 'Conspiracy to Assault', New Statesman, 25 February 1983; quote from GLC, Ethnic Minorities Committee, 'Newham 8 Defence Campaign', Funding Application, 22 April 1985, LMA, GLC/DG/PRE/49/50.
[101] Glynn, Class, Ethnicity and Religion in the Bengali East End, 124.
[102] GLC, Ethnic Minorities Committee, 'Tower Hamlets Association for Racial Equality', Funding Application, 22 April 1985, LMA, GLC/DG/PRE/49/50.

abuse and [spitting] at the victims', with the police saying that 'they were too busy with the Libyan Embassy siege to worry about "minor neighbourly disputes"'. A week later, another attack happened, but this time, led by a Bangladeshi woman confronting the attackers, '[t]he racists retreated'. The Federation called a meeting with the Race and Housing Action Team and then a public meeting to put pressure on the police to take action.[103]

As a landlord, the GLC viewed the problem of racial harassment with deep concern. In addition to supporting broader programmes of anti-racism (as spearheaded by the GLC through London), its Housing Committee discussed a variety of ways to solve the problem. This included intensifying sanctions against tenants who committed racial harassment or abuse, such as placing such sanctions within tenancy agreements, withdrawing tenancies from perpetrators, or allocating older properties to them. As for the victims of racial harassment, though the GLC did not want to create 'no-go' zones, it did agree that it should be up to families to decide whether they requested transfers out of afflicted estates and that such transfers be given high priority. As for other legal means to combat racial harassment, the GLC wanted the police to view the problem with greater gravity, especially not forcing the victims of racial harassment to pursue private prosecutions. If this was going to be the case, the GLC considered using its own funds to support such private prosecutions.[104] There was also some discussion of allowing ethnic minority tenants to transfer to estates with larger ethnic minority populations, such as Coventry Cross, where 17 per cent of the tenancies were held by Bangladeshi families.[105]

Fighting racial harassment against Bangladeshi people also attracted the efforts of some left-wing groups. ELWAR sought to protect and pro-mote the presence of Bangladeshi people on white estates. In so doing, it attacked the GLC for its 'divisive policies' of anti-racism which, ELWAR maintained, blamed 'white workers for the growth of racism' without

---

[103] Nadira Hura and Kumar Nurshid, 'Bangladeshis Fight Back', *East End News* 64 (June 1984).

[104] See GLC, Housing Committee Minutes, 24 July 1984, LMA, GLC/MIN/089/004.

[105] GLC, Report by Head of Housing Services, 'Race and Housing Advisory Group – Report', 17 September 1984, LMA, GLC/DG/PRE/108/02.

providing 'any of the workers in East London with the housing or the services they need'.[106] Keith Tompson, a member of ELWAR, published a powerful account of racial harassment, *Under Siege* (1988). But it is not clear how much purchase ELWAR had within the Bangladeshi community.[107] Bangladeshi community leaders looked to work within the local Labour Party in East London.[108] When the Home Affairs Committee heard evidence about the place of Bangladeshis in Britain, one local councillor, of Bangladeshi origin, made the case that this was the beginning of a major change in society and politics: 'This country is no more a white man's country; it is a multicultural and multiracial society now. This building so far has been a white man's club but next election you will see so many black faces here.'[109]

White resentment also had powerful political manifestations. In Tower Hamlets, the local Liberal Party exploited the issue.[110] In 1986, the Liberals took control of Tower Hamlets Council. The party indicated its support for the sentiments of white tenants and its antipathy to the Bangladeshi community. It argued that Bangladeshi migrants had made themselves intentionally homeless by coming to Britain. A plan was mooted to house homeless people on a 'ship moored on the Thames'.[111] A prominent local Liberal travelled to Bangladesh to announce that the borough could take no more migrants. The council cut funding to Bangladeshi organizations such as THARE and the Race and Housing Action Team.[112] It also reinstituted the 'sons and daughters' scheme; even though the actual number of people housed under this scheme was low, it disproportionately benefited white tenants. In 1990, a fake Labour pamphlet was circulated suggesting that the party would make Bangladeshis a priority. In such ways, 'the Liberals made discriminatory procedures the centre of their community politics' in Tower Hamlets.[113]

---

[106] Letter to *East London Advertiser*, 21 November 1984.
[107] Glynn, *Class, Ethnicity and Religion in the Bengali East End*, 135.
[108] Glynn, Class, Ethnicity and Religion in the Bengali East End, ch. 7.
[109] Home Affairs Committee, *The Bangladeshis in Britain: Volume II*, 26.
[110] Glynn, *Class, Ethnicity and Religion in the Bengali East End*, 157.
[111] Sarah Glynn, 'Playing the Ethnic Card: Politics and Segregation in London's East End', *Urban Studies* 47/5 (2010): 999, doi: 10.1177/0042098009353630.
[112] Patrick Curry, 'Tower Hamlets Tragedy', *New Statesman*, 11 December 1987.
[113] Glynn, 'Playing the Ethnic Card', 1000.

This helped create a particularly toxic situation in the eastern part of the borough, the Isle of Dogs, an area already challenged by the Docklands development and high unemployment. The Liberal Democrats (as they were known after 1988) campaigned there under the slogan 'Island homes for Island People' and helped establish a campaign to end 'discrimination against locals'. Tapping into the sense of white grievance was not a political strategy limited to the Liberal Democrats. In September 1993, in a local by-election, the BNP won the Millwall ward, the far-right's first electoral victory in Britain.[114]

There was, therefore, no quick resolution to the problem of racial harassment and violence. Racism in these ways found institutional form in local politics. Racial harassment and violence of the kind found on the Lincoln Estate in 1984 continued to be an ongoing issue in everyday life in London. In 1993, the murder of Stephen Lawrence led to a major examination of the problem of racist violence and policing. The Macpherson Report recommended that greater priority be given to 'racist incidents', a commitment the GLC and parliament's Home Affairs Committee had been asking of the police since 1986. In 1998, the Crime and Disorder Act made 'racially or religiously aggravated' crime a formal offence. This included not only physical assault and criminal damage to property but also the causing of 'fear or provocation of violence...intentional harassment, alarm or distress'.[115] Of course, the problem is still a prominent one. Between October 2015 and October 2016 there were 1,290 recorded religious and racist hate crimes, 206 homophobic hate crimes, 40 anti-Semitic crimes, and 84 anti-Muslim crimes in the Metropolitan Police area.[116] What happened on the Lincoln Estate was but one example of the continuing problem of fear and hatred in modern Britain.

London, 1984: Conflict and Change in the Radical City. Stephen Brooke, Oxford University Press.
© Stephen Brooke 2024. DOI: 10.1093/9780191895395.003.0009

[114] See *Observer,* 13 February 1994.
[115] Under terms of 1986 Public Order Act: http://www.legislation.gov.uk/ukpga/1998/37/part/II/crossheading/raciallyaggravated-offences-england-and-wales.
[116] http://www.met.police.uk/crimefigures/boroughs/ht_month%20-%20mps.htm.

9

Westminster and Broadwater Farm

On 16 May 1984, the House of Commons debated the third reading of the Police and Criminal Evidence bill (PACE). This established the framework for police procedure well into the twenty-first century, consolidating an untidy collection of older laws. One was 'sus'—stop under suspicion—which had been established in 1824 through the Vagrancy Act. The enactment of PACE formalized the police power to stop-and-search. Police were permitted to stop-and-search 'any person or vehicle' as long as a police officer had 'reasonable grounds for suspecting he [*sic*] will find stolen or prohibited articles.'[1] 'Reasonable grounds' were not defined. The Home Office believed not only that it was a critical 'initiative…to fight crime' but also that it would encourage 'effective policing with the consent and cooperation of society at large.'[2] In the parliamentary debate on the third reading of the Bill, Leon Brittan, the Home Secretary, insisted that '[t]he police need the power to stop-and-search for weapons if they are to respond properly to the appalling incidents of street violence which we read of daily in the newspapers', linking this, in particular, to the problems of the 'inner cities.'[3] PACE came into force in October 1984.

PACE is an overlooked legacy of the Thatcher years. It continues to structure everyday policing in Britain, particularly in terms of the power to stop-and-search. But stop-and-search, whether in the form of sus or under the terms of PACE, has also structured the relationship between the Metropolitan Police and the Black community, and it is an understatement to say that that relationship has been toxic. In July 2023,

---

[1] *United Kingdom Public General Acts*, C. 60, Police and Criminal Evidence Act 1984, Part 1, Sections 1.2, 1.3.

[2] Quoted in Robert Reiner, 'PACE: Review Essay', *British Journal of Criminology* 26/3 (1986): 300, doi: 10.1093/oxfordjournals.bjc.a047613.

[3] *Parliamentary Debates* (Commons), Volume 60, 16 May 1984, col. 381.

for example, the Home Secretary announced her support for increasing the use of stop-and-search, which, as both the government and the Metropolitan Police acknowledge, is used disproportionately against Black people, who are seven times more likely to be stopped and searched by the Met.[4] In some respects, PACE is one of the important and problematic legacies of 1984.

A few months before the enactment of PACE and a world of power away from Westminster, the GLC's Ethnic Minorities Committee considered an application from the Broadwater Farm Youth Association (BFYA). Broadwater Farm was a housing estate in Tottenham, built in the 1960s and 1970s. By the 1970s, the estate was caught in a 'spiral of deterioration', and it was heavily policed, using 'hard policing' such as sus.[5] Young Black people on the estate felt the sharp edge of sus on a daily basis. In 1983, a spate of burglaries led to the white-dominated tenants' association to propose the establishment of a mini police station on the estate. This alarmed many Black residents. Fearing that an embedded police presence on the estate would simply make an already bad situation for young Black people worse, Dolly Kiffin, a dressmaker and mother, called a meeting in her front room.[6] The result was the BFYA, which recognized that one of the critical issues shaping the lives of Black youth on Broadwater Farm estate was the 'racist and sexist attitude towards them by many in the community and the police in particular'. A particular point of resentment was how young people were subject to stop-and-search. The BFYA sought to provide cultural, leisure, and training opportunities for 'disillusioned and alienated' youth on the estate. It had already established a day-care centre, workshops on sewing and photography, and a weekday meal service for the elderly. The BFYA asked for £24,000 for four full-time workers and one part-time worker. The Ethnic Minorities Committee called it an 'an oasis of hope in an otherwise depressing environment'.[7] The BFYA association was also a

[4] *Guardian*, 19 June 2023.

[5] Lord Gifford, *The Broadwater Farm Enquiry: An Independent Enquiry into the Disturbances of October 1985 at the Broadwater Farm Estate Tottenham* (London: Broadwater Farm Enquiry, 1986) [hereafter *Gifford Report*], para. 2.18.

[6] *Gifford Report*, 2.33; see also Les Levidow, 'Broadwater Farm: a "criminal estate"? An interview with Dolly Kiffin', *Race & Class* 29/1 (1987): 79, doi: 10.1177/030639688702900106.

[7] GLC, Ethnic Minorities Committee, 'Broadwater Farm Youth Association', Funding Application, 9 July 1984, LMA, GLC/DG/PRE/49/30.

direct reaction to the kind of policing pursued by the Met in London in the 1970s and 1980s which profoundly affected Black people.

A year after the enactment of PACE and the application of the BFYA to the Ethnic Minorities Committee, the two worlds of Westminster and Broadwater Farm came into disastrous collision. On 5 October 1985, a young Black motorist, Floyd Jarrett, an active member of the BFYA, was stopped by police on Rosebery Avenue, Tottenham, under the terms of PACE. The premise for the search was that the tax disc for Jarrett's BMW coupe had expired at the end of August. One of the police then checked the national computer database for the car number. At trial two months later, the policeman was asked by a solicitor why he had done this:

'Would you have checked me out if I had been driving with a tax disc five weeks out of date?' The officer said no. Mr Solley asked if he could give any reason, other than that he was a Black man driving a flashy-looking car (a BMW Coupe). He could give no reason.[8]

What we would now call racial profiling clearly shaped Jarrett's stop. The computer check failed to reveal that the car had been stolen or involved in any crime, but there was a discrepancy (a 'U' rather than a 'W') between the plate number on the BMW and that on the computer database. On this basis, the officers decided to arrest Jarrett on suspicion of theft. He responded by running across the road. He was apprehended, taken to the police station, and charged with assault. Further investigation showed that there were no grounds for thinking that the car was stolen, and Jarrett was later acquitted of assault.

This incident, in most respects, simply followed a depressingly familiar narrative of the policing Black people faced every day in the 1980s under the terms of sus or PACE: an arbitrary stop; 'suspicion' based upon nothing but the racial identity of the individual; and a 'knock-on' charge provoked by the initial stop. But on 5 October 1985, this narrative took an even darker turn. While Jarrett was being held at Tottenham police station, an off-duty detective inspector, Michael Randall, decided to escalate the situation. He claimed to know Jarrett (something Jarrett

---

[8] *Gifford Report*, para. 4.7.

denied) and to know that he handled stolen goods. On this basis, the detective got a warrant to search the home of Jarrett's mother, Cynthia, even though Jarrett did not live at his mother's house. At 5.45 p.m., police arrived at Cynthia Jarrett's home. Because they had taken Jarrett's keys, they did not knock, but simply let themselves in.

Cynthia Jarrett was 48 years old in 1985. She had come to London from Jamaica in 1958, worked at a plastics factory until it closed in 1983, and brought up her children and grandchildren in Tottenham. Jarrett was deeply agitated by police entering her home on 5 October. She was at home with three of her grandchildren and her daughter. The police did what they called a speculative search, with no particular stolen goods defined in the warrant. In the course of this search—the account is disputed—either Cynthia Jarrett was shoved by Michael Randall or fell over accidentally. Cynthia Jarrett had advanced heart disease. She had a massive heart attack, probably provoked by her anxiety and the fall. Ten minutes after the police had arrived at Cynthia Jarrett's home, the emergency services had to be called. Within half an hour, Cynthia Jarrett was pronounced dead. Floyd Jarrett was released from Tottenham police station around 7 p.m., six hours after he had been stopped on Rosebery Avenue. He was then told that his mother had had a heart attack.

As news of Cynthia Jarrett's death spread that night and the next day, anger grew among the Black community. One member said, 'there is no way we can accept the death of a Black mother within our community'.[9] This came only a week after another Black mother, Cherry Groce, had been shot by police during a search of her home in Brixton. On Sunday, 6 October, a demonstration of about 100 people gathered outside Tottenham police station. Meetings at two local organizations, the West Indian Centre and the BFYA, saw expressions of 'deep anger', sadness, and shock.[10] As the afternoon wore on, there were increasing reports of unrest on Broadwater Farm Estate. Bottles were thrown at beat officers. In the early evening, three transit vans of police appeared. This infuriated youths on the estate, who tried to prevent the vans from entering by banging on the sides of the vehicles. Police in riot gear came out, using

[9] *Gifford Report*, para. 5.1.   [10] *Gifford Report*, paras. 5.9, 5.10.

Figure 9.1   Police at Broadwater Farm, 6 October 1985.
Credit: Trinity Mirror/Mirrorpix/Alamy Stock Photo.

truncheons to push back the youths and allegedly using racist language. Cars were overturned and set on fire. Bricks and petrol bombs fashioned out of milk bottles were thrown at the police. Police cars were attacked with machetes. Within ten minutes, barricades of burning vehicles had been established at the entrances to the estate. The police responded with 'massive force' (see Figure 9.1).[11] For the next three and a half hours, there was intense fighting on the estate between youths and the police. Some gunshots were fired at police; one officer was hit. Up to 2,000 police were eventually deployed at Broadwater Farm that night. The Broadwater Farm disturbance had begun with one death and ended with another. PC Keith Blakelock had been accompanying firemen trying to bring a hose up a stairwell in one of the estate's blocks when his party came under attack by a group of youths. Blakelock slipped, was quickly surrounding by youths, and was murdered.

The Broadwater Farm disorder was, with Brixton before and the 2011 disorders (the last triggered by a police shooting near Broadwater

---

[11] *Gifford Report*, para. 5.35.

Farm), one of the most serious episodes of violent civil unrest in British history. All of this violent unrest began, in one way or another, with a police stop of a young Black man. Against what the Home Office had articulated in 1984, there could be no illusion that policing was accompanied by the 'consent and co-operation of society at large'.[12] On 18 October 1985, Father Lamont Phillips, curate at St Paul the Apostle church, Tottenham, in north London, addressed the funeral service for Cynthia Jarrett. Phillips quoted Jeremiah 29:7: 'seek the peace of the city'.[13] This hope was set against a bleak vision of contemporary Britain: '[o]urs is a violent country...shades of the rainbow of violence that overshadows our beloved country'.[14]

The contrasting events in 1984—between the enactment of PACE and how it was perceived and played out in Black communities—illustrate one of the deepest tensions in contemporary British society, around the policing of racialized communities. The present chapter examines this question through the prism of PACE in 1984, Broadwater Farm before the disorders, and the divisions created by policing in Black communities. It also looks briefly at the aftermath of the unrest, arguing that there was no sense that the different visions of policing, one established by PACE in 1984 and the other held by Black communities, showed promise of coming together. This was a factor in the lead-up to one of the most important turning points in race and policing in Britain in the late twentieth century and, indeed, one of the most important turning points in exposing the state of racism in Britain—the racist murder of Stephen Lawrence in 1993 and the subsequent Macpherson Report, which stated that the Metropolitan Police were institutionally racist.

9.1

The violent unrest in Brixton in 1981 and Broadwater Farm in 1985 was triggered by encounters between young Black men and the Metropolitan Police. These encounters were shaped by a climate of distrust between

[12] Quoted in Reiner, 'PACE: Review Essay', 300.
[13] *King James Bible* (Oxford: Oxford University Press, 1997).
[14] *The Times*, 19 October 1985.

the police and the Black community, a climate emerging from racist patterns of policing. Those patterns were themselves moulded by race relations in Britain since 1948, but they were also rooted in nearly two centuries of a particular legal framework. In 1824, the Vagrancy Act had given newly formed police forces the power to arrest under suspicion, something intended to pre-empt criminal behaviour—in the nineteenth century directed against working-class people. By the 1970s, Section 4 of the Vagrancy Act, known as 'sus', was a cornerstone of everyday policing. Sus was a policing tactic particularly used in areas of London with significant Black populations, disproportionately against young Black men.[15] In addition to everyday street policing, the Met also used special anti-street crime squads that would descend upon particular neighbourhoods (and especially those with a large Black population); one such squad, the Special Patrol Group, was referred to as an 'Army of Occupation' in Lambeth in the 1970s.[16] The practice of sus on the street was matched by the prosecution of the charge in the courts. Sus charges were heavily reliant on police evidence alone, meaning there were few acquittals. The police also relied upon conspiracy charges to discipline large groups of Black youth. The street was the main arena of conflict between youth and the police, but there were predictably other spaces that attracted police attention, such as dance halls and clubs, and other venues that also invited police intervention, such as shebeens and private parties. As Rob Waters has pointed out, street festivals, in particular the Notting Hill Carnival, also became the focus of confrontations between the police and Black youth.[17]

The discriminatory practice of sus revealed in different ways the connections between racism and policing. In the first place, there was an issue with the Metropolitan Police as an institution. In the 1970s, the Met was overwhelmingly white. Racist attitudes, particularly against Black people, were 'pervasive...accepted and even fashionable' according to a

---

[15] See Paul Lawrence, 'The Vagrancy Act (1824) and the Persistence of Pre-emptive Policing in England since 1750', *British Journal of Criminology* 57/3 (2017): 513–31, doi: 10.1093/bjc/azw008.

[16] Quoted in Robin Bunce and Paul Field, *Renegade: Darcus Howe and the Fight for Black British Civil Rights* (London: Bloomsbury, 2021), 207–8.

[17] Waters, *Thinking Black*, 171.

Policy Studies Institute report in 1985.[18] Street encounters between Black people and the police made such racism a feature of everyday life in many Black communities in London. The police harassment of the Mangrove restaurant in 1970, which led to public protests and a series of trials, revealed the problem of racist policing on a larger, national stage.

But the problem of racism and policing went beyond the Met itself. As Stuart Hall and others argued, in the 1970s street crime or 'mugging' became identified, through the media and other forms of public discourse, with Black people, particularly with Black youth. Black communities were criminalized in this way, portrayed as a threat to order and to the nation and as a cipher for a larger 'crisis' of post-war British society. Policing that crisis, as Hall argued, depended upon policing race.[19]

By the time of the Brixton disorders in 1981, tensions between the police and the Black community in London had been brewing for nearly twenty years.[20] In 1972, a Select Committee on Race Relations and Immigration heard considerable evidence of the tensions created by sus; one Community Relations Committee in Islington said that Black youth 'feel that they are being harassed by the police to the point that they fear the police'.[21] Seven years later, the Institute of Race Relations told another government enquiry, the Royal Commission on Criminal Procedure, that, through sus, 'criminal procedure is being used to harass a whole community' as 'an everyday occurrence, a matter of routine'.[22] In 1983, the Policy Studies Institute published a major examination of *Police and People in London*. A particular focus of the study was the relationship between Black people and the police, based in part upon extended interviews with a group of young Black men and women. What this revealed was sobering, but unsurprising—that '[a]ll contact with the police was negative'—underlining to young Black people the equation between the racism of the police and the racism of British

[18] See D. J. Smith and J. Gray, *Police and People in London* (London: Gower/Policy Studies Institute, 1985).

[19] See Stuart Hall et al., *Policing the Crisis* (London: 1979).

[20] Waters, *Thinking Black*, 167.

[21] *Select Committee on Race Relations and Immigration, 1971–2, Police/Immigrant Relations*: Volume 3, *Evidence, Documents and Index* (London: HMSO, 1972), 588.

[22] *Police Against Black People* (1979), in Institute of Race Relations, *Policing Against Black People* (London: Institute of Race Relations, 1987), 2, 30.

society: '[t]he police are racist and society is racist'; police were the 'symbols of *white* authority'.[23] Sus was the main form of encounter between Black people and the police. 'Clifton', one of the interviewees, suffered a typical experience:

> Clifton was stopped and searched by the police on at least two occasions during the period of research, once by uniformed officers and once by plain clothes officers. The first occurred at about 7.45 am near to Earl's Court while Clifton was making his way to work. The police officers told him that there had been a burglary in the neighbourhood and they wanted to search him. Clifton had informed them that he was on his way to work and pointed to his workplace which was two hundred yards down the road. He showed them his holdall bag in which he had his tools and his lunchtime sandwiches. The police insisted upon searching him and went through his holdall, his jacket and trousers pocket and his hair and tam (woollen hat). He became incensed with they opened his lunchbox, looked through his sandwiches and threw them on the ground. They then left him and went on their way.[24]

Another story, this time involving some of the youths who were eventually involved in the Broadwater Farm disorders, similarly shows the way arbitrary police stops could, in a moment, derail young men's lives. In his book on the murder of Keith Blakelock and the 'Tottenham Three', David Rose uses the stories of three Black youths growing up in Tottenham in the 1960s and 1970s—Winston Silcott, Stafford Scott, and Delroy Lindo—to show the effects of social deprivation and policing practices on the lives of young Black men. Winston Silcott grew up as the child of hard-working, religious immigrants from Montserrat. He was a serious child, but experiences at school proved alienating. Silcott was accused by a teacher, for example, of stealing a bottle of perfume he had bought as a gift for his mother. His friend Stafford Scott was a good student but was discouraged by his teachers from pursuing O and A levels.

---

[23] Stephen Small, *Police and People in London*, Volume II: *A Group of Young Black People* (London: Policy Studies Institute, 1983), 104, 110, 4.
[24] Small, *Police and People in London*, 104–5.

Scott also fell foul of the police in other ways. In the late seventies, he was at Bow Street Court to hear a case against one of his friends. The friends went to Covent Garden during one of the trial breaks; they were followed by four detectives and arrested under suspicion of crime, a charge that was upheld in court. Each was fined £40. For Scott, this charge proved calamitous for his future plans, meaning that he could not join the RAF. Silcott also experienced the hard consequences of sus. He was once charged by police with having faulty brakes on his bicycle and fined £15. These proved formative experiences for the two boys. Eventually, they drifted into petty crime. They were caught for trying to sell stolen goods, and Silcott was sent to borstal for a few months and Scott for three years. Their friend Delroy Lindo eventually ended working with the BFYA. As an adult, he continued to experience the sharp end of policing. As a driver, he was regularly stopped by the police. He saw this as a continuation of the racial socialization of his childhood: 'It was a way of keeping up the pressure, making sure we still knew our place.' All of these experiences, according to Stafford Scott, left Black youth with a 'well-founded grudge' against the police.[25]

By the 1980s, policing was 'the central political issue for many black Britons'.[26] Alarmed at the treatment faced by their children from the police on a daily basis, Black parents came together to challenge sus. In 1975, the Black Parents Movement was established, with policing as one of its main concerns. Three years later, the Black People's Organizations Campaign Against SUS followed. Particular individuals were instrumental in calling attention to the problem of sus, such as Mavis Best, a mother in Peckham who spearheaded the Scrap Sus campaign; Martha Osamor in Tottenham; and a young lawyer working in the Paddington Law Centre, Paul Boateng. The demand was a very clear one: to scrap sus in order to allow Black people the same respect and freedom in daily life as other people. As one mother told a public meeting on SUS about her son: 'I want him to be able to walk down the street like any other decent person.'[27] This campaign did gain some traction, even before

---

[25] David Rose, *A Climate of Fear: The Murder of PC Blakelock and the Case of the Tottenham Three* (London: Bloomsbury, 1992), 39, 24.

[26] Waters, *Thinking Black*, 167.

[27] See 'Breaking Point' (n.d.), https://www.youtube.com/watch?v=lRbcFNhDFeA (accessed 15 December 2022).

Brixton, in the review of criminal procedure. As shown in Chapter 2 ('Anti-Racist Year'), working against sus was also a common theme in the efforts of Black community organizations.

Two events in 1981 highlighted the problem of policing for Black people. The first was the New Cross tragedy. On 18 January 1981, thirteen young people died as a result of a fire during a birthday party.[28] New Cross had seen considerable National Front activity, and the immediate suspicion was that the fire was a racist arson attack. But the Metropolitan Police found no definitive evidence of arson in its investigation, a conclusion that infuriated a grieving Black community. There was frustration and anger at what was perceived to be the Met's disinterest in taking the tragedy seriously, its heavy-handed treatment of victims of the fire, and the lack of sympathy from government, particularly compared to the gestures made to Irish people after a fire in Dublin around the same time. At a public meeting in Lewisham, the local police commander was reviled as a 'murderer'.[29] The New Cross fire led to the organization of a mass protest, the first of its kind by the Black community in Britain—the Black People's Day of Action. This was the product of the New Cross Massacre Action Committee, which had been established by, among others, the activists John La Rose and Darcus Howe. The march brought together a wide range of Black organizations, not only in London but nationwide. On Monday, 2 March 1981, about 20,000 demonstrators began the Day of Action on New Cross Road, making their way through south London, across Blackfriars Bridge (the first protest to do so since the 1848 Chartist demonstrations), and on to Fleet Street, where they were met by a torrent of often racist abuse from office workers, some of whom were working for the media.[30] Clashes with police occurred along the route, with twenty-five people eventually charged.

The second major event in 1981 was, of course, the violent civil unrest in Brixton in early April. The disorders were sparked by a heavy police

[28] Humphrey Brown, Peter Campbell, Steve Collins, Patrick Cummings, Gerry Francis, Andrew Gooding, Lloyd Hall, Rosaline Henry, Patricia Johnson, Glenton Powell, Paul Ruddock, Yvonne Ruddock, and Owen Thompson; the fire claimed a fourteenth victim, when one of the survivors, Anthony Berbick, committed suicide.

[29] Quoted in Bunce and Field, *Renegade*, 189.

[30] See Bunce and Field, *Renegade*, 199–201.

presence in the Brixton area, notably with what was dubbed Swamp 81, an intense action headed by the Special Patrol Group. The two immediate causes of the unrest were the police taking a young man to hospital, mistakenly apprehended as being taken into police custody, and the use of sus against a taxi driver on suspicion of drugs possession. The violence lasted two days, then spread to other urban areas within Britain. The New Cross tragedy and the Brixton disorders illustrated that the problem of the Met's policing of Black communities was twofold: the over-policing of Black communities through something like sus, and the under-policing of Black communities when those communities were faced with racial or police violence.

The Scarman Report that followed the Brixton unrest eschewed accusing the police of institutional racism but did underline the damage that the heavy and often discriminatory use of sus was doing to relations between the Black community and the police, and recommended its abolition. A 1980 parliamentary Select Committee had already recognized the need to repeal sus, but the aftermath of the Brixton disorders hastened that action. The Criminal Attempts Act which came into law in August 1981 abolished Section 4 of the Vagrancy Act. But the practice continued. In 1983 alone, it was estimated that the Metropolitan Police did about 780,000 stop-and-searches. In the aftermath of Brixton, the evidence continued to show that stop-and-search was used disproportionately against young Black men. Throughout the 1980s, policing in London came under sharp scrutiny, prompted by the intersection between race and policing. David McNee, the Met's Commissioner, said, in the immediate wake of Brixton, '[t]he greatest problem I will have in my commissionership, and that my successor and probably his successor will have, is getting on with the ethnic minorities in this great city.'[31] Ironically, the abolition of sus laid the groundwork for its rearticulation in 1984 with PACE.

Between 1981 and 1984, there was little improvement in the relations between the Met and Black people in London. There were episodes when, indeed, that relationship became worse. In 1983, for example, a young Black man, Colin Roach, died from a shotgun wound suffered

---

[31] Quoted in Paul Gilroy, 'Police and Thieves', in *The Empire Strikes Back,* 141.

inside Stoke Newington police station. In the years that followed, there were several demonstrations organized by the Roach Family Support Committee and the Hackney Black People's Association to demand a formal enquiry into the circumstances of Colin's death. Nearly a hundred people were arrested over the course of these demonstrations. At one point, Hackney Council refused to pay the police precept (in effect, defunding the police) as 'an expression of anger at the state of policing in Hackney'.[32]

The coming to power of the GLC further intensified the problem of how the Met policed Black communities, particularly because the incoming Labour administration was committed to making the Met more accountable, a policy which lay behind much of the right-wing reaction to the GLC in 1981. The GLC's Police Committee and its Police Committee Support Unit worked on this issue within County Hall and published *Policing London,* a publication which kept up steady pressure on the question. The Police Committee and the Ethnic Minorities Committee were also committed to funding local organizations interested in police accountability. In January 1984, for example, the Police Committee articulated its support for, and made grants to, a number of 'defence' committees, such as the Roach Family Support Committee and the Stoke Newington and Hackney Legal Defence Campaigns, to oppose 'aggressive police methods'.[33] There were also grass-roots monitoring organizations in Southall and Newham, part of whose aims were to track police actions on the ground. The Community Alliance for Police Accountability was one of the more active organizations in this regard, working in Tower Hamlets 'against the excesses, prejudices and non-responses of the police'.[34] Thus, a critical response to how sus was used on the ground to police Black communities was the extension of local democratic control over the police.

In the wake of Brixton and the election of the Labour GLC, therefore, there were contrasting visions of how policing worked on the ground in

[32] *Hackney Gazette* (London), 25 February 1983.
[33] GLC, Ethnic Minorities Committee, 'Police Working Group Request for Funds for Defence Funds', 13 January 1984, LMA, GLC/DG/PRE/49/19.
[34] GLC, Ethnic Minorities Committee, 'Community Alliance for Police Accountability', Funding Application, 19 March 1984.

relation to race. Despite the Scarman Report and the abolition of the historical sus laws, there was little indication from either the Met or the government that stop-and-search would be changed or that hard policing would be abandoned. The experiences of Brixton and New Cross had only served to make Black communities more frustrated with the police. Stop-and-search, or whatever form of everyday policing the Met adopted, added to a toll of humiliation and anger that the Black community faced. Finally, the political solution taken up by local government and activist groups was to insist upon democratic accountability—greater control of the police by local bodies.

9.2

In 1982, the Conservative government introduced what it called the Police and Criminal Evidence Bill. This was an attempt to clarify the powers of the police, and it set a more comprehensive framework for policing. The 1982 version was tilted towards the police, but it faced considerable opposition from the Labour Party and civil liberties groups. This bill was allowed to fall with the election of June 1983 and, after that Conservative victory, the new Home Secretary Leon Brittan presented a new version of PACE. This version proved more amenable to opinion in the centre, but the bill nonetheless faced a great deal of debate and revision. At the report stage, there were 170 government amendments, and the committee stage took 159 sittings, both record numbers for that time. This was, in large part, about the complexity of codifying complex police practices. Particular issues attracted attention, such as a provision for holding suspects for ninety-six hours, the appropriateness of intimate body searches, and the establishment of a Police Complaints Board. It is important to note that throughout the debate on PACE in 1983 and 1984, outside of minority communities, stop-and-search garnered majority support among the British public. In January 1984, 66 per cent of those polled supported the police practice of stop-and-search.[35]

[35] *The Times*, 9 January 1984.

With regard to the existing practice of sus, it was the first section of PACE that was relevant. The new law gave police the right to 'search any person or vehicle...for stolen or prohibited articles' and could 'detain a person or a vehicle' towards that end if the police had 'reasonable grounds for suspecting that he [sic] will find stolen or prohibited articles'.[36] This superseded the 1824 Vagrancy Act. There was some reform of this power, such as making uniformed police officers identify themselves to those stopped-and-searched, but the power to stop-and-search remained largely as it had been, reliant upon a policeman deciding that there were reasonable grounds, with little definition of what those reasonable grounds were, or, more to the point, what they were not—in other words, tempered by racial profiling.

Outside of Westminster, there was significant opposition to the continuation of stop-and-search in this form. In 1983, the CRE asked the government to drop stop-and-search powers on the grounds of what would later be called racial profiling.[37] As suggested in Chapter 5 ('Gay's the Word'), the gay and lesbian community was opposed to PACE in the form it took in 1984. 'The Bill', GALOP stated, 'brings us closer than ever before to a police state. By harassing us, the police can drive us back into the ghetto.'[38] The GLC's Police Committee argued that the Bill 'can and will affect everyone's civil liberties – at home, in the streets, and inside the police station.'[39]

When the Bill finally came to the Commons for its third and final reading in May 1984, it was surprising that there was so little reference to the racial issues around stop-and-search. Given the controversies around gay politics, it is perhaps less surprising that there was no reference to the possible effect of the Bill on gay and lesbian life.

Introducing the Bill, Brittan played up the problems in the 'inner cities' as justifying robust stop-and-search powers: '[t]he police need the power to stop and search for weapons if they are to respond properly to the appalling incidents of street violence which we read of daily in the

---

[36] Police and Criminal Evidence Act, UK General Acts c. 60, 2 (a), 2 (b), and 3.
[37] *The Times*, 29 April 1983.
[38] Quoted in GLC, *Gays and the Police Bill* (London: GLC, 1984).
[39] GLC, *Gays and the Police Bill*.

newspapers'.[40] But he disavowed that it would be used in a 'random or discriminatory manner'.[41] The Labour and SDP–Liberal Alliance opposition did object to what the Labour Shadow Home Secretary, Gerald Kaufman, called the 'intolerably wide stop and search powers', but there were few specific references to how these affected the Black community in particular.[42] The Labour MP Clare Short criticized the bill for encouraging a 'repressive police force' and made the argument for democratic control of policing, but only Alf Dubs, Labour MP for Battersea, highlighted the particular problem stop-and-search had for Black people: '[t]he power to stop and search, which was discussed in detail in the House yesterday, is one provision which will lessen the willingness of the public to co-operate with the police and which will have a particularly damaging effect on the attitude of young people, especially young blacks.'[43]

Thus, while in communities and on the streets perhaps the most controversial aspect of policing was the relationship between stop-and-search and race, something that had sparked violent unrest in Brixton and elsewhere in 1981, in the Commons in 1984 this was hardly mentioned explicitly as an issue.

9.3

To understand the tensions around policing in the Black community, it is worth looking in greater detail at a particular community, in this case Broadwater Farm. As already suggested, the state of conditions on the estate had been articulated in the 1984 application to the GLC's Ethnic Minority Committee.

In 1965, a contract was awarded to build a housing estate on what had been allotment land to the east of Lordship Recreation Ground in Haringey. The new estate was completed in 1973 with several tower

---

[40] *Parliamentary Debates* (Commons), Volume 60, 16 May 1984, c. 381.

[41] *Parliamentary Debates* (Commons), Volume 60, 16 May 1984, c. 382.

[42] *Parliamentary Debates* (Commons), Volume 60, 16 May 1984, c. 384.

[43] Clare Short, in *Parliamentary Debates* (Commons), Volume 60, 16 May 1984, cs. 405–6; Alf Dubs in *Parliamentary Debates* (Commons), Volume 60, 16 May 1984, c. 407.

blocks, an arresting ziggurat-shaped central block, and raised connecting walkways. The estate lacked some amenities, such as health facilities, and it was also disadvantaged by poor public transport connections with the neighbourhood outside of the estate. Nonetheless, the initial response from new residents was positive. The flats were 'spacious, peaceful, and above all warm'.[44] Dolly Kiffin remarked:

> There was a lot of peace there. The front room was quite big, and it was warm for the kids...It was all nice and clean. And especially at night when you sit on the patio and look over, it's a beautiful sight.[45]

But soon after its completion Broadwater Farm was caught in a 'spiral of deterioration'.[46] It became associated with 'problem families', a category that included one-parent families and the homeless.[47] By 1980, only seven years after the estate's completion, a Department of Environment report discussed the possibility of demolishing it.[48] The local press also painted a depressing, lurid, and often racist picture of the estate. The *Hornsey Journal* offered a 'scarifying picture of life on one of the borough's modern tower blocks', where '[t]he sight of unmarried West Indian mothers walking about the estate' inflamed 'racial tension'. The estate was portrayed as 'classic breeding-ground for anti-social behaviour in the young children...Individual and gang vandalism, assault and intimidation are high'.[49] Similarly, the *Tottenham Weekly Herald* claimed that '[f]ear haunts the gloomy passages, lifts and entrances of Broadwater Farm Estate'.[50] Well before 1985, therefore, Broadwater Farm had become a space infused with dread and fear, and that fear was tied to race. In the aftermath of the Broadwater Farm disorder, a young man remarked, '[y]ou won't understand what happened here until you know

---

[44] *Gifford Report*, para. 2.7.   [45] *Gifford Report*, para. 2.8.
[46] *Gifford Report*, para. 2.18.   [47] *Gifford Report*, para. 2.16.
[48] *Gifford Report*, para. 2.16.
[49] Quoted in Dominic Severs, 'Rookeries and No-go Estates: St Giles and Broadwater Farm, or middle-class fear of "non-street" housing', *Journal of Architecture* 15/4 (2010): 476, doi: 10.1080/13602365.2010.507526.
[50] *Gifford Report*, paras. 2.20, 2.21.

what it feels like to be black'.[51] What it felt like to grow up on the Broadwater Farm estate in the 1970s and 1980s was shaped by generation, deprivation, and racism, particularly from the police and media.

The situation at Broadwater Farm in the year of the Brixton unrest mirrored the deprivation on other estates and in other neighbourhoods in London, particularly for Black people:

> The young men, many of them unemployed, had nothing to do. The old people were afraid of them, the police suspected them. The young women with children were isolated and lonely. The teenagers had the use of a flat in Hawkinge block which operated on three evenings a week, but nothing more. The physical appearance of the estate was run down and ill maintained.[52]

Race was a clear dividing line in this. The tenants' association on Broadwater Farm was dominated by white tenants up to 1981, and often felt like an unwelcome space for Black people. It was suggested that a former leader of the association was a member of the National Front.[53] Older white tenants and pensioners on the estate were frightened of young people. As already mentioned, in 1983 a spate of burglaries led to the tenants' association proposing to have a mini police station on the estate. This alarmed many Black residents, fearing that it would simply make worse the relations between youth and the police.

At this point, Dolly Kiffin called a meeting in her front room, to see if any young people wanted to form an association that would 'see if life could be changed on the Broadwater Farm'.[54] The result was the Broadwater Farm Youth Association. The BFYA was committed to improving the lives of Black youth on the estate through self-help, noting that the 'main obstacle' facing Black youth was 'lack of training and employment opportunities, lack of recreational and cultural venues and a racist and sexist attitude towards them by many in the community

---

[51] Quoted in John Clare, 'The Ratchet Advances Another Turn', in John Benyon and John Solomos (eds.), *The Roots of Urban Unrest* (Oxford: Pergamon Press, 1987), 64.

[52] *Gifford Report*, para. 2.30.

[53] 'Broadwater Farm: a "criminal estate"? An interview with Dolly Kiffin', 79.

[54] *Gifford Report*, para. 2.33.

and the police in particular'.[55] The BFYA had, therefore, a clear political aim growing out of the situation in Broadwater Farm, to mitigate the effects of racism, not least that from the police. With a small grant of £300 from Haringey Council, the new BFYA took over a disused fish and chip shop on the estate. With its motto 'Success Through Caring', the association offered a place to go for those aged between 8 and 30. Eventually the centre was regularly offering lunches to sixty to seventy pensioners, which helped build a better relationship between older white people and Black youth.[56] Aided by grants from Haringey and the GLC, the BFYA organized two childcare facilities, a recurring summer festival at Lordship Lane, a laundrette, a hairdressing salon, a photographic workshop, a sewing workshop, and a food co-op. Kiffin and another founder of the BFYA, Clasford Stirling, were invited to a garden party at Buckingham Palace in recognition of their work, and this contact led to a visit by the Princess of Wales in February 1985.

But the success of the BFYA did not improve the poor relations between the Black community and the police. The legacy of humiliation and anger from years of hard policing left the BFYA leadership reluctant to cooperate with the police. The police refused to accept any increased monitoring of their work by Haringey Council. Younger beat officers were particularly resistant to any compromise of their tactics.[57] Crime remained at a high level, particularly in burglary and the trafficking in drugs. Arrests on the estate would sometimes result in vigorous protests when hundreds of people demonstrated outside Tottenham Police Station or took part in physical attacks on police offices on the estate.

In 1984 and 1985, the evidence from Broadwater Farm suggested a very deep division about policing on the estate. A locally produced broadsheet appearing after the disorders argued that, before October 1985, the police were resentful of the success of the BFYA, particularly of 'the success of the youths who proved that they could take control of their own lives', and it alleged that the police had contingency plans for

---

[55] GLC, Ethnic Minorities Committee, 'Broadwater Farm Youth Association', Funding Application, 9 July 1984.
[56] Tony Moore, *The Killing of Constable Keith Blakelock* (London: Waterside Press, 2015, e-book edition), location 690.
[57] Moore, locs. 1019, 1136.

taking control of the estate.[58] The police perspective, unsurprisingly, was completely at odds with this. After the violent events of early October, a journal reflecting the police perspective stated that the image of Broadwater Farm 'as a beehive of flourishing rehabilitation and positive community involvement... cloaks the ugly reality of criminal gangs ruling the estate, robbing and terrorising the inhabitants'. When Dolly Kiffin left the estate to go on holiday in the summer of 1985, the article went on, criminal activity increased and the BFYA occupied a compromised position, itself not respecting licensing hours, and (to the police a particular provocation) some of their members attended a festival on the estate in 'combat dress'.[59]

Even before the events of 5 and 6 October 1985, therefore, anger and tension structured the relationship between the Black community and the police. The Leader of Haringey Council, Bernie Grant, remarked that economic deprivation underlay the situation at Broadwater Farm, but that economic deprivation 'rarely leads to a revolt of the kind we saw on Broadwater Farm. Something else is needed to trigger such an angry reaction. That "something else" is oppressive policing... Policing which is frankly racist'.[60]

The violence provoked by Cynthia Jarrett's death has already been described. Its aftermath saw an overwhelming police presence on the estate. Up to 200 police were on the estate the next day, and it was estimated that up to 2,000 police were deployed on the estate in the following weeks and months. Only after a year—in September 1986—did policing levels drop to normal levels on the estate, and a police van was removed.[61] That massive police presence shaped life on the estate, as discussed below.

The other explicit result of the disorders was the media treatment of the estate and its characterization of the unrest. One author has characterized this as 'demonization' and the 'racist criminalization of the black

[58] Handbill, 'Haringey Ghost Town', [n.d., 1985], George Padmore Institute, London, LRA/6/8/2.

[59] 'The "Battle" of Broadwater Farm', *Police*, November 1985, 12, 14, Black Cultural Archives, RC/RF/16/17/C/1.

[60] Bernie Grant Papers, Bernie Grant Statement to Haringey Council, 14 October 1985, Bishopsgate Institute Archives, BG/P/4/6/4.

[61] *The Times*, 13 September 1986.

community'.[62] National newspapers such as the *Daily Express, Mail, Mirror,* and *Sun* all contributed to a picture of Broadwater Farm and the disorders that stressed its alien and horrifying nature. 'Riot' and 'rioters' were the terms dominating such coverage. The *Daily Express* suggested, falsely, that the disorder was begun by '[s]treet-fighting experts trained in Moscow and Libya'.[63] The *Daily Star's* headline 'Red Butchers' carried on this theme.[64] Kenneth Newman added fuel to this fire by suggesting, again falsely, that the disorders had been the work of '[g]roups of trotskyites [sic] and anarchists.... They are both Black and White and come from within and outside London, operating in areas of ethnic concentration'.[65] Other papers, like the *Daily Mail,* focused on racial tensions within the estate, suggesting that it was a place of white victim-ization: 'A daily war [is] being waged against White families by the younger members of a burgeoning Black community', and 'White people there do feel they are living in an alien and terrifying land and nobody will even listen to them, let alone help them'.[66] An independent enquiry chaired by Lord Gifford was set up with the help of Haringey Council; that enquiry heard complaints that any accounts of racial cooperation went unreported by the press.

In these ways the Broadwater Farm disorders were quickly fitted into a framework dominated by particular ideas of race and politics. They were riots emanating from racial animosity, on the part of Black people, which made white Britons victims, whether in terms of everyday vio-lence against the residents of Broadwater Farm or against the police. They were riots imported from hostile foreign powers such as the Soviet Union or Libya and cloaked in hostile foreign ideologies. This placed the riots not within an understanding of domestic politics or the conse-quences of racial difference in a racist society, but as a threat to the nation and national order. Thinking of Stuart Hall's work on policing, Black youth became the cipher of the crisis of the national or social order.

---

[62] Michael Rowe, *The Racialisation of Disorder in Twentieth Century Britain* (Aldershot: Ashgate, 1998), 135.

[63] Quoted in Martin Loney, 'Imagery and Reality in the Broadwater Farm Riot', *Critical Social Policy* 6/17 (1986): 83, doi: 10.1177/026101838600601706.

[64] Loney, 'Imagery and Reality in the Broadwater Farm Riot', 82.

[65] *Gifford Report*, para. 6.2.   [66] Quoted in *Gifford Report*, para. 6.3.

In this way, the national crisis or the urban crisis could be read in the figure of the Black rioter. In the context of the 1980s, the rioters of Brixton, Toxteth, St Paul's, Handsworth, and Tottenham joined Irish republicans and striking miners as the 'enemies within'. This is not to excuse the violence of the disorders. It is, however, to understand that the Broadwater Farm disturbances were almost immediately placed within a long-standing framework. The Gifford Report said that '[t]he racist theme which appears in some of the reports which we have quoted...was reinforced by headlines about "hyenas", "butchers" and "monsters".'[67]

In the initial days after the disturbance, before the search for Blakelock's killer began in earnest, this invective was focused on one figure—the Leader of Haringey Council, Bernie Grant. Grant had necessarily carried a great deal of authority within Broadwater Farm before the unrest of October 1985. He had found it hard, for example, in the wake of Cynthia Jarrett's death, to gain much standing with the young people of the estate. But his response to the riots was immediately controversial. In addition to suggesting that Blakelock might have been killed by another policeman and refusing to condemn the actions of rioters, Grant said the following: '[t]he reason Sir Kenneth Newman is threatening the use of rubber bullets is because on Sunday night the police got a bloody good hiding. The police will not accept that Black youths can successfully organize themselves and outsmart them and outmanoeuvre them.'[68]

These remarks were widely condemned. Within Haringey Council there was an emergency meeting of employees represented by the National Association of Local Government Officers (NALGO) that week, demanding Grant's resignation, believing that he had 'agree[d] with attacks on the police and members of the public or condone the burning down of people's houses', while at the same time criticizing the policies of the Thatcher government which had caused social deprivation in the borough.[69] NALGO also dissociated itself from the remarks,

[67] *Gifford Report*, para. 6.4.   [68] *Gifford Report,* para. 6.6.
[69] Bernie Grant Papers, Mass Meeting, Parkview Depot, 11 October 1985, Bishopsgate Institute, BG/P/4/6/4, Part 2.

as well as dissociating itself from the Home Secretary and the Police Commissioner.

A week after the disorder, on 14 October 1985, Grant explained his remarks. The Council passed a motion that 'violence is unacceptable, whether it occurs through police insensitivity, Government indifference or public disorders':

> … petrol bombing, shooting and stone throwing are no answer to the legitimate grievances of black and white people in Tottenham. The only solution is a political one – to end this Government's policies of misery at the next General Election by replacing it with a Labour Government.[70]

He did admit that 'things could have been better said', but said that in his original remarks 'I have been trying to articulate the perceptions of those young black people who *do* see the police as their enemy'. Nonetheless, he criticized violence: '[y]ou can't fight hatred with hatred'. The result would be that '[t]he State's response will always escalate. Next time, rubber bullets and CS gas will be used. The time after that, the Army will be brought in.'[71]

The army remark was apposite. After the disorders, the estate 'had the feeling of being under occupation'.[72] Police vans were parked on The Avenue running near the estate every day. Far more police than usual patrolled the estate. Searches and arrests shaped everyday life. The aftermath of the disorders resulted in an escalating series of arrests. By the end of November, 141 had been arrested; by the end of May, 359. Of these, fifty-six were charged with affray and seven with riot. Eighteen per cent of the arrests were of juveniles, only 9 per cent of women. The majority of those arrested, 71 per cent, were Black. For the people of Broadwater Farm, the police took a forceful approach to the policing of the estate after the unrest with arrests, smashing doors, and doing

---

[70] Bernie Grant Papers, Special Meeting of Haringey Council, 14 October 1985, Bishopsgate Institute, BG/P/4/6/4, Part 2.

[71] Bernie Grant Papers, Special Meeting of Haringey Council, 14 October 1985, Bishopsgate Institute, BG/P/4/6/4, Part 2.

[72] Rose, *A Climate of Fear*, 111.

aggressive searches; there were many allegations of harsh treatment during detention, including a refusal to allow suspects to see solicitors. Among other things, the police were looking for weapons, including guns. The focus of the investigation was also, understandably, the murder of Keith Blakelock. The police's prime suspect was Winston Silcott, who was arrested in the week following the disturbance, wrongfully convicted, and then had his sentence quashed with two other suspects.

The raids and searches of the estate in the aftermath were examples of heavy policing, designed to humiliate and frighten, often done with armed officers:

> [The police] said, 'It's your bastard's birthday tomorrow, isn't it?' I said, 'What do you mean by that' and they said, 'It's your little bastard's birthday, open the door, we've got a warrant for your arrest'. When I opened the door the sledgehammer was coming back on the door. They grabbed me, they put me to spread out on the wall, and they searched me. All I had on was my tee shirt and my knickers…it's not affected me, it's my daughter, because she saw everything that happened and she was screaming, literally screaming when she saw, especially when the gun was at my head, you know, she was really, really screaming.[73]

The police damaged personal possessions, food, and furniture in their searches. Once under arrest, suspects were treated heavily by the police. Often the suspects were teenagers. Some were denied access to legal advice. Others were denied access to their parents. One of the counsel for suspects remarked that 'It was just complete chaos, like a madhouse…'. Another said that the way questioning was done closed down the estate's community: 'The police frightened the living daylights out of everybody. That's why they were faced with the so-called wall of silence. People were simply terrified.'[74]

Outside the estate, the wake of the disorder also saw a division among the wider public over policing on racial grounds. A poll suggested that over a quarter of Black and Asian people felt the violence by what were

---

[73] Quoted in Rose, *A Climate of Fear*, 111.   [74] Rose, *A Climate of Fear*, 114, 115.

termed 'rioters' was justified; a majority of those polled also believed that the policing of ethnic minority people was biased. By contrast, nearly half of Londoners polled felt that the policing of the 'riot' had not been hard enough, and 57 per cent agreed that CS gas and rubber bullets should have been used.[75]

9.4

The enactment of PACE in October 1984, as argued at the beginning of this chapter, was one of the most important legacies of 1984, in that it confirmed police practices, in the form of stop-and-search, that perpetuated a toxic relationship between the Met and racialized communities. This chapter has charted how that practice affected Black people and how, through the local example of Broadwater Farm, it had helped to create an environment of tension, humiliation, resentment, and fear between Black people and the police. With tragic inevitability, this exploded into large-scale violence in October 1985. Understanding the relationship between the police and Black people is a critically important way of understanding the contours of Black life in the late twentieth century.

Of course, the difficult truth is that this has not changed very much. Indeed, the state of policing in 1984, as formalized by PACE, has kept a particular situation in stasis since. To be sure, the murder of Stephen Lawrence and the subsequent report on the institutional racism of the Metropolitan Police cemented the importance of the issue in contemporary political culture. But the tragedies persist, and the tensions persist around policing. In 2001, the poet Benjamin Zephaniah articulated that repetitive persistence in his poem 'The One Minutes of Silence':

> I have stood for so many minutes of silence in my time
> I have stood many one minutes for
> Blair Peach,
> Colin Roach
> And

---

[75] *The Times*, 14 October 1985.

Akhtar Ali Baig
And every time I stand for them
The silence kills me.
...
I spend hours considering our trials and
Tribulations,
I seem to have spent a lifetime
Thinking about death;
...
I've spent hours
Standing for minutes
Pondering the meaning of life
The reason for death
And considering my time and space.[76]

As Zephaniah suggests in his poem, there is also a sense that these events become references to one another, a kind of unfolding and ever-increasing litany of the tragic cost of racism. That trajectory flows forward to the murder of Stephen Lawrence in 1993, to the 1999 Macpherson Report's critique of the Met's handling of that investigation, and, sadly, to the present day. As Stuart Hall suggested in 1999, on the occasion of the publication of the Macpherson Report, these private and public tragedies are evidence of how 'black people have been the subject of racialized attack, had their grievances largely ignored by the police, and have been subjected to racially-inflected practices of police...a catalogue of disasters, marked by mistrust, prejudice and disrespect, often leading to tragedy'.[77] In 1984, the enactment of PACE and how that kind of policing landed on Black communities did little if anything to disrupt that narrative.

London, 1984: Conflict and Change in the Radical City. Stephen Brooke, Oxford University Press.
© Stephen Brooke 2024. DOI: 10.1093/9780191895395.003.0010

[76] Benjamin Zephaniah, 'The One Minutes of Silence', in Courttia Newland and Kadija Sesay (eds.), *IC3: The Penguin Book of New Black Writing in Britain* (London: Penguin, 2001), 141.
[77] Hall, 'From Scarman to Stephen Lawrence', 188.

Conclusion

1 April 1986: The GLC is abolished. There is a drinks party at County Hall and then, in a final gesture of defiance to Westminster, a fireworks display at midnight illuminates the Thames.

22 May 2023: Calthorpe Community Garden, founded in 1984, lies between Grays Inn Road, Sidmouth Street, and King's Cross Road. To the east, Mount Pleasant Royal Mail sorting office, where some of the books seized from Gay's the Word were held in 1984, is now an enormous building site, being redeveloped into a 'mixed use residential-led scheme comprising of 700 apartments, as well as commercial and retail uses'.[1] By contrast, Calthorpe Community Garden describes itself as an 'inner city community garden and centre', existing 'to improve the physical and emotional wellbeing of those who live, work or study in Camden and surrounding areas'.[2] On the Monday that I walk by, it is offering a programme of tai chi for beginners, gardening, walking football, and cooking. There is a plaque outside the garden (Figure 10.1), which reads:

> This community garden was opened by The Worshipful The Mayor of Camden, King's Cross Ward Councillor, Barbara Hughes, in September 1984 following a successful campaign by local people against a proposed office development.
>
> We are committed to continue providing open green space and positive leisure activities for the local community and visitors to our garden.

Forty years ago, Matrix consulted with the Calthorpe Garden project about the design and construction of a single-storey building. But

---

[1] https://www.sweco.co.uk/projects/mount-pleasant-sorting-office/.
[2] https://www.calthorpecommunitygarden.org.uk/our-philosophy.

Figure 10.1 Calthorpe Community Garden plaque, 2023.
Author photo.

funding proved difficult, and the Matrix design remained unbuilt.[3] One can assume that, at least in part, the lack of funding was due to the abolition of the GLC and the drying up of alternative local authority funds

[3] See http://www.matrixfeministarchitecturearchive.co.uk/calthorpe/.

after 1986. Like other campaigns in Coin Street and the Docklands, Calthorpe Community Garden was, in 1984, an attempt to etch out a space against the encroachment of the neoliberal city in the material shape of offices.

The proximity of Calthorpe Community Garden to the redevelopment of the Mount Pleasant sorting office is a reminder of the tensions and resonances that could be seen in 1984 and that persist to the present day, in a city in which an oasis of alternative culture and community exists within a larger landscape shaped by the market. The present book, as suggested above, is not intended as a linear history of London in the 1980s, nor does it present a linear analysis of how one city became another. What it offers instead is an exploration of a particular moment in London's history, the strengths and conflicts of which have been carried forward to the present day. That ambiguous legacy can be read spatially in the juxtaposition of Calthorpe Community Garden and the Mount Pleasant development. Contemporary London is a neoliberal city, but one haunted, in some corners, by the afterlives of its social democratic past.

The arc of London's development in the age of neoliberalism is both similar and different to other global cities such as New York and Paris.[4] We can see, for example, a similar trajectory of gentrification and the high concentration of capital changing both the material space of the city (in terms of things such as redevelopment, housing, and retail and cultural spaces) and its accessibility to all its citizens. Echoes of the alienation this causes resound not only in places like London but in Paris and New York as well.[5] But at least in terms of a comparison with global cities such as Paris and New York, what made London exceptional between the 1980s and the present day was the presence of a defiantly social democratic local government early in that period. Paris did not have a socialist mayor until 2001. In London, the counterweight to a central government pursuing a neoliberal agenda was a dynamic local

---

[4] See Saskia Sassen, *The Global City* (Princeton: Princeton University Press, 2001); Fainstain, Gordon, and Harloe (eds.), *Divided Cities*.

[5] On Paris, see Éric Hazan, *Paris in Turmoil: A City Between Past and Future*, trans. David Fernbach (London: Verso, 2022).

political actor that explored new forms of democratic activism and intervention.

In 1984, as already noted, Stuart Hall believed London was the main battleground for a 'direct confrontation' between the 'two essential conflicting principles of English political life...the camp of the profit motive and possessive liberalism...and the camp of collective social need and the public interest'.[6] It is largely the 'camp of the profit motive and possessive liberalism' that has been left standing today.

A journey through some of the sites explored in the present book nearly forty years after 1984 reveals the nature of that victory. Where the Dalston Children's Centre used to operate, terraced houses have risen in price by over 700 per cent. 'Boutique' is the adjective that can be applied to many businesses in the area: boutique hotels, boutique clothing stores, boutique bars. But even hipster angels may be hearing valedictory bells, rung by the unsleeping wraiths of the market. Zed Nelson's recent documentary about Hoxton, *The Street* (2019), is an exploration not only of the encroachment upon a working-class community by a hipster capitalism marked by small, but expensively sourced, batches of coffee, beer, and cheese ad infinitum but also of the encroachment upon that hipster world by luxury housing developments. Cowcross Street in Farringdon, once home to the London Lesbian and Gay Centre, is now lined with cafes and bars that lead from the newly opened Elizabeth Line (a public–private funding project) to Clerkenwell's chic design stores and workspace studios. Spitalfields is still home to a market, but now one that services the office workers employed in financial services nearby. 'Docklands' now has one meaning, not two, a shorthand for temples of international finance and tower blocks of expensive flats, many of which are empty, furnished shells in which to invest spare capital.

On this journey, there remain continuities with the 1980s. Inequality and deprivation are but two. The Lincoln Estate, though refurbished in the 1990s, continues to be an area of considerable poverty.[7] Broadwater

[6] Hall, 'Face the Future', 37.
[7] https://www.standard.co.uk/news/dispossessed/meet-the-gangs-buster-who-chose-to-live-on-crimeridden-estate-in-bow-9176565.html.

Farm is still afflicted by high crime rates and poverty, and after the 2017 Grenfell Tower tragedy it was also the focus of concern about the safety of building materials used in its construction. Questions over the exercise of state power through policing also remain in other ways. The police shooting of Mark Duggan in Tottenham in 2011 led to serious rioting across London and the rest of the UK. Before the disorders began, there had been a protest march from Broadwater Farm to Tottenham station. Women's safety in the city is a point of serious concern, particularly after revelations about the levels of misogyny and violence emanating from the Metropolitan Police themselves.

The most recent survey of London conducted by the GLC's successor organization, the Greater London Authority, concluded that London's current economic state could be described as 'prosperity'. But it is a harsh prosperity. London is also a city where '[i]ncome inequality' is 'stark, with the richest tenth of Londoners having almost 10 times the income of the poorest tenth.[8] Economic changes that were first clear in the 1980s were the norm in 2023: service, not production, employed the majority of those working; most job growth in 2023 was in low-paying jobs. The counterpoint to this was massive increases in property and rental costs. Since the turn of the twenty-first century, property prices have trebled, far outpacing increases in salaries and wages.[9] The contraction, if not extinction, of social housing provision has seen an increase in private renting and substantial rises in rental costs. All of this has meant that living in contemporary London seems, to many, more and more untenable: 'recent polls show that 52% of Londoners struggled to meet essential food and shopping needs, while 47% of renters think they will struggle to pay their rent in the next six months, and 40% think they will struggle with their energy bills.[10] Poverty has also persisted amid the 'prosperity' of London: 'one in six Londoners were classed as in persistent poverty between 2017 and 2021', and 'three in four children in poverty are in persistent poverty'—about 24 per cent of all children.[11]

[8] City Intelligence/GLA, *The State of London: A Review of London's Economy and Society* (London: GLA, June 2023), 10.
[9] See, for example, https://www.london.gov.uk/sites/default/files/house-prices-in-london.pdf.
[10] City Intelligence/GLA, *The State of London*, 8.
[11] City Intelligence/GLA, *The State of London*, 87.

This is in stark contrast to the London of the super-rich.[12] Some views of London dwell upon the often nightmarish ascent of neoliberalism and the wounds of austerity that produce this social chasm—*London's Overthrow* (2012), in the words of China Miéville.[13]

What is different between 1984 and the present is that there is little in the way of an alternative, at least in terms of state power. In 2016, Rowan Moore remarked that London 'looks like a city where market forces are running riot and where government bodies are enfeebled and reactive'.[14] The Grenfell Tower fire of the following year tragically bore out this statement. The fire was a terrible summation of the human cost of inequality, neglect, and lack of responsibility in London, deepened first by neoliberalism and then, after 2010, by austerity. Paul Gilroy has recently stressed the connections between the Grenfell Fire and the tragedies of the 1980s:

> Corruption, cruelty, complicity, disdain and disrespect feature here as both causes and effects. All have been harnessed to the machinery of rapacious, unregulated capitalism and then projected through the frames of xenophobia and racist common sense. This mixture has produced unwelcome and unsettling echoes of the indifference and loathing that defined official (non)responses to the deadly fire at 439 New Cross Road in 1981.[15]

'Who is London for?' asked Anna Minton in 2017. Not, it appears, ordinary Londoners. In 1984, there were alternatives that offered a different answer to this question, in part centred in local democracy, in part centred in community organizations and activism, and, in part, generated by individuals helped by that local democracy and that activism. A claim to the city, to defining who London might be for, could and was made by a wide variety of people in 1984. What is the legacy of that moment? At the beginning of this book, I suggested that it might be

[12]   See Caroline Knowles, *Serious Money* (London: Penguin, 2022).
[13]   China Miéville, *London's Overthrow* (London: Westbourne Press, 2012).
[14]   Rowan Moore, *Slow Burn City* (London: Picador, 2016), 3.
[15]   Paul Gilroy, 'Never Again Grenfell', Serpentine Gallery (2023), https://www.serpentine-galleries.org/art-and-ideas/never-again-grenfell/.

difficult to accord the term success or even longevity to the alternative moments and spaces of 1984. To varying degrees, they were foreclosed, whether it was because of the inexorable progress of finance and neo-liberalism or the abolition of the GLC and the power of an antipathetic central government.

Is the present book, then, a history of failure, capturing the last breath of what James Vernon has called the 'brief life of social democracy'?[16] In some ways it is. There is no way of denying the dominance of the neo-liberal city, a development which extinguished many of the alternative possibilities of London in 1984.

But it is also more complicated than that. This book has argued that, first of all, even as the short life of social democracy was expiring in the 1980s, London witnessed a radical and expansive redefining of what the 'social' in social democracy might mean—in this case, an understanding of the 'social' that included the claims of gender, race, and sexuality—and a similarly expansive exploration of new ideas of 'democracy', embracing, for example, decentralization or the allocation of central resources to the community. The last gasp of social democracy was less a gasp than a sometimes discordant, but nonetheless rich, chorus of new voices and new possibilities.

The life of social democratic London may have been short, ended by abolition in 1986, but we can still see and feel its afterlives and hear echoes of that chorus. Some of the alternative spaces and causes documented in this book pushed through, and even flourished, in the late twentieth and early twenty-first century. Gay's the Word recently celebrated its fortieth anniversary as a central institution in queer life in London. Pride and the Notting Hill Carnival are extraordinarily popular demonstrations of London's diversity, a diversity which began to gather strength, support, and acceptance in the last blush of social democracy in the 1980s. The architects of Matrix went on to pursue many of that organization's original aims, albeit in different forms. And, of course, what seemed controversial and groundbreaking in 1984 has become part of mainstream political and social discourse: anti-racist initiatives, gender equality, rights for LGBT+ people. The questions that animated

---

[16] Vernon, 'The Local, the Imperial, and the Global', 418.

1984 continue to animate the contemporary city. And the afterlives of 1980s London still run through that city—some, like Pride, in the form of a spectacle; others, like Calthorpe Community Garden, with a quieter, but no less powerful, presence.

In *Rebel Cities* (2013), David Harvey reinterpreted Henri Lefebvre's reflections on the 'right to the city' in the light of early twentieth-century neoliberalism, seeing in a variety of global anti-capitalist protests a reassertion of that claim to urban space. Harvey revived Lefebvre's idea of heterotopic spaces in the city, as 'something different' to neoliberalism: '[t]his "something different" does not necessarily arise out of a conscious plan, but more simply out of what people do, feel, sense, and come to articulate as they seek meaning in their lives'.[17] London in 1984 was a kind of heterotopia, forged through what a local democracy did and what the people of Matrix, Gay's the Word, the Anti-Apartheid Movement, the Joint Docklands Action Group, the Dalston Children's Centre, the Broadwater Farm Youth Association, and many others attempted to create. That London was made not only of offices but of many diverse and often humble spaces—community gardens, activist centres on a local street, a small bookshop, a women's centre, a childcare centre—all contributing to the 'rowdy exuberance' Patrick Wright evoked in 1991.[18] That city was not without conflict and tension, but it did reflect London's dynamism and diversity and enhanced Londoners' freedom and equality. Democracy of different sorts and across different registers formed that city, as did the desire to create new communities and new ways of living in the city.

The most compelling valediction for the London of 1984 and the best epitaph for this book comes from Stuart Hall—less a tribute to what had been and more a longing for what might have been. In 1988, Hall reflected on the demise of the GLC, tracing London's possible alternative trajectory without abolition. As an alternative future, he imagined a social ethos developing from the GLC's failed transport policy, 'a fare's fair society', an ethos animating a different, fairer, and freer London, a

---

[17] David Harvey, *Rebel Cities* (London: Verso, 2013), xiii; see also Henri Lefebvre, *Writings on Cities*, trans. Eleonore Kofman and Elizabeth Lebas (Oxford: Blackwell, 2000), ch. 14.

[18] Wright, *A Journey Through Ruins*, 18–19.

city in which ordinary people could see themselves and claim a space. Hall envisioned a London populated by 'all sorts of ordinary people, with different tastes, purposes, destinations, desires...enabled by a system of public intervention...to enlarge their freedoms to move about the city...to see and experience new things, to go into places hitherto barred to them...in safety and comfort'.[19] In Hall's vision of 1980s London, the answer to the question 'Who is London for?' would be 'All Londoners'.

London, 1984: Conflict and Change in the Radical City. Stephen Brooke, Oxford University Press.
© Stephen Brooke 2024. DOI: 10.1093/9780191895395.003.0011

[19] Stuart Hall, 'Introduction: Thatcherism and the Crisis of the Left', in *The Hard Road to Renewal*, 13.

Bibliography

Primary Sources

Unpublished Archival Sources

Archbishop of Canterbury's Commission on Urban Priority Areas, Lambeth Palace Archives and Library, London

Bernie Grant Papers, Bishopsgate Institute Archives, London

Black Cultural Archives, Brixton, London

Campaign for Homosexual Equality Papers, Hall-Carpenter Archives, London School of Economics, London

Defend Gay's the Word Campaign Archives, Bishopsgate Institute Archives, London

Gay Rights Working Party Papers, Hall-Carpenter Archives, London School of Economics

George Padmore Institute, London

Greater London Council, Papers, London Metropolitan Archives, Islington, London

Makanji Papers, Bishopsgate Institute Archives, London

Margaret Thatcher Foundation Archives, https://www.margaretthatcher.org/archive

Interviews

Jos Boys

Fran Bradshaw

Helen Brown

Julia Dwyer

Benedicte Foo

Liz Khan

Manju Mukherjee

Suzy Nelson

Nina Nissen

Anna Sherwin

Anne Thorne

Online Archival Sources

Anti-Apartheid Movement Archives, https://www.aamarchives.org

Garland Archives of Gender and Sexuality, https://www.gale.com/primary-sources/archives-of-sexuality-and-gender

Lesbians and Policing Project, Glasgow Women's Library Archives, GL1534LP, https://archive.womenslibrary.org.uk/the-lesbians-and-policing-project-lespop

Contemporary Newspapers and Journals
Body Politic, Toronto
Daily Express, London
Daily Mail, London
Daily Telegraph, London
East London Advertiser, London
East End News, London
Gay News, London
Guardian, London
Hackney Gazette, London
Lesbian and Gay Socialist, London
London Labour Briefing, London
Mail on Sunday, London
Marxism Today, London
New Left Review, London
New Socialist, London
New Statesman, London
Observer, London
Searchlight, London
Spare Rib, London
Spectator, London
Evening Standard, London
Sun, London
The Times, London
Town and Country Planning, London

Government Publications

Government Reports
Commission for Racial Equality. *Annual Report of the Commission for Racial Equality 1980.* London: HMSO, 1981.
Commission for Racial Equality. *Annual Report of the Commission for Racial Equality 1981.* London: HMSO, 1982.
Home Affairs Committee*Racial Attacks and Harassment. .* London: HMSO, 1986.
Home Affairs Committee. *Racial Attacks and Harassment.* London: HMSO, 1989.
Home Affairs Committee. *The Bangladeshis in Britain: Volume I.* London: HMSO, 1986.
Home Affairs Committee. *The Bangladeshis in Britain: Volume II.* London: HMSO, 1986.
Select Committee on Race Relations and Immigration, 1971–2, Police/Immigrant Relations: Volume 3, *Evidence, Documents and Index.* London: HMSO, 1972.
The Swann Report: Education for All. London: HMSO, 1985.
Walmsley, Roy. *Personal Violence: Home Office Research Study 89.* London: HMSO, 1986.

Parliamentary Acts

Police and Criminal Evidence Act 1984.
Race Relations Act 1976.

Parliamentary Debates

House of Commons Debates. Fifth Series.
House of Lords Debates. Fifth Series.

Printed Primary Sources

Alexander, Sally. 'Women, Class and Sexual Difference', *History Workshop Journal* 17/1 (Spring 1984): 125–41, doi: 10.1093/hwj/17.1.125.

Benn, Melissa, and Worpole, Ken. *Death in the City.* London: Canary Press, 1986.

Bethnal Green and Stepney Trades Council. *Blood on the Streets.* London: Bethnal Green and Stepney Trades Council, 1978.

Bracewell, Michael. *Souvenir.* London: White Rabbit, 2021.

Carby, Hazel, L. 'White Women Listen! Black Feminism and the Boundaries of Sisterhood', in Centre for Contemporary Cultural Studies, *The Empire Strikes Back.* London: Hutchinson, 1982.

Carvel, John. *Citizen Ken.* London: Chatto & Windus/Hogarth Press, 1984.

Centre for Contemporary Cultural Studies. *The Empire Strikes Back: Race and Racism in 70s Britain.* London: Routledge, 1982.

City Intelligence/GLA. *The State of London: A Review of London's Economy and Society.* London: GLA, 2023.

Cockburn, Cynthia. *The Local State.* London: Pluto Press, 1977.

Commission for Racial Equality. *Brick Lane and Beyond.* London: CRE, 1979.

Commission for Racial Equality. *Race and Council Housing in Hackney.* London: CRE, 1984.

Creation for Liberation. *Catalogue.* London: Creation for Liberation, 1983.

Dalston Children's Centre. *Annual Reports, 1981–3,* https://hackneyhistory.word-press.com/2017/08/09/dalston-childrens-centre-19823/.

Dalston Children's Centre/Centerprise. *Breaking the Silence: Writing by Asian Women.* London: DCC/Centerprise, 1984.

Davidoff, Leonore. 'The separation of work and home', in S. Berman (ed.), *Fit Work for Women.* London: Croom Helm, 1979.

Edinburgh Weekend Return Group. *In and Against the State.* London: Pluto Press, 1979.

Forrester, Andrew, Lansley, Stewart, and Pauley, Robin. *Beyond Our Ken: A Guide to the Battle for London.* London: Fourth Estate, 1985.

Gifford, Lord. *The Broadwater Farm Enquiry: An Independent Enquiry into the Disturbances of October 1985 at the Broadwater Farm Estate Tottenham.* London: Broadwater Farm Enquiry, 1986.

Gilroy, Paul. *There Ain't No Black in the Union Jack*. Chicago: University of Chicago Press, 1987, 1991.

Greater London Council. *Policing London*. London: GLC, 1981–6.

Greater London Council. *East London File*. London: GLC, 1983.

Greater London Council. *Ethnic Minorities and the Abolition of the GLC*. London: GLC, 1984.

Greater London Council. *Gays and the Police Bill*. London: GLC, 1984.

Greater London Council. *There is an Alternative*. London: GLC, 1984.

Greater London Council. *London Industrial Strategy*. London: GLC, 1985.

Greater London Council. *The GLC Women's Committee, 1982–6: A Record of Change and Achievement for Women in London*. London: GLC, 1986.

Greater London Council/Gay Working Group. *Changing the World*. London: GLC, 1985.

Hall, Stuart. 'Face the Future', *New Socialist* 19 (September 1984).

Hall, Stuart. *The Hard Road to Renewal*. London: Verso, 1988.

Hall, Stuart, et al. *Policing the Crisis: Mugging: The State, and Law and Order*. London: Macmillan, 1978.

Harrison, Paul. *Inside the Inner City*. Harmondsworth: Penguin, 1983.

Harvey, David. *Rebel Cities*. London: Verso, 2013.

Hayden, Dolores. *The Grand Domestic Revolution*. Cambridge, MA: MIT Press, 1981.

Hazan, Éric. *Paris in Turmoil: A City Between Past and Future*, trans. David Fernbach. London: Verso, 2022.

Hollinghurst, Alan. *The Swimming Pool Library*. New York: Vintage, 1989.

Independent Committee of Inquiry. *Policing in Hackney 1945–84: A Report Commissioned by the Roach Family Support Committee*. London: Karia Press/ Roach Family Support Committee, 1989.

Institute of Race Relations. *Policing Against Black People*. London: Institute of Race Relations, 1987.

Joint Docklands Action Group. *Docklands in Danger*. London: JDAG, 1980.

Joint Docklands Action Group for the Campaign to Restore Democracy in Docklands. *Docklands Fights Back*. London: JDAG, 1983.

Knowles, Caroline. *Serious Money*. London: Penguin, 2022.

Lefebvre, Henri. *Writings on Cities*, trans. Eleonore Kofman and Elizabeth Lebas. Oxford: Blackwell, 2000.

Le Grand, Julian, and Estrin, Saul (eds.). *Market Socialism*. Oxford: Oxford University Press, 1989.

Levidow, Les. 'Broadwater Farm: a "criminal estate"? An interview with Dolly Kiffin', *Race & Class* 29/1 (1987): 77–85, doi: 10.1177/030639688702900106.

Livingstone, Ken. *You Can't Say That*. London: Faber & Faber, 2011.

London Docklands Development Corporation. *Annual Reports*, 1981–6.

London Labour Party. *A Socialist Policy for the GLC—Labour's London Manifesto 1981*. London, 1981.

McCutcheon, Martine. *Who Does She Think She Is? My Autobiography*. London: Arrow, 2000.

Mackintosh, Maureen, and Wainwright, Hilary (eds.). *A Taste of Power*. London: Verso, 1987.

Market Nursery. *Not So Much a Nursery*. London: n.d. [late 1970s].

Matrix. *Making Space: Women and the Man-Made Environment*. London: Verso, 1984, 2022.

Matrix. *A Job Designing Buildings*. London: Matrix/GLC, 1986.

Matrix. *Building for Childcare*. London: Matrix/GLC, 1986.

Miéville, China. *London's Overthrow*. London: Westbourne Press, 2012.

Minton, Anna. *Big Capital: Who is London For?* London: Penguin Random House, 2017.

Moore, Tony. *The Killing of Constable Keith Blakelock*. London: Waterside Press, 2015, e-book edition.

Mulgan, Geoff, and Worpole, Ken. *Saturday Night or Sunday Morning?* London: Comedia, 1986.

Newham Docklands Forum. *The People's Plan for the Royal Docks*. London: Newham Docklands Forum/GLC PPU, 1983.

Oldfield Ford, Laura. *Savage Messiah*. London: Verso, 2011.

Phillips, Deborah. *What Price Equality? A report on the allocation of GLC housing in Tower Hamlets: Housing Research and Policy Report No. 9*. London: GLC, 1986.

Rowbotham, Sheila. *Hidden from History*. London: Pluto Press, 1973.

Rowbotham, Sheila. *Dreams and Dilemmas*. London: Virago, 1983.

Rowbotham, Sheila. *Dreams and Dilemmas*. London: Virago, 1988.

Rowbotham, Sheila. *Promise of a Dream*. London: Penguin, 2000.

Rowbotham, Sheila, Segal, Lynne, and Wainwright, Hilary. *Beyond the Fragments*. London: Merlin Press, 1979.

Runnymede Trust and Radical Statistics Race Group. *Britain's Black Population*. London: Heinemann, 1980.

Seaborne, Mike. *The Isle of Dogs: Before the Big Money*. London: Hoxton Mini Press, 2018.

Sivanandan, Ambalavaner. *A Different Hunger*. London: Pluto, 1982, 3–55.

Sivanandan, Ambalavaner. *Communities of Resistance: Writing on Black Struggles for Socialism*. London: Verso, 1990.

Small, Stephen. *Police and People in London, Volume II: A Group of Young Black People*. London: Policy Studies Institute, 1983.

Smith, David. *Police and People in London*. London: Policy Studies Institute, 1983.

Smith, David J., and Gray, Jeremy. *Police and People in London*. London: Gower/Policy Studies Institute, 1985.

Stevenson, Drew. 'Taking Liberties at Coin Street', *Town and Country Planning* 51 (September–October 1982): 204–6.

Tenants Tackle Racism: An Account of a Series of Workshops Held in Stepney. London: no publisher, 1985.

Thomas, June. 'Gagging Gay's the Word', *Off Our Backs* 15/4 (April 1985): 3.

Thomson, David. *In Camden Town*. London: Hutchinson, 1983.

Thorn, Tracey. *Bedsit Disco Queen*. London: Virago, 2014.

Tompson, Keith. *Under Siege: Racial Violence in Britain Today*. Harmondsworth: Penguin, 1988.

Tower Hamlets Federation of Tenants Associations. *Get Together and Get Things Done*. London: Tower Hamlets Federation of Tenants Associations, 1984.

Townsend, Peter, with Corrigan, Paul, and Kowarzik, Ute. *Poverty and Labour in London*. London: Low Pay Unit/Poverty Research London, 1987.
Wright, Gwendolyn, *Moralism and the Model Home*. Chicago: University of Chicago Press, 1980.
Wright, Patrick. *A Journey Through Ruins: The Last Days of London*. Oxford: Oxford University Press, 1991; 2009 edition, 18–19.
Zephaniah, Benjamin. 'The One Minutes of Silence', in Courttia Newland and Kadija Sesay (eds.), *IC3: The Penguin Book of New Black Writing in Britain*. London: Penguin, 2001, 141.

Online Primary Sources

Interviews: Digital and Online

Lewis, Gail, interviewed by Rachel Cohen, British Library, *Sisterhood and After*, Interview 4.
Wainwright, Hilary, interviewed by Claire Perrault, 'The GLC Story Oral History Project', 2 April 2017, http://glcstory.co.uk/listen-to-interviews/.
Wilson, Amrit, interviewed by Margaretta Jolly, British Library, *Sisterhood and After*, Interview 7.
Wong, Ansel, interviewed by Zahra Dalilah, GLC Story Oral History Project, 16 February 2017, http://glcstory.co.uk/wp-content/uploads/2017/03/AnselWong transcript.docx.pdf.

Other online resources

'Activism and the Under-Fives', http://radicalhistorynetwork.blogspot.ca/2016/01/activism-and-under-fives-meeting-report.html.
BFI, *Somewhere in Hackney*, 1980, https://player.bfi.org.uk/free/film/watch-somewhere-in-hackney-1980-online.
'Breaking Point'. n.d. https://www.youtube.com/watch?v=lRbcFNhDFeA.
Conservative Party General Election Manifesto, 1983, http://www.conservative-manifesto.com/1983/1983-conservative-manifesto.shtml.
'Docklands Armada, 1985', photographs by Mike Seaborne, http://www.80sislandphotos.org.uk/docklands-armada-1985/.
Fox, Anna. 'Work Stations', https://annafox.co.uk/photography/work-stations-2/.
Hackney Flashers. 'Who's Holding the Baby?'. 1978. exhibition, https://hackney-flashers.co.uk/whos-holding-the-baby-1978/#:~:text=The%20resulting%20project%20%27Who%27s%20Holding,this%20had%20on%20women%27s%20lives
Jagonari Centre, 'A Short History of the Jagonari Centre', https://eastendwomensmuseum.org/blog/2020/9/2/jago-nari-jago-banhishikha-a-short-history-of-the-jagonari-centre-in-whitechapel.
Jagonari Centre, 'Building of the Month', https://c20society.org.uk/building-of-the-month/jagonari-asian-womens-education-centre-whitechapel-london.
Mangrove Steelband, https://mangrovesteelband.wordpress.com/history.
Matrix Open Feminist Architecture Archive, http://www.matrixfeministarchitecturearchive.co.uk/jagonari/.

Mukherjee, Manju, https://www.ahackneyautobiography.org.uk/people/manjula-mukherjee.

Pinnock, Agostinho. Stephen Lawrence Centre, 'Unsettled Multiculturalisms', https://www.youtube.com/watch?v=7K7s8-U5T3I&t=2010s.

'Selous Street', https://theconversation.com/how-resistance-led-to-londons-selous-street-becoming-mandela-street-100770.

Sutherland, Allan. 'The Other Tradition: From Personal Politics to Disability Arts', 2006, http://citeseerx.ist.psu.edu/viewdoc/download?doi=10.1.1.548.565&rep=rep1&type=pdf.

Taylor, Sarah, 'Queer Neighbourhoods: Lesbian Squats in London Fields', https://eastendwomensmuseum.org/blog/category/Protest.

'The People's Armada to Parliament', http://cspace.org.uk/archive/docklands-community-poster-project/armada-2/.

Wainwright, Hilary. 'The Economics of Labour: Robin Murray, Industrial Strategy and the Popular Planning Unit', https://robinmurray.co.uk/glc-ppu.

Worpole, Larraine, https://www.ahackneyautobiography.org.uk/people/larraine-worpole.

https://www.hackneygazette.co.uk/news/22941133.parent-power-radical-stoke-newington-nursery-sandbrook-going-strong-40-years/.

Secondary Sources

Books

Aikens, Nick, and Robles, Elizabeth (eds.). *The Place is Here: The Work of Black Artists in 1980s Britain*. Berlin/Eindhoven: Sternberg Press/Van Abbemuseum, 2019.

Back, Les. *New Ethnicities and Urban Culture*. New York: St. Martin's Press, 1996.

Barker, Martin. *The New Racism*. London: Junction Books, 1981.

Ben-Tovim, Gideon, Gabriel, John, Law, Ian, and Stredder, Karen. *The Local Politics of Race*. London: Macmillan, 1986.

Boase, Massimi, and Pollitt. *How the Left Learned to Love Advertising*. London: BMP, 2000.

Bowling, Benjamin. *Violent Racism*. Oxford: Oxford University Press, 1998.

Brooke, Stephen. *Sexual Politics*. Oxford: Oxford University Press, 2011.

Brown, Wendy. *Undoing the Demos: Neoliberalism's Stealth Revolution*. New York: Zone Books, 2015.

Brownill, Sue. *Developing London's Docklands*. London: Chapman, 1990.

Bunce, Robin, and Field, Paul. *Renegade: Darcus Howe and the Fight for Black British Civil Rights*. London: Bloomsbury, 2021.

Burkett, Jodi. *Constructing Post-Imperial Britain*. Houndmills: Palgrave Macmillan, 2013.

Butler, David, and Butler, Gareth. *British Political Facts*. London: Macmillan, 1994.

Connell, Kieran. *Black Handsworth: Race in 1980s Britain*. Berkeley: University of California Press, 2019.

Cook, Chris, and Stevenson, John. *The Longman Handbook of Modern British History 1714–1987,* 2nd edition. Harlow: Longman, 1988.

Cook, Matt. *Queer Domesticities: Homosexuality and Home Life in Twentieth-Century London*. Basingstoke/New York: Palgrave Macmillan, 2014.

Curran, James, with Gaber, Ivor, and Petley, Julian. *Culture Wars: The Media and the British Left*. Edinburgh: Edinburgh University Press, 2005.

David, Jonathan, and McWilliam, Rohan (eds.). *Labour and the Left in the 1980s*. Manchester: Manchester University Press, 2018.

Davies, Aled, Jackson, Ben, and Sutcliffe-Braithwaite, Florence (eds.). *The Neoliberal Age? Britain since the 1970s*. London: UCL Press, 2021.

Davis, John. *Reforming London*. Oxford: Oxford University Press, 1988.

Davis, John. *Waterloo Sunrise*. New Haven: Yale University Press, 2022.

Deakin, Nicholas, and Edwards, John. *Enterprise Culture and the Inner City*. London: Routledge, 1993.

Dench, Geoff, Gavron, Kate, and Young, Michael. *The New East End: Kinship, Race and Conflict*. London: Profile Books, 2006.

Denney, Geoff, Leonard, Max, Stoll, Tamara, et al. *The Rio Tape/Slide Archive: Radical Community Photography in Hackney in the 80s*. London: Isola, 2020.

Dubow, Saul. *Apartheid 1948–1994*. Oxford: Oxford University Press, 2014.

Durham, Martin. *Sex and Politics*. Basingstoke: Macmillan, 1991.

Edelman, Murray. *Constructing the Political Spectacle*. Chicago: University of Chicago Press, 1988.

Edgerton, David. *The Rise and Fall of the British Nation*. London: Penguin, 2019.

Egan, Daniel. *The Politics of Economic Restructuring in London, 1981–6*. Lewiston: Edwin Mellen, 2001.

Eley, Geoff. *Forging Democracy*. Oxford: Oxford University Press, 2002.

Fieldhouse, Roger. *Anti-Apartheid*. London: Merlin Press, 2005.

Foot, Michael. *Aneurin Bevan*, Volume 1. London: MacGibbon & Kee, 1962.

Foster, Janet. *Docklands: Cultures in Conflict, Worlds in Collision*. London: UCL Press, 1999.

Gilroy, Paul. *Postcolonial Melancholia*. New York: Columbia University Press, 2005.

Glynn, Sarah. *Class, Ethnicity and Religion in the Bengali East End*. Manchester: Manchester University Press, 2014.

Grandy, Christine. *What the Audience Wants: Film, Television, and Audience Racism in Twentieth-century Britain*. Forthcoming.

Hall, Suzanne. *City, Street and Citizen*. New York: Routledge, 2012.

Hammond-Perry, Kennetta. *London is the Place for Me*. Oxford: Oxford University Press, 2016.

Hamnett, Chris. *Unequal City: London in the Global Arena*. London: Routledge, 2003.

Harvey, David. *A Brief History of Neoliberalism*. Oxford: Oxford University Press, 2005.

Hatherley, Owen. *A Guide to the New Ruins of Great Britain*. London: Verso, 2011.

Hughes, Colin, and Wintour, Patrick. *Labour Rebuilt*. London: Fourth Estate, 1990.

Husbands, Christopher T. *Racial Exclusionism and the City: The Urban Support of the National Front*. London: George Allen & Unwin, 1983.

Inglehart, Ronald. *The Silent Revolution*. Princeton: Princeton University Press, 1977.

Jackson, Ben, and Saunders, Robert (eds.). *Making Thatcher's Britain*. Cambridge: Cambridge University Press, 2012.

Jennings, Rebecca. *Tom Boys and Bachelor Girls: A Lesbian History of Postwar Britain*. Manchester: Manchester University Press, 2013.

Jerram, Leif. *Streetlife*. Oxford: Oxford University Press, 2011.

Joyce, Patrick. *The Rule of Freedom*. London: Verso, 2003.

Keith, Michael. *Race, Riots and Policing: Lore and Disorder in a Multi-racist Society*. London: UCL Press, 1993.

Keith, Michael, and Pile, Steve (eds.). *Place and the Politics of Identity*. London: Routledge, 1993.

Kelliher, Diarmaid. *Making Cultures of Solidarity: London and the 1984–5 Miners' Strike*. London: Routledge, 2021.

Kershen, Anne. *Strangers, Aliens and Asians*. London: Routledge, 2005.

Lansley, Stewart, Goss, Sue, and Wolmar, Christian. *Councils in Conflict: The Rise and Fall of the Municipal Left*. Houndmills: Macmillan, 1989.

Lawrence, Jon. *Me, Me, Me?*. Oxford: Oxford University Press, 2019.

Lent, Adam. *British Social Movements since 1945: Sex, Colour, Peace and Power*. New York: Palgrave Macmillan, 2001.

McKibbin, Ross. *Ideologies of Class*. Oxford: Oxford University Press, 1988.

McSmith, Andy. *No Such Thing as Society*. London: Constable, 2011.

Massey, Doreen. *Space, Place and Gender*. Oxford: Polity Press, 1994.

Massey, Doreen. *World City*. Cambridge: Polity Press, 2007.

Matera, Marc. *Black London*. Berkeley: University of California Press, 2015.

Moore, Rowan. *Slow Burn City*. London: Picador, 2016.

Moran, Leslie, Skeggs, Beverley, with Tyrer, Paul, and Corteen, Karen. *Sexuality and the Politics of Violence and Safety*. London: Routledge, 2004.

Murphy, Colm. *Futures of Socialism*. Cambridge: Cambridge University Press, 2023.

Ortolano, Guy. *Thatcher's Progress*. Cambridge: Cambridge University Press, 2019.

Ost, David. *The Defeat of Solidarity*. Ithaca: Cornell University Press, 2005.

Owusu, Kwesi. *The Struggle for Black Arts in Britain*. London: Comedia, 1986.

Payling, Daisy. *Socialist Republic: Remaking the British Left in 1980s Sheffield*. Manchester: Manchester University Press, 2023.

Pearson, David G. *Race, Class and Political Activism: A Study of West Indians in Britain*. Farnborough: Gower, 1981.

Pennybacker, Susan D. *From Scottsboro to Munich: Race and Political Culture in 1930s Britain*. Princeton: Princeton University Press, 2009.

Peplow, Simon. *Race and Riots in Thatcher's Britain*. Manchester: Manchester University Press, 2019.

Randall, Vicky. *The Politics of Child Daycare in Britain*. New York: Oxford University Press, 2000.

Rayside, David. *On the Fringe: Gays and Lesbians in Politics*. Ithaca: Cornell University Press, 1998.

Renton, David. *Never Again: Rock Against Racism and the Anti-Nazi League 1976–1982*. London: Routledge, 2019.

Riaz, Ali. *Islam and Identity Politics Among British Bangladeshis*. Manchester: Manchester University Press, 2013.

Robinson, Lucy. *Gay Men and the Left in Britain*. Manchester: Manchester University Press, 2007.

Robinson, Lucy. *Now That's What I Call a History of the 1980s: Pop Culture and Politics in the Decade that Shaped Modern Britain.* Manchester: Manchester University Press, 2023.

Rose, David. *A Climate of Fear: The Murder of PC Blakelock and the Case of the Tottenham Three.* London: Bloomsbury, 1992.

Rosenwein, Barbara. *Emotional Communities in the Early Middle Ages.* Ithaca: Cornell University Press, 2006.

Rossol, Nadine. *Performing the Nation in Interwar Germany.* London: Palgrave Macmillan, 2010.

Rowe, Michael. *The Racialisation of Disorder in Twentieth Century Britain.* Aldershot: Ashgate, 1998.

Sassen, Saskia. *The Global City.* Princeton: Princeton University Press, 2001.

Schlögel, Karl. *In Space We Read Time.* Trans. Gerrit Jackson. New York: Bard Graduate Centre, 2016.

Schofield, Camilla. *Enoch Powell and the Making of Postcolonial Britain.* Cambridge: Cambridge University Press, 2013.

Schwartz, Vanessa. *Spectacular Realities: Early Mass Culture in Fin de Siècle Paris.* Berkeley: University of California Press, 1998.

Scott Brown, Timothy. *West Germany and the Global Sixties: The Anti-Authoritarian Revolt 1962-78.* Cambridge: Cambridge University Press, 2013.

Seyd, Patrick. *The Rise and Fall of the Labour Left.* London: Macmillan, 1987.

Skinner, Rob. *The Foundations of Anti-Apartheid.* Basingstoke: Palgrave Macmillan, 2007.

Slobodian, Quinn. *Globalists: The End of Empire and the Birth of Neoliberalism.* Cambridge, MA: Harvard University Press, 2018.

Smith, Anna Marie. *New Right Discourse on Race and Sexuality.* Cambridge: Cambridge University Press, 1994.

Stein, Marc. *City of Sisterly and Brotherly Loves: Lesbian and Gay Philadelphia, 1945-72.* Chicago: University of Chicago Press, 2000.

Sternberg, Robert J., and Sternberg, Karin. *The Nature of Hate.* Cambridge: Cambridge University Press, 2008.

Stewart, Graham. *Bang!* London: Atlantic, 2013.

Stoller, Sarah. *Inventing the Working Parent: Work, Gender, and Feminism in Neoliberal Britain.* Cambridge, MA: MIT Press, 2023.

Sutcliffe-Braithwaite, Florence. *Class, Politics and the Decline of Deference in England, 1968-2000.* Oxford: Oxford University Press, 2018.

Thomlinson, Natalie. *Race, Ethnicity and the Women's Movement in England, 1968-1993.* Houndmills: Palgrave Macmillan, 2016.

Thörn, Håkan. *Anti-Apartheid and the Emergence of a Global Civil Society.* Houndmills: Palgrave Macmillan, 2006.

Thornley, Andrew. *Urban Planning under Thatcher.* London: Routledge, 1993.

Turner, Alwyn W. *Rejoice! Rejoice!* London: Aurum, 2010.

Vernon, James. *Distant Strangers.* Berkeley: University of California Press, 2014.

Vernon, James. *Modern Britain 1750 to the Present.* Cambridge: Cambridge University Press, 2017.

Vinen, Richard. *Thatcher's Britain*. London: Pocket Books, 2009.

Wainwright, Hilary. *A Tale of Two Parties*. London: Hogarth Press, 1987.

Walkowitz, Judith. *City of Dreadful Delight*. Chicago: University of Chicago Press, 1992.

Waters, Rob. *Thinking Black*. Berkeley: University of California Press, 2018.

Wetherell, Sam. *Foundations: How the Built Environment Made Twentieth-Century Britain*. Princeton: Princeton University Press, 2020.

White, Jerry. *London in the Twentieth Century*. London: Bodley Head, 2017.

Whitehorse, Wes. *GLC: The Inside Story*. London: James Lester, 2000.

Wickham-Jones, Mark. *Economic Strategy and the Labour Party*. New York: St. Martin's Press, 1996.

Williams, Elizabeth M. *The Politics of Race in Britain and South Africa: Black British Solidarity and the Anti-Apartheid Struggle*. London: I. B. Tauris, 2015.

Zachernuk, Philip. *Colonial Subjects*. Charlottesville: University Press of Virginia, 2000.

Articles

Ahmed, Sara. 'The Organization of Hate', *Law and Critique* 12/3 (2001): 345–65, doi: 10.1023/a:1013728103073.

Andrews, Aaron, Kefford, Alistair, and Warner, Daniel. 'Community, culture, crisis: the inner city in England, c. 1960–90', *Urban History* 20/2 (June 2023): 202–13, doi: 10.1017/S0963926821000729.

Ashe, Stephen, Virdee, Satnam, and Brown, Lawrence. 'Striking back against racist violence in the East End of London, 1968–1970', *Race & Class* 58/1 (2016): 34–54, doi: 10.1177/0306396816642997.

Atashroo, Hazel A. 'Weaponising Peace: The Greater London Council, Cultural Policy and "GLC Peace Year 1983"', *Contemporary British History* 33/2 (2019): 170–88, doi: 10.1080/13619462.2018.1519420.

Beckles, Colin A. '"We Shall Not Be Terrorized Out of Existence": The Political Legacy of England's Black Bookshops', *Journal of Black Studies* 29/1 (1998): 52–72, doi: 10.1177/002193479802900104.

Brooke, Stephen. 'Living in "New Times": Historicizing 1980s Britain', *Historical Compass* 12/1 (2014): 20–32.

Brooke, Stephen. 'Sexual Rights, Human Rights, the Material and the Post-Material in Britain, 1970 to 2010', *Revue Française de Civilisation Britannique* 14/3 (2015): 114–28.

Brooke, Stephen. 'Space, Emotions and the Everyday: The Affective Ecology of 1980s London', *Twentieth Century British History* 28/1 (2017): 110–42.

Brown, Geoff. 'Not Just Peterloo: The Anti-Apartheid March to the Springbok Match, Manchester, 26 November 1969', *Socialist History* 56 (2019): 19–42.

Bruley, Sue. 'Consciousness Raising in Clapham: Women's Liberation as 'Lived Experience' in South London in the 1970s', *Women's History Review* 22/5 (2013): 717–38, doi: 10.1080/09612025.2013.769378.

Burrows, Roger, and Knowles, Carolyn. 'The "Haves" and the "Have Yachts": Social-Spatial Struggles in London between the "Merely Wealthy" and the "Super-Rich"', *Cultural Politics* 15/1 (2019): 72–87, doi: 10.1215/17432197-7289528.

Callaghan, John. 'Rise and Fall of the Alternative Economic Strategy: From Internationalization of Capital to Globalization', *Contemporary British History* 14/3 (2000): 105–30: doi 10.1080/13619460008581596.

Campsie, Alexandre. '"Socialism will never be the same again": Re-imagining British left-wing ideas for the "New Times"', *Contemporary British History* 31/2 (June 2017): 166–88, doi: 10.1080/13619462.2017.1306211.

Church, A. 'Urban Regeneration in London Docklands: A Five-Year Policy Review', *Environment and Planning C: Government and Policy* 6/2 (1988): 197–208, doi: 10.1068/c060187.

Cook, Matt. 'Archives of Feeling: The AIDS Crisis in Britain 1987', *History Workshop Journal* 83/1 (2017): 51–78, doi: 10.1093/hwj/dbx001.

Crook, Sarah. 'The Labour Party, Feminism, and Maureen Colquhoun's Scandals in 1970s Britain', *Contemporary British History* 34/1 (2019): 71–94, doi: 10.1080.13619462.2019.1624166.

Curtis, S. E., and Ogden, P. E. 'Bangladeshis in London: A challenge to welfare', *Revue Européenne des Migrations Internationales* 2 (1986): 135–50.

Delap, Lucy. 'Feminist Bookstores, Reading Cultures and the Women's Liberation Movement, c. 1974–2000', *History Workshop Journal* 81/1 (2016): 171–96, doi: 10.1093/hwj/dbw002.

Francis, Mathew. '"A Crusade to Enfranchise the Many": Thatcherism and the "Property-Owning Democracy"', *Twentieth Century British History* 23/2 (June 2012): 275–97, doi: 10.1093/tcbh/hwr032.

Glynn, Sarah. 'Playing the Ethnic Card: Politics and Segregation in London's East End', *Urban Studies* 47/5 (2010): 991–1013, doi: 10.1177/0042098009353630.

Goodyer, Ian. 'Rock Against Racism: Multiculturalism and Political Mobilization, 1976–81', *Immigrants and Minorities* 22/1 (2010): 44–62, doi: 10.1080/02619288.2003.9975053.

Grote, Janie. 'Matrix: A Radical Approach to Architecture', *Journal of Architecture and Planning Research* 9/2 (1992): 159.

Hall, Stuart. 'From Scarman to Stephen Lawrence', *History Workshop Journal* 48 (1999): 187–97, doi: 10.1093/hwj/1999.48.187.

Hall, Stuart. 'The Neoliberal Revolution', *Cultural Studies* 25/6 (October 2011): 705–28, https://www.tandfonline.com/doi/abs/10.1080/09502386.2011.619886.

Hermance, Ed. 'Giovanni's Room in the LGBT* Movement', *QED: A Journal in GLBTQ Worldmaking* 1/2 (Summer 2014): 91–110, doi: 10.14321/qed.1.2.0091.

Hilton, Matthew. 'Politics is Ordinary: Non-Governmental Organisations and Political Participation in Contemporary Britain', *Twentieth Century British History* 22/2 (2011): 230–68, doi: 10.1093/tcbh/hwr002.

Hilton, Matthew, Moores, Chris, and Sutcliffe-Braithwaite, Florence. 'New Times Revisited: Britain in the 1980s', *Contemporary British History* 31/2 (June 2017): 145–65, doi: 10.1080/13619462.2017.1306214.

Husbands, Christopher T. 'East End Racism 1900–1980', *London Journal* 8/1 (1982): 3–26, doi: 10.1179/ldn.1982.8.1.3.

Husbands, Christopher T. 'Attitudes to Local Government in London: Evidence from Opinion Surveys and the GLC By-Elections of 20 September 1984', *London Journal* 11/1 (1985): 59–74, doi: 10.1179/ldn.1985.11.1.59.

Keith, Michael. 'Urbanism and City Spaces in the Work of Stuart Hall', *Cultural Studies* 23/4 (2009): 538–58, doi: 10.1080/09502380902950989.

Kelliher, Diarmaid. 'Solidarity and Sexuality: Lesbians and Gays Support the Miners 1984–5', *History Workshop Journal* 77/1 (2014): 240–62, doi: 10.1093/hwj/dbt012.

Langhamer, Claire. '"Who the Hell are Ordinary People?" Ordinariness as a Category of Historical Analysis', *Transactions of the Royal Historical Society* 28 (2018): 175–95, DOI: 10.1017/S0080440118000099.

Lawrence, Paul. 'The Vagrancy Act. 1824. and the Persistence of Pre-emptive Policing in England since 1750', *British Journal of Criminology* 57/3 (2017): 513–31, doi: 10.1093/bjc/azw008.

Llewelyn, Matthew P., and Rider, Toby C. 'Sport, Thatcher and Apartheid Politics: the Zola Budd Affair', *Journal of Southern Africa Studies* 44 (2018): 575–92, doi: 10.1080/03057070.2018.1464297.

Loney, Martin. 'Imagery and Reality in the Broadwater Farm Riot', *Critical Social Policy* 6/17 (1986): 81–6, doi: 10.1177/026101838600601706.

Matera, Marc, Natarajan, Radhika, Hammond-Perry, Kennetta, Schofield, Camilla, and Waters, Rob. 'Introduction: Marking Race', *Twentieth Century British History* 34/3 (2023): 407–14, doi: 10.1093/tcbh/hwad036.

May, Jon. 'Globalization and the Politics of Place: Place and Identity in an Inner London Neighbourhood', *Transactions of the Institute of British Geographers* 21 (1996): 194–215, doi: 10.2307/622933.

Moores, Chris. 'Opposition to the Greenham Peace Camps in 1980s Britain: RAGE Against the "Obscene"', *History Workshop Journal* 78/1 (August 2014): 204–27, doi: 10.1093/hwj/dbt038.

Moores, Chris. 'Thatcher's Troops? Neighbourhood Watch Schemes and the Search for "Ordinary" Thatcherism in 1980s Britain', *Contemporary British History* 31/2 (June 2017): 230–55, doi: 10.1080/13619462.2017.1306203.

Murphy, Colm. 'The "Rainbow Alliance" or the Focus Group? Sexuality and Race in the Labour Party's Electoral Strategy, 1985–7', *Twentieth Century British History* 31/2 (2020): 291–315, doi: 10.1093/tcbh/hwz015.

Nolan, Peter, and O'Donnell, Kathy. 'Taming the Market Economy? A Critical Assessment of the GLC's Experiment in Restructuring for Labour', *Cambridge Journal of Economics* 11/3 (1987): 251–63, doi: 10.1093/oxfordjournals.cje.a035029.

Offer, Avner. 'The Market Turn: from social democracy to market liberalism', *Economic History Review* 70/4 (November 2017): 1051–71, doi/10.1111/ehr.12537.

Parkinson, Michael. 'The Thatcher Government's Urban Policy, 1979–89: A Review', *Town Planning Review* 60/4 (November 1989): 421–40.

Payling, Daisy. '"Socialist Republic of South Yorkshire": Grassroots Activism and Left-Wing Solidarity in 1980s Sheffield', *Twentieth Century British History* 25/4 (2014): 602–27, doi: 10.1093/tcbh/hwu001.

Pike, Karl. 'Mere theology? Neil Kinnock and the Labour Party's aims and values, 1986–8', *Contemporary British History* 34/1 (January 2020): 95–117, doi: 10.1080/13619462.2019.1636650.

Price, Richard. 'One Big Thing: Britain, Its Empire, and Their Imperial Culture', *Journal of British Studies* 45/3 (2006): 602–27, doi: 10.1086/503593.

Reiner, Robert. 'PACE: Review Essay', *British Journal of Criminology* 26/3 (1986): 299–302, doi: 10.1093/oxfordjournals.bjc.a047613.

Rieger, Bernhard. 'Making Britain Work Again: Unemployment and the Remaking of British Social Policy in the Eighties', *English Historical Review* 133/568 (June 2018): 634–66, doi: 10.1093/ehr/cey087.

Robinson, Emily, Schofield, Camilla, Sutcliffe-Braithwaite, Florence, and Thomlinson, Nathalie. 'Telling Stories about Post-war Britain: Popular Individualism and the "Crisis" of the 1970s', *Twentieth Century British History* 28/2 (June 2017): 268–304, doi: 10.1093/tcbh/hwx006.

Saumarez Smith, Otto. 'The Inner City Crisis and the End of Urban Modernism in 1970s Britain', *Twentieth Century British History* 27/4 (December 2016): 578–98: doi: 10.1093/tcbh/hww032.

Schofield, Camilla. 'In Defence of White Freedom: Working Men's Clubs and the Politics of Sociability in Late Industrial England', *Twentieth Century British History* 38/1 (2023): 1–37, doi: 10.1093/tcbh/hwad038.

Schofield, Camilla, and Jones, Ben. '"Whatever Community Is, This is Not It": Notting Hill and the Reconstruction of "Race" in Postwar Britain', *Journal of British Studies* 58/1 (January 2019): 149, doi: 10.1017/jbr.2017.174.

Schregel, Susanne. 'Nuclear War and the City: Perspectives on Municipal Interventions in Defence. Great Britain, New Zealand, West Germany, USA, 1980–1985', *Urban History*, 42/4 (November 2015): 564–83, doi:10.1017/S0963926815000565.

Schwarz, Bill. '"The only white man in there": the re-racialisation of England, 1956–68', *Race & Class* 38 (1996): 65–78, doi: 10.1177/030639689603800105.

Setch, Eve. 'The Face of Metropolitan Feminism: The London Women's Liberation Workshop, 1969–79', *Twentieth Century British History* 13/2 (June 2002): 171–90, doi: 10.1093/tcbh/13.2.171.

Severs, Dominic. 'Rookeries and No-go Estates: St Giles and Broadwater Farm, or middle-class fear of "non-street" housing', *Journal of Architecture* 15/4 (2010): 449–97, doi: 10.1080/13602365.2010.507526.

Short, J. R., and Bassett, Keith. 'Housing Action Areas', *Area* 10/2 (1978): 153–7.

Spry Rush, Ann. 'Imperial Identity and Colonial Minds: Harold Moody and the League of Coloured Peoples, 1931–50', *Twentieth Century British History* 13/4 (2002): 356–83, doi: 10.1093/tcbh/13.4.356.

Sutcliffe-Braithwaite, Florence. 'Neo-Liberalism and Morality in the Making of Thatcherite Social Policy', *Historical Journal* 55/2 (June 2012): 497–520, doi: 10.1017/S0018246X12000118.

Sutcliffe-Braithwaite, Florence. 'Discourses of "Class" in "New Times"', *Contemporary British History* 31 (2017): 294–317, doi: 10.1080/13619462.2017.1306199.

Vernon, James. 'The Local, the Imperial and the Global: Repositioning Twentieth-Century Britain and the Brief Life of its Social Democracy'. *Twentieth Century British History*, 21/3 (2010): 405–18, doi: 10.1093/tcbh/hwq026.

Vernon, James. 'Heathrow and the Making of Neoliberal Britain', *Past and Present* 252 (2021): 213–47, doi: 10.1093/pastj/gtaa022.

Walkowitz, Judith. 'Feminism and the Politics of Prostitution in King's Cross in the 1980s', *Twentieth Century British History* 30/2 (June 2019): 231–63, doi: 10.1093/tcbh/hwz011.

Wall, Christine. 'Sisterhood and Squatting in the 1970s: Feminism, Housing and Urban Change in Hackney', *History Workshop Journal* 83 (2017): 79–97, doi: 10.1093/hwj/dbx024.

Waters, Chris. '"Dark Strangers in Our Midst": Discourses of Race and Nation in Britain, 1947–63', *Journal of British Studies* 36 (1997): 207–38, doi: 0.1086/386134.

Watt, Paul. 'Respectability, Roughness and "Race"', *International Journal of Urban and Regional Research* 30/4 (2006): 776–97, doi: 10.1111/j.1468-2427.2006.0 0688.x.

Weedon, Chris, 'Migration, Identity, and Belonging in British Black and South Asian Women's Writing', *Contemporary Women's Writing* 2/1 (2008): 17–35, doi: 10.1093/cww/vpn003.

Wetherell, Sam. 'Painting the Crisis: Community Arts and the Search for the "Ordinary" in 1970s and '80s London', *History Workshop Journal* 76 (2013): 235–49, 10.1093/hwj/dbt008.

Wetherell, Sam. 'Freedom Planned: Enterprise Zones and Urban Non-planning in Post-War Britain', *Twentieth Century British History* 27/2 (June 2016): 266–89, doi: 10.1093/tcbh/hww004.

Whittall, Daniel. 'Creating Black Places in Imperial London: The League of Colonial Peoples and Aggrey House, 1931–43', *London Journal* 36/3 (2011): 225–46, doi: 10.1179/174963211X13127325480316.

Williams, Elizabeth. 'Anti-Apartheid: The Black British Response', *South African Historical Journal* 64/3 (2012): 685–706, doi: 10.1080/02582473.2012.675809.

Wolmuth, Philip. 'Radical Losses', *British Journal of Photography* (June 2010): 87–8.

Chapters in Books

Back, Les, and Keith, Michael. 'Reflections: Writing Cities', in Hannah Jones and Emma Jackson (eds.), *Stories of Cosmopolitan Belonging*. Abingdon: Routledge, 2014, 15.

Cadart, Marie-Luare. 'Des "crèches sauvages" à la structuration au réseau associative. 1968–1986', in *Des Parents dans les Crèches, Utopie ou Réalité*. Toulouse: ERES, 2006, 11–24.

Castells, Manuel, and Murphy, Karen. 'Organization of San Francisco's Gay Community', in Norman I. Fainstein and Susan S. Fainstein (eds.), *Urban Policy Under Capitalism*. Beverly Hills: Sage, 1982, 237–59.

Clare, John. 'The Ratchet Advances Another Turn', in John Benyon and John Solomos (eds.), *The Roots of Urban Unrest*. Oxford: Pergamon Press, 1987, 61–8.

Conekin, Becky. '"Here is the Modern World Itself": The Festival of Britain's Representations of the Future', in Becky Conekin, Frank Mort, and Chris Waters (eds.), *Moments of Modernity*. London: Rivers Oram, 1999, 228–46.

Cook, Matt. 'From Gay Reform to Gaydar, 1967–2006', in Matt Cook (ed.), *A Gay History of Britain*. Oxford: Greenwood, 2007, 179–214.

Cook, Matt. 'Capital Stories: Local Lives in Queer London', in Matt Cook and Jennifer V. Evans (eds.), *Queer Cities, Queer Cultures*. London: Bloomsbury, 2014.

Curran, James. 'The Boomerang Effect: the Press and the Battle for London, 1981–6', in James Curran, Anthony Smith, and Pauline Wingate (eds.), *Impacts and Influences*. London: Methuen, 1987, 113–40.

Dabney Pennybacker, Susan. 'A Cold War Geography: South African Anti-Apartheid Refuge and Exile in London, 1945–94', in Nathan Riley Carpenter and Benjamin N. Lawrence (eds.), *Africans in Exile: Mobility, Law and Identity*. Bloomington: Indiana University Press, 2018, 185–99.

Davis, John. 'From GLC to GLA: London Politics from Then to Now' in Joe Kerr and Andrew Gibson (eds.), *London from Punk to Blair*. London: Reaktion, 2012, 97–105.

Dwyer, Julia, and Thorne, Anne. 'Evaluating Matrix: Notes from Inside the Collective', in Doina Petrescu (ed.), *Altering Practices: Feminist Politics and Poetics of Space*. London: Routledge, 2007, 42–3.

Fainstein, Susan, and Young, Ken. 'Politics and state policy in economic restructuring', in Susan Fainstein, Ian Gordon, and Michael Harloe (eds.), *Divided Cities*. Oxford: Blackwell, 1992, 215–24.

Kean, Hilda. 'The Transformation of Political and Cultural Space', in Joe Kerr and Andrew Gibson (eds.), *London from Punk to Blair*. London: Reaktion, 2012, 141–50.

Keith, Michael. '"Policing a Perplexed Society?" No-go areas and the mystification of police-black conflict', in Ellis Cashmore and Eugene McLaughlin (eds.), *Out of Order: Policing Black People*. London: Routledge, 1991, 189–214.

Lysaght, Karen, and Basten, Anne. 'Violence, Fear and "the Everyday": Negotiating Spatial Practice in the City of Belfast', in Elizabeth A. Stanko (ed.), *The Meanings of Violence*. London: Routledge, 2003, 224–42.

Mercer, Kobena. 'Welcome to the Jungle: Identity and Diversity in Postmodern Politics', in Jonathan Rutherford (ed.), *Identity: Community, Culture, Difference*. London: Lawrence & Wishart, 1990, 259–85.

Phillips, Mike. 'The State of London', in Joe Kerr and Andrew Gibson (eds.), *London from Punk to Blair*. London: Reaktion, 2012, 151–8.

Phizacklea, Annie, and Miles, Robert. 'Working Class Racist Beliefs in the Inner City', in Robert Miles and Annie Phizacklea (eds.), *Racism and Political Action in Britain*. London: Routledge & Kegan Paul, 1979, 93–128.

Schwarz, Bill. 'Where horses shit a hundred sparrows feed: Docklands and East London during the Thatcher years', in John Corner and Sylvia Harvey (eds.), *Enterprise and Heritage*. London: Routledge, 1991, 75–90.

Segal, Lynne. 'Jam Today: Feminist Impacts and Transformations in the 1970s', in Black, Lawrence, Pemberton, Hugh, and Thane, Pat. (eds.), *Reassessing 1970s Britain*. Manchester: Manchester University Press, 2013, 149–66.

Spence, Jo. 'Women's Collective Work 1974 Onwards', in *Putting Myself in the Picture*. Seattle: Real Comet Press, 1988, 166–77.

Theodore, Nik, Peck, Jamie, and Brennen, Neil. 'Neoliberal Urbanism: Cities and the Rule of Markets', in Gary Bridge and Sophie Watson (eds.), *The New Blackwell Companion to the City*. Oxford: Wiley-Blackwell, 2011, 15–25.

Unpublished Dissertations

Atashroo, Hazel A. 'Beyond the "Campaign for a Popular Culture": Community Art, Activism and Cultural Democracy in 1980s London', PhD thesis, University of

Southampton, Faculty of Business, Law and Art, Winchester School of Art (2017), 173, https://eprints.soton.ac.uk/414571/1/17._Final_submission_of_thesis.pdf.

Bianchini, Franco. 'Cultural Policy and Political Strategy: The British Labour Party's Approach to Arts Policy, with Particular Reference to the 1981–86 GLC Experiment', PhD dissertation, University of Manchester (1996), 184, https://eprints.soton.ac.uk/414571/1/17._Final_submission_of_thesis.pdf.

Index

Note: Figures are indicated by an italic "*f*", following the page number.

Because the index has been created to work across multiple formats, indexed terms for which a page range is given (e.g., 52–53, 66–70, etc.) may occasionally appear only on some, but not all, of the pages within the range.